In Search of Pluralism

The John M. Olin Critical Issues Series

Published in cooperation with
the Harvard University Russian Research Center

In Search of Pluralism: Soviet and Post-Soviet Politics, edited by Carol R. Saivetz and Anthony Jones

Soviet Social Problems, edited by Anthony Jones, Walter D. Connor, and David E. Powell

The Nationalities Factor in Soviet Politics and Society, edited by Lubomyr Hajda and Mark Beissinger

The Soviet Union in the Third World, edited by Carol R. Saivetz

In Search of Pluralism

Soviet and Post-Soviet Politics

EDITED BY

Carol R. Saivetz
HARVARD UNIVERSITY

Anthony Jones
NORTHEASTERN UNIVERSITY

Westview Press
BOULDER · SAN FRANCISCO · OXFORD

The John M. Olin Critical Issues Series

Published in 1994 in the United States of America by Westview Press, Inc., 5500 Central Avenue, Boulder, Colorado 80301-2877, and in the United Kingdom by Westview Press, 36 Lonsdale Road, Summertown, Oxford OX2 7EW

Library of Congress Cataloging-in-Publication Data
In search of pluralism : Soviet and Post-Soviet politics / edited by
    Carol R. Saivetz, Anthony Jones.
        p.   cm. — (The John M. Olin critical issues series)
    Includes index.
    ISBN 0-8133-1952-8 — ISBN 0-8133-1953-6 (pbk.)
        1. Soviet Union—Politics and government—1985–1991—Congresses.
2. Former Soviet republics—Politics and government—Congresses.
3. Pluralism (Social sciences)—Soviet Union—Congresses.
4. Pluralism (Social sciences)—Former Soviet republics—Congresses.
I. Saivetz, Carol R.   II. Jones, Anthony, 1940–   .   III. Series.
JN6511.I5   1994
306.2'0947—dc20   93-6430
                                                                                          CIP

Printed and bound in the United States of America

The paper used in this publication meets the requirements
of the American National Standard for Permanence of Paper
for Printed Library Materials Z39.48-1984.

10   9   8   7   6   5   4   3   2   1

Contents

Acknowledgments — ix

Introduction, *Anthony Jones and Carol R. Saivetz* — 1

1 Pluralism, Civil Society, and Post-Soviet Politics, *Stephen White* — 5

2 Pluralism and the New Press in Russia, *Mervyn Matthews* — 27

3 Pluralism and Politics in an Urban Soviet: Donetsk, 1990–1991, *Theodore H. Friedgut* — 45

4 How Democratic Are Local Russian Deputies? *Jeffrey W. Hahn* — 62

5 Prospects for Political Pluralism in Central Asia, *Peter Clement* — 86

6 Pluralism Versus Corporatism: Government, Labor, and Business in the Russian Federation, *Elizabeth Teague* — 109

7 State, Property, and Political Society in Postcommunist Russia: In Search of a Political Center, *Michael E. Urban* — 125

8 Conclusion: Today's Russia, Pluralism, and Social Science Theory, *Anthony Jones and Carol R. Saivetz* — 151

About the Book — 161
About the Editors and Contributors — 163
Index — 165

Acknowledgments

We wish to thank the John M. Olin Foundation for its generous support of the Olin Critical Issues Seminar Series at the Harvard University Russian Research Center, at which preliminary versions of the chapters in the book were presented. We would also like to thank Vladimir Brovkin, Timothy Colton, Nicholas Daniloff, Mark Beissinger, Steven Burg, Walter Connor, and David Powell for serving as discussants at the seminar sessions and for offering comments on the papers presented. In addition, we would like to express our appreciation to our friends and colleagues at the Russian Research Center. Finally, we wish to thank Amy Randall, Michele Wong Albanese, and Alan Fortescue for their invaluable assistance in putting the series together and in preparing the manuscript.

Carol R. Saivetz
Anthony Jones

Introduction

Anthony Jones and Carol R. Saivetz

In the winter of 1990–1991, conservative forces in the Soviet Union appeared to be ascendant: Plans to move quickly to a market economy (the Shatalin 500-Day Plan) had been rejected, and the independence movements in Lithuania and Latvia had been put down in bloody confrontations. Then, in spring 1991, Soviet President Mikhail S. Gorbachev opted to restart the reform process. It seemed that glasnost and perestroika were back on track and that democratization was proceeding: Political groups were active within and outside of Parliament, and there was public debate about the appropriate way to move from a centrally planned to a market economy. Although Gorbachev faced serious economic, political, and ethnic problems, the mood among reform-minded people was decidedly positive.

It was in this political and economic climate that we began to organize the John M. Olin Critical Issues Seminar for the 1991–1992 academic year. As we looked at the USSR it appeared that although full democracy had certainly not been achieved, there was nevertheless evidence of a fledgling, yet developing, pluralism. (Even Gorbachev and several other Politburo members began using the phrase "socialist pluralism.") Hence the title of our series and of this book, *In Search of Pluralism: Soviet and Post-Soviet Politics*.

What began as a relatively straightforward enterprise, to describe and evaluate the forms in which pluralist tendencies were developing, became more complicated as 1991 unfolded. With the abortive August 1991 coup, the disintegrative tendencies in Soviet society accelerated, culminating in the creation of the Commonwealth of Independendent States (CIS) and finally in Gorbachev's resignation as president of the USSR on Christmas Day. These events altered the framework for our study: The circumstances of the search for pluralism changed, and consequently the tasks of the participants became considerably more complicated.

A fundamental problem confronting those who would assess political trends in the late-Soviet and post-Soviet periods is the inadequacy of the models with which Soviet specialists have been working for so long.[1] Ideas about the nature of the Soviet polity and society have been evolving since the 1930s, yet there was no firm agreement among scholars as to what the Soviet "model"—if there was one—actually was. The earliest and most influential political model was totalitarianism.[2] Based on six characteristics—an official ideology, a single mass party led by a dictator, pervasive terror, monopoly control of the media, control of the

1

armed forces, and a centrally planned economy—the model took as its fundamental assumption the denial of pluralist elements in Soviet society. Following the death of Stalin, however, this approach was subjected to increasing criticism on the grounds that it posited a continuation of institutionalized terror and that it required the presence of a powerful political dictator. Additionally, the totalitarian model failed to consider the role of social structure and seemed to obscure both obvious and subtle changes in post-Stalinist Soviet politics.

Among the other approaches to the study of Soviet politics were political-economy theories, industrial society models, and bureaucratic studies.[3] The political-economy models were for the most part Marxist in orientation and were concerned more with the question of ownership of productive property and the nature of classes in the USSR than they were with evaluating the presence or absence of pluralistic elements. Industrial society theorists looked at Soviet politics in the context of developmental issues and the problems of highly industrialized societies. They started from the position that there are similar dynamics at work in all industrial societies and that these dynamics tend to create similar pressures for institutional changes.[4] Finally, other paradigms were suggested by Alfred Meyer's concept of the "USSR Incorporated," in which he saw the Soviet Union as one large corporate entity.[5] Although this model had limitations, it highlighted the hierarchical nature of the Soviet polity and recognized intense politics at the highest levels.[6]

Still other important approaches assumed the presence of a degree of pluralism in the USSR and looked for evidence that there were interest groups competing for access to valued resources and struggling to define and influence policy. Applying Western ideas about the operation of interest groups, scholars produced a number of works that not only sought to undo the notion that Soviet society was unique but also manifested much greater sensitivity to the nuances of Soviet politics.[7] Each of these approaches to the study of Soviet politics clearly has its limitations; yet each provides some insight into the USSR. By the 1980s, there were, for example, a number of interesting case studies of how groups, cliques, and individuals tried to influence political decision making. Yet, there was no systematically developed model of political pluralism in the Soviet Union.

Without such a conceptual framework, the dramatic changes that occurred in the late-Soviet period and the continuing political upheaval in the former Soviet Union present serious challenges to contemporary scholars. It is not clear on what we should focus, and why. Should we concentrate on political infighting at the "center" or give most attention to events at the grass roots? Are current notions of political parties and interest groups adequate to describe political phenomena in the late- and now post-Soviet periods? Will pluralism emerge on the foundations of preexisting interests and groups, or is it developing de nouveau? As several of our contributors point out, there are political *groups* operating, but can they be described as *parties?* How do they compete for power? What interests do they represent? And to whom are they accountable? We must also raise questions about the environment in which these groups operate. For example, how are divergent opinions articulated? Are these opinions and views tolerated by the competing groups and the general public? What is the political/institutional framework in which groups compete?

All of our contributors offer assessments of the rudimentary pluralism that seems to be emerging in parts of the former Soviet Union, but they caution that this nascent pluralism should not be confused with full democratization or democracy. Stephen White, after assessing previous models of Soviet society, explores what he calls the Gorbachev revolution from above and its relation to the populist revolution from below. Within that context, he analyzes the institutional changes that have occurred thus far, as well as electoral reform. He also discusses the impact that glasnost has had on the emerging political process—a theme taken up in the chapter by Mervyn Matthews. Matthews describes changes in the official media and the growth of the independent press. He analyzes the tenuous and still murky relationship between the authorities and the press and speculates on what the consequences of commercialization may be for the "health" of an independent press.

Theodore Friedgut, in his case study of Donetsk, and Jeffrey Hahn, in his analysis of the Yaroslavl' soviet, discuss the effects of the institutional and electoral reforms, and of the freeing of the press, on local politics. Friedgut cautions against confusing pluralism with "fragmentation." He argues: "The stability of any system will quite naturally depend on the ratio between activity restrained with common accepted norms and that unrestrained by such norms." In Yaroslavl', local deputies debate issues but seem disinclined to carve out distinct legislative roles. As Hahn illustrates, there are rudiments of competitiveness and representativeness, but thus far not a truly pluralistic system.

Although most of the chapters deal with Russia and Ukraine, we thought it important to raise these same questions with regard to the Central Asian republics of Kazakhstan, Kyrgyzstan, Tajikistan, Turkmenistan, and Uzbekistan. Peter Clement, in his chapter on Central Asia, describes the situation regarding parties and groups there; in contrast to Russia or Ukraine, independent groups are weak and seem to have a far smaller role in the newly created governing institutions. Clement argues that traditional patterns of clientelism and clan rule are far stronger than any nascent pluralism.

Elizabeth Teague directly addresses the interrelationship between economics and politics in her chapter on labor-management relations. She argues that the transition in Russia is complicated by the highly centralized nature of the Soviet system. As her discussion shows, this is manifested in labor-management negotiations in which it is not always clear who is representing whom. Thus, she concludes that neocorporatism may be a more appropriate model than pluralism for the study of post-Soviet politics. Michael Urban approaches the interconnectedness between economics and politics differently. He sees attitudes toward state and property as the defining axes of political life in Russia today. Yet, in many respects, these attitudes prevent the coalescence of a single political center in this transitional period. In the conclusion, the editors discuss the theoretical issues raised by the contributors and suggest directions for future research.

The assessments offered in this volume are preliminary at best, given the dramatic and unceasing changes in the late-Soviet and post-Soviet periods. Moreover, we should bear in mind the difficulties inherent in this endeavor. We have no distance from events: We must analyze on the spot ongoing political infighting, constantly changing political configurations, and the unending search for new political institutions. Too much of our information is fragmentary. In addition, our task is made more difficult, ironically, by the surfeit of information coming from the former Soviet Union—much of it contradictory.

From now on, we must not allow the information overload to divert us from what should be our main task: to make scholarship on the new Russia and the other successor states more consciously theoretical than was true of our analyses of the USSR. The chapters offered in this volume take us, we think, in the direction of a more theoretically based enterprise.

Notes

1. Alex Inkeles, "Models and Issues in the Analysis of Soviet Society," *Survey,* July 1966, pp. 3–17.

2. See, for example, Carl J. Friedrich and Zbigniew Brzezinski, *Totalitarian Dictatorship and Autocracy* (Cambridge: Harvard University Press, 1956), and Michael Curtis, *Totalitarianism* (New Brunswick, N.J.: Transaction Books, 1979).

3. For an elaboration and discussion of industrial society models, see Anthony Jones, "Models of Socialist Development," *International Journal of Comparative Sociology,* December 1983, pp. 86–98.

4. For the best, as well as some of the earliest, analysis of the USSR as an industrial society, see the work of Alex Inkeles, especially his *Social Change in Soviet Russia* (Cambridge: Harvard University Press, 1968). For a survey of the ideas underlying the industrial society model, see Anthony Jones, "Modernization Theory and Socialist Development," in Mark Field, ed., *The Social Consequences of Modernization in Communist Societies* (Baltimore: Johns Hopkins University Press, 1976).

5. Alfred Meyer, "The USSR Incorporated," in Donald W. Treadgold, *The Development of the USSR: An Exchange of Views* (Seattle: University of Washington Press, 1964).

6. Leslie Holmes, *Politics in the Communist World* (Oxford: Oxford University Press, 1986), p. 392.

7. The best example of this literature is H. Gordon Skilling and Franklyn Griffiths, eds., *Interest Groups in Soviet Politics* (Princeton: Princeton University Press, 1971).

CHAPTER 1

Pluralism, Civil Society, and Post-Soviet Politics

Stephen White

Pluralism may be defined as the "diffusion and dispersal of power in a political system from central authorities to more or less autonomous groups, organizations and individuals, typically expressed in the establishment of 'bargaining' rather than 'command' relationships between them."[1] It was not, until at least the 1960s, a model that appeared to have any direct bearing upon a political system of the Soviet type. Rather, it appeared Soviet and East European systems were best conceptualized as totalitarian ones, based upon the dominant authority of a communist party. In systems of this kind political power was highly centralized, not dispersed. There was no scope for autonomous group activity of the kind familiar in the West; such bodies as trade unions and women's committees, on the contrary, were expected to act as "transmission belts," ensuring the implementation of party directives among their respective memberships. There was virtually no private sphere in which citizens could pursue their literary, sporting, religious, or other interests; all areas were politicized and (generally speaking) were either banned or compulsory. Within the dominant party, moreover, political power was itself highly centralized. Each level of the party leadership was directly subordinate to the level above it, according to the principle of "democratic centralism," and the national leadership, at the top, could call on the means of coercion to protect its dominant position.[2]

In fact, this may not have been an adequate account of the Soviet system even in the Stalin era. It made unrealistic assumptions about the information that was available to the central leadership, exaggerated the range of its control outside the major urban areas, and neglected the extent to which organized groups (such as the army or police) could act to protect their interests.[3] It was not until the 1960s, however, that the totalitarian model began to appear positively misleading, as patterns of political development in the communist world began to diverge and as at least a few Soviet-type systems (notably those of Yugoslavia and Czechoslovakia) attempted to reconcile communist rule with a wider range of human and civil liberties. Soviet authority was reimposed through the Brezhnev Doctrine of the 1970s, but in the late 1980s and early 1990s the countries of Central and Eastern Europe moved still further, from communist to democratic rule and from central planning to the market.[4] Under Mikhail S. Gorbachev's leadership, the Soviet Union accepted these changes, reconsidered the history of its relationship with the countries concerned, and moved toward a "humane, democratic socialism" that seemed to owe much to earlier Eastern European experience. By late 1991, in the aftermath of the attempted coup and with the Communist Party suspended, it began to appear that the Soviet Union itself was engaged in a similar process of transition.

In general, social scientists had a rather patchy record of predicting and explaining changes of this kind. Andrzej Korbonski, for instance, writing in 1988, thought the East European situation "not unprecedented" and foresaw no "radical changes" in the Soviet–East European relationship in the near future.[5] Others, however, had written about the "demise of communism" before it had actually occurred,[6] and still others had suggested that the Soviet system in particular would not withstand the fall in economic growth rates that it had experienced in the late 1970s and early 1980s. For example, in 1984 R. V. Burks argued that "all the ingredients for some kind of explosion are increasingly in place"; and for Richard Pipes the Soviet Union already fit V. I. Lenin's definition of a "revolutionary situation."[7] Apart from these short-run predictions there was an influential orthodoxy, developed after the collapse of totalitarian approaches, that suggested political changes of this kind were more or less inevitable as the countries concerned acquired economic maturity—in other words, as they "modernized." One form of this newer orthodoxy was "convergence," by which both East and West would move toward an economic and political system that reconciled the two extremes. More influential, however, was the view that Soviet-type systems would necessarily move toward political pluralism of a Western kind. In this chapter I consider this theory more closely, and then examine its bearing upon recent and prospective developments in what used to be the Soviet Union.

Modernization, Pluralism, and Political Transition

Modernization approaches are in many ways a direct descendant of the evolutionary theories of the nineteenth century and earlier. These theories saw mankind as progressing through successive stages of social organization until some final state of near-perfection was attained.[8] Auguste Comte, in one of the earliest such formulations, spoke of this change as one from a theological or military stage of social development to one that was scientific or rational in character. Henry Maine, in his *Ancient Law* of 1861, saw the change as one from "status" to "contract"; and Ferdinand Toennies, in his *Gemeinschaft und Gesellschaft* (1887), saw the transition as one from a "community" mode of social organization toward an industrial-capitalist society based upon "association." Karl Marx and Friedrich Engels, writing at this time, were strongly influenced by U.S. anthropologist Lewis Henry Morgan. Morgan's *Ancient Society,* published in 1877, sought to establish that all societies passed (in the words of its subtitle) in a "Line of Human

Progress from Savagery Through Barbarism to Civilization" (in which civilization was identified as the urban United States of his time). Marx and Engels were themselves persuaded to set forth a five-stage sequence of modes of production, leading finally from capitalism to socialism. Optimistic, unilinear assumptions of this kind have underpinned more recent conceptualizations of political change, among them political modernization.

These types of evolutionary theories may conveniently be approached through the work of their principal modern exponent, Talcott Parsons.[9] Parsons, explicitly drawing upon Charles Darwin, argued that social systems could be classified in terms of their development through a series of "evolutionary universals," that is to say, "a complex of structures and associated processes the development of which so increases the long-run adaptive capacity of living systems in a given class that only systems that develop the complex can attain certain higher levels of general adaptive capacity." As a society emerged from the primitive level, Parsons suggested, it would tend to evolve a system of social stratification based upon functional differentiation and achievement rather than upon kinship and ascription. A specialist political function would emerge that was independent of religious authority for its legitimation. An administrative bureaucracy and a market system would come into existence, as would an independent judicial system, which was a prerequisite for the remaining evolutionary universal, "democratic association with elective leadership and fully enfranchised membership." Parsons, a member of the Russian Research Center at Harvard, argued more specifically that what he called communist totalitarian systems would prove incapable of competing with liberal-democratic regimes in the long run. He believed they would be compelled to make adjustments in the direction of electoral democracy and a plural party system if they were not to regress into less advanced forms of social organization.

The theory of political modernization in relation to the Soviet Union and other communist systems was developed by a number of other writers, many of whom acknowledged their debt to Parsons.[10] Like Parsons, modernization theorists assumed that communist systems, variously conceptualized as "mobilizing" or "modernizing regimes," would manifest the same linkages between socioeconomic change and the polity as did political systems elsewhere. Robert Dahl summed up these linkages as follows: A high socioeconomic level and competitive politics were associated; not only competitive politics but also pluralist democracy were associated with relatively high levels of socioeconomic development; and the higher the socioeconomic level the more competitive the political system, and vice versa. "Because of its inherent requirements," Dahl wrote, "an advanced economy and its supporting social structures automatically distribute political resources and political skills to a vast variety of individuals, groups and organizations." Among these skills and resources are knowledge, income, esteem, the ability to organize and communicate, and access to organizations, experts, and elites. These resources could be used to negotiate for individual or group advantages and to ensure that when conflicts arose, as they were bound to do, they were resolved by negotiation and bargaining rather than by compulsion and coercion. The monopoly of political power enjoyed by the rulers of communist states, Dahl concluded, was therefore undermined by the programs of social and economic development that they themselves had sponsored. Dahl argued that the transition from Stalinism was already a "profound step towards liberalization"; further moves in this direction were inescapable as a centrally dominated political system became increasingly difficult to reconcile with the pluralistic pressures of a modern economy and society.[11]

The same view has been taken by a wide variety of other writers. For instance, in one of the earliest such statements, Alexander Eckstein maintained that communist systems were quite functional in response to a rapid rate of economic and social development; but mobilization would soon exhaust its usefulness and technical specialists and other groups would begin to demand the political influence to which their skills appeared to entitle them.[12] Merle Fainsod spoke of the "emergence over time of a looser, more pragmatic, and pluralistically based party" in which the various interests of an industrial society could find free expression.[13] Samuel Huntington thought the party would become the "aggregator and regulator of competing specialist interests" in the manner of a "modern pluralist democracy"; Roy Medvedev, writing in the 1970s, saw pluralization as an "inevitable tendency"; and Karl Deutsch, writing earlier, identified an "automatic trend towards pluralization."[14] Gabriel Almond, in perhaps the most far-reaching of such prognostications, spoke of the "pluralistic pressures of a modern economy and society" and identified a "secular trend in the direction of decentralization and pluralism." Already, Almond wrote, Russian successes in science, education, technology, economic productivity, and national security had produced some decentralization of the political process. "I fail to see," he went on, "how these decentralizing, pluralistic tendencies can be reversed, or how their spread can be prevented."[15]

Conceptualizations of this kind lost something of their force during the 1970s as Khrushchevian innovation was replaced by Brezhnevite stagnation and as Soviet control was reasserted throughout the bloc. The changes of the Gorbachev era, however, restored them to good health. The Soviet leadership made it clear that they would not necessarily sustain East European communist authorities if they failed to develop their own bases of support. They emphasized, indeed, that these authorities should not have intervened to overthrow the Alexander Dubcek leadership in 1968 and that a common commitment to socialism did not exclude conflicts of interest among the states in question.[16] Denied the Soviet support that had previously sustained them, communist regimes collapsed throughout Eastern and Central Europe in the late 1980s. In 1991 the institutions that had underpinned the bloc as a whole—Comecon and the Warsaw Treaty Organization—followed them into oblivion. The Soviet system itself, under the impact of domestic pressures, increasingly accommodated a variety of political forces, and by late 1991 it was moving toward a postcommunist future and a mixed economy with substantial private and foreign ownership. The "iron law of pluralism," however belatedly, appeared to be asserting itself.[17]

Several writers, among them Moshe Lewin, spelled out the implications of social and economic change for the distribution of political authority in the Gorbachev era. Lewin had earlier argued that the increasing influence of the Communist Central Committee was the "inevitable result of a deep structural transformation of the whole social setting," leaving the party "more than ever a bargaining-and-brokerage type of organization."[18] By the Gorbachev years, Lewin went on, Soviet society had come to need a state that could "match its own complexity." Urban society had become a kind of "system maker," influencing the political and economic system alike. The whole country had become more urbanized, educated, professionally differentiated, and culturally diverse. A huge class of educated specialists and a complex structure of elites had emerged, and reflecting this, a civil society, independent of the state, had also appeared, which marked the "start of a new age."[19] For Lucian Pye, similarly, the pluralizing changes of the Gorbachev era were a "vindication of modernization theory" and a reflection of the "inevitable growth in the complexities of societies." The information revolution, the emergence of a middle class, and the growth of a technically educated population had necessarily created "new centers of power, leading to drastically altered attitudes about the nature of authority."[20] The bureaucracy, in Isaac Deutscher's words, in effect, had been "educating its own gravediggers."[21]

Pluralism and the Gorbachev Revolution

The changes of the Gorbachev era had certainly led, by the early 1990s, to a political system that was quasi-pluralistic in character.[22] In the first place, there was a far-reaching reform of what used to be the Soviet state. This included the reform of the electoral system, mentioned briefly in Gorbachev's report to the 27th Party Congress in 1986 and then considered more directly at the January 1987 Central Committee plenum, at which the slogan of "democratization" was officially launched. In the discussion there was no shortage of evidence that the existing system had long ago ceased to convince Soviet electors that they wielded effective influence over the deputies that spoke in their name. There was no choice of candidates, for a start. Since the very first years of Soviet rule, in fact, there had never been more candidates than seats available. In 1984, at the last national elections of this kind, only 1,499 candidates were in contention for the 1,500 seats available because one of the candidates had died shortly before the poll, leaving no time to secure a replacement.[23] Candidates who had little previous identification with the constituency were often nominated, and it was difficult to vote against them because to do so it was normally necessary for voters to make use of a screened-off booth at the side of the polling station. At the 1984 elections, if the official results were to be believed, only .01 percent of the electorate failed to vote, and only .05 percent failed to approve the single list of candidates.[24]

The January 1987 plenum had approved a limited experiment in electoral choice at the local elections the following June. Then, in December 1988, an entirely new electoral law was adopted that provided for—though it did not actually require—an unlimited choice of candidates. The right to nominate candidates was extended to voters' meetings of five hundred or more; and deputies were not allowed to combine their representative duties with service in government (how could they be expected to hold themselves to account?). Moreover, deputies were expected to live or work in their own constituency, and they were required to present "programs" of their future activity to the electorate (otherwise what would be the point of a choice of candidates?). Voters, for their part, had to pass through a booth or room before casting their vote, ending the discredited practice of earlier years.[25] The general elections in March 1989, which were the first to be conducted on the basis of the new law, saw nearly two candidates nominated for each of the seats available, with a choice in about three-quarters of them. The results were still more remarkable, with at least thirty-eight leading party officials defeated throughout the country, even when (in some cases) they were standing unopposed.[26] There was a still greater degree of choice in the republican and local elections that took place in 1990, and the results gave majorities to nationalist movements in the three Baltic republics, in Georgia, and in Armenia.[27]

The process of political reform also extended to the Soviet state. The central objective here was "All power to the Soviets!" This time the reforms were to be in real rather than in formalistic terms and this, generally, meant a shift of executive authority from party to state institutions. The soviets, in Gorbachev's view, had served as the basis of a system of genuinely socialist democracy during the early postrevolutionary years, but they had then fallen victim to bureaucratization and overdetailed regulation by party committees.[28] One of the problems the Central Committee identified in their January 1987 discussion was the largely honorific nature of the deputy's mandate. Candidates were nominated, in many cases, because of the official position they held. Workers and collective farmers were added to the ballot to substantiate the claim that these were institutions of popular democracy; and very few places were left for experts and specialists who had a decisive contribution to make to the success of perestroika. The Soviet parliament, the Supreme Soviet, held sessions twice a year for just a few days at a time, giving deputies, however they were selected, little opportunity to question ministers or to influence the direction of public policy. Members largely agreed that deputies should be chosen for their political qualities, not because of their social origin, and that at least a substantial proportion of them should exercise their duties on a full-time basis.[29]

These and other elements of a Soviet "parliamentarianism" were approved by the Party Conference and then passed into law in December 1988. Local soviets, it was made clear, should be elected for five years at a time to allow deputies a reasonable opportunity to learn how to carry out their responsibilities. Officials at all levels were to be elected on a competitive basis for a maximum of two consecutive terms. A new supreme assembly was established, a Congress of USSR People's Deputies, made up of representatives from public organizations as well as from ordinary constituencies. The Congress would elect a new style Supreme Soviet, which would meet for up to eight months of the year, working through an elaborate system of committees and commissions.[30]

In an unprecedented move the new Parliament voted down six of the names originally proposed for membership in the new Council of Ministers. It established an organizational base, with a library and electronic services, and began to develop a network of deputy groups. One of the first was the Inter-Regional Deputies' Group, in effect a radical caucus, under the joint direction of Boris Yeltsin and other reformers. By 1991 there were twenty-three active deputies' groups. The committees of the new Parliament alone had held 1,250 meetings in their first two years.[31] Costs of the new Supreme Soviet rose from 7 million rubles a year before the reforms to 222 million rubles a year after them.[32]

The process of reform naturally concerned the Communist Party, until the late 1980s the core of the entire system. In the first place, Communist Party members called for the party to democratize its own activities and to allow members a greater degree of influence upon the policies that were made in their names. There had been "definite deformations in the party itself," Gorbachev told the Party Conference in 1988. Democratic centralism had degenerated into bureaucratic centralism, the rank and file had lost control over the leaders that were supposed to speak for them, and an atmosphere of comradeship had been replaced by one of subordination and command. Previously, party officials had been protected from criticism, and had come to believe they were irreplaceable. By the late 1980s many had lost contact with party members and with the public at large, and this had often ended in their "political and moral degeneration."[33] In their concluding resolutions, the delegates of the Party Conference agreed with Gorbachev that a "profound democratization" of party life was necessary and that there should "never again" be a recurrence of the deformations that had marked the Stalin and Brezhnev years. The officials concurred that the branches should be more independent; members should be chosen on the basis of their moral and political qualities, not because of their social origins; meetings should be more critical and constructive; and—a matter of "prime importance"—all posts up to the Central Committee–level should be filled by means of secret and competitive ballots and for a maximum of two consecutive five-year terms.[34] These and other reforms were gradually implemented over the months and years that followed.

Competitive elections to party positions had, in fact, already begun to take place in February 1987; a local party secretary in the Kemerovo region was chosen by secret ballot over a competing candidate.[35] Further changes to the party followed in September 1988 when the Central Committee approved six new commissions, each of them chaired by a senior member of the leadership. The commissions had parallel organizations at the local level and had expanded considerably in October 1990. They were intended to involve members of the Central Committee in high-level policy formation.[36] The Central Committee apparatus was reduced in scope and in the number of its members.[37] The reformed body now provided much more information to its members than ever before: about party finances, for instance, or about party history and membership.[38] Television cameras were now to be admitted into Central Committee meetings, and in 1990, for the first time, two journalists were allowed to attend and to report on a meeting of the Secretariat.[39]

The 28th Party Congress, which met in July 1990, consolidated these changes by approving a new set of party rules that permitted the formation of platforms or opinion groups among the membership. The new regulations gave a greater degree of independence to branches and to republican organizations and permitted members and branches at all levels to form horizontal links (previously regarded as incompatible with democratic centralism).[40]

There were further changes in the relationship between the Communist Party of the Soviet Union (CPSU) and society in the early 1990s, and there were additional alterations in the party's own operation. In a dramatic move in February 1990, the Central Committee approved Gorbachev's proposal that the party should abandon the constitutionally guaranteed monopoly that it had acquired in 1977. This was, as Gorbachev explained, simply a recognition that any real monopoly of this kind had already disappeared. Gorbachev was still concerned that the party play a "consolidating" role in Soviet political life and that it remain the "political leader" of society as a whole.[41] Gorbachev asked the delegates to the 28th Party Congress in July 1990 what such an "updated CPSU" would look like. It would be a party of the "socialist choice and communist perspective," committed at the same time to the common ideals of humanity. It would be one "freed of its ideological blinkers and dogmatism," promoting its policies through dialogue and cooperation with other "progressive" social and political forces. It would be a tolerant party, based upon a recognition of the rights of minorities and "total freedom of debate" and upon the independence of party organizations within a common program and statute.[42] The party's earlier "monolithic unity" had, in fact, already disappeared, with a series of revolts against local officials, a dramatic fall in membership, and with the secession of at least one republican party organization and the formation of about ten organized groupings within its ranks, ranging from neo-Stalinists to Social Democrats.[43]

In the former Soviet Union electoral choice, a working Parliament, and a democratized Communist Party that no longer exercised a political monopoly were among the necessary conditions for a pluralist order; but these were not sufficient. Particularly important among those requirements that remained was a free press (or at least a relatively autonomous one). As Gorbachev told the Central Committee that had elected him, "the better the people are informed, the more consciously they act, [and] the more actively they support the party, its plans and programmatic objectives."[44] The new policy of glasnost embraced an honest scrutiny of the Soviet past, including what Gorbachev described in November 1987 as the "wanton repression" of the 1930s, and it encompassed a more objective treatment of Old Bolsheviks such as Nikolai Bukharin and Leon Trotsky. The quality of public information improved, with the return—for the first time since the 1920s—of the collection and dissemination of official data on crime, abortion, suicide, and judicial execution. Disasters were finally acknowledged, such as the earthquake that had devastated Ashkhabad in 1948. The government even recognized the occurrence of a shooting at Novocherkassk in 1962 and divulged that twenty-four demonstrators had been killed and thirty-nine had been wounded.[45]

The leadership, in keeping with the new policy of freedom of the press, began to allow the publication of previously banned works of Russian writers; notable among them was Boris Pasternak's *Doctor Zhivago*. The work of recent émigrés followed, including, beginning in 1989, that of Aleksandr Solzhenitsyn. Later, foreign works were permitted, too. In 1990 the military-historical journal published extracts from Hitler's *Mein Kampf;* the foreign literature journal published Henry Miller's *Tropic of Cancer;* and a Kazakh journal, *Prostor,* even began to publish the work of the Marquis de Sade. The party organizational journal, meanwhile, was publishing Dale Carnegie's *How to Win Friends and Influence People*—to no very obvious effect.

The legislation that was supposed to protect these new freedoms was finally approved in June 1990. The result of a lengthy and sometimes acrimonious process of negotiation, the new press law did at least proclaim the right of all Soviet citizens to "express opinions and beliefs [and] to seek, select, receive, and disseminate information and ideas in any form."[46] The government abolished censorship, at least in principle, apart from a limited number of cases, including those concerned with the disclosure of state secrets or ones involving appeals for the violent overthrow of the state and social system. It also prohibited any media monopoly (again in principle) and gave individuals and political parties, as well as state bodies, the right to establish their own publications. All means of communication had to be registered with the authorities, however, and there were criminal penalties for the "abuse" of freedom of speech or for the dissemination of information that did not "correspond to reality." State control over printing presses and stocks of paper, in any case, meant that many of the rights provided in the new law were somewhat academic. This legislation, nonetheless, did provide a formal basis for a wider range of opinion in the Soviet media than had ever existed previously: There was *Tema,* the "voice of Soviet lesbians and homosexuals," and *Ekos,* the first Soviet "green" journal, as well as many publications that catered to business, religious, and other interests.[47] About 8,000 newspapers and journals had been registered under the new law by spring 1991; of these, about half were entirely new.[48]

The new press legislation was one of a series of laws that were intended to establish a secure foundation for a range of political freedoms. Gorbachev, a lawyer by training, told interviewers from *Der spiegel* that perestroika was as much a "legal revolution as a reform of the political system."[49] He set out the main elements of his thinking on this point in *Perestroika,* published in 1987. Democracy, he argued, "cannot exist and develop without the rule of law, because law is designed to protect society from abuses of power and guarantee citizens and their organizations and work collectives their rights and freedoms. This is the reason we have taken a firm stand on the issue. And we know from our own experience what happens when there are deviations from these principles."

Gorbachev felt that law, equally, should not be overprescriptive: It was better to follow the principle of "everything which is not prohibited by law is permitted." Important steps in this direction had already been taken, including passing legislation permitting appeals against the actions of officials and establishing a procedure for submitting important questions of public life to a process of national discussion. But much more remained to be done, including the adoption of measures that would guarantee the independence of judges and secure the "most strictly democratic principles" in the work of the courts.[50]

These principles found expression during 1988 in an entirely new concept, the "socialist rule-of-law state" (*sotsialisticheskoe pravovoe gosudarstvo*); first mentioned at a meeting between Gorbachev and media workers in May 1988, it was given more prominence in the theses that were published by the Central Committee in advance of the Party Conference. In turn, it became the centerpiece of a resolution adopted at the conference itself. This resolution called for "large-scale legal reform" over the coming years, including a review of existing codes of law, greater safeguards for the independence of judges, and an extensive program of legal education for the population as a whole.[51]

The process of reform was carried further in the constitutional amendments that the Supreme Soviet adopted in December 1988. In perhaps the most notable of these changes, an amendment established the twenty-three-person Committee of Constitutional Supervision, elected by the Congress of People's Deputies from "specialists in politics and law." This committee became responsible for ensuring the constitutionality of governmental decisions and draft legislation. The aim, Gorbachev indicated, was a "socialist system of checks and balances," designed to protect society from abuses of official power.[52] Legislation that concerned the courts, introduced in 1989, for the first time established the principle of the presumption of innocence. In 1991 the committee approved a new criminal code that reduced the number of offenses for which custodial sentences were mandatory, restricted the death penalty to "exceptional" cases, and made no reference to "anti-Soviet agitation and propaganda."[53]

All of these changes took place within the framework of a conception of "humane, democratic socialism," which was itself conceived of as a part of a broader process of the advance of civilization. Gorbachev resisted the adoption of a program that was like a "railway timetable," full (as Nikita Khrushchev's 1961 Party Program had been) of dates and stages by which this forward movement was to be accomplished. Speaking to the 28th Party Congress in July 1990 Gorbachev insisted that the ideology of socialism could not be set down in a textbook, in a kind of updated Stalinist *Short Course;* it could only be formed as the society itself developed and became part of the "general progress of civilization."[54] The Party Congress approved a programmatic declaration, "Towards a Humane, Democratic Socialism," which reflected these guidelines; in turn, it was superseded by the draft of an entirely new Party Program, published in summer 1991, after some months of open and private discussion. The program committed the party to social progress, humanism, and democracy, and more particularly to the separation of powers, the rule of law, and the amendment of existing legislation on human rights so that it corresponded to international norms. Communism remained, but as no more than a "historical perspective"; in effect, it was, as Leningrad leader Boris Gidaspov put it, the "inscription on a gravestone."[55]

The term "pluralism" originally had been a pejorative one, applicable to capitalist rather than socialist society. Gorbachev, from July 1987, began to suggest a very different conceptualization. The term first appeared in his discussion with media workers, in which he had urged them to ensure that "socialist pluralism, so to speak, was present in every publication."[56] When he was speaking to a group of French visitors two months later, Gorbachev described them as a "pluralistic complex" and went on to agree that Soviet society was increasingly pluralistic, provided only that it was described as "socialist."[57] In February 1988 Gorbachev spoke approvingly to the Central Committee of the "socialist pluralism of opinions" that they had begun to experience, and he even made positive references, later in the year, to a "pluralism of opinions" and a "pluralism of interests."[58] Gorbachev made further supporting references to pluralism, "socialist" or otherwise, at the 19th Party Conference in summer 1988.[59] At a meeting in Poland, Gorbachev even attempted to explain what he meant by the term—at any rate, he understood it to mean the opposite of "uniformity" or "spiritual unification."[60] In early 1989 Gorbachev was still opposed to "political pluralism," together with a multiparty system and private property.[61] But in summer 1989 at the First Congress of People's Deputies, there were again positive references to the "pluralism of opinions."[62] The 1991 Party Program showed that the transformation of thinking was complete: It referred to "political and ideological pluralism" as one of the features of the humane and socialist society that the party would seek to establish in the future.[63]

From Communism to Pluralism?

If the Gorbachev reforms had represented a "revolution from above," the attempted coup of August 1991 and the developments that followed it took the form of a "revolution from below."[64] The new union treaty, ready for signature on August 20, was swiftly superseded; the Commonwealth of Independent States (CIS) that replaced it in December was a loose and perhaps temporary association. All of the republics of the Soviet Union (apart from Russia) declared their formal independence. The three Baltic republics had their independence acknowledged by what were then still the Soviet authorities as well as by the international community. The USSR armed forces and the interior ministry were depoliticized,[65] and the KGB was restructured and placed under new management.[66] A series of newspapers and journals seized the opportunity to become independent of their institutional sponsors, and many also changed their names—the party theoretical journal, for instance, moved improbably from *Kommunist* to *Svobodnaya mysl'* (Free thought). Above all, the Communist Party was suspended, its property was confiscated, and its activity was banned in most of the republics.[67] The Congress of People's Deputies, in what proved to be its last meeting, adopted the "Declaration of the Rights and Freedoms of the Individual," which came close to a bill of rights.[68] In December 1991 Gorbachev resigned, and the Soviet Union was formally dissolved. Now, at last, the way seemed open to a new and genuinely pluralist political system.

There were certainly parallels between these developments and their counterparts in East-Central Europe.[69] In almost every case, a fall in economic growth rates had led to tensions and had placed an intolerable strain upon the "social contract" by which the regimes concerned traded a restricted range of political rights for a secure and steadily improving standard of living.[70] Soviet economic decline had reached a critical stage by the early 1990s: There was an unprecedented decrease in national income in 1990 and in 1991 a fall of about 15 percent, with a further 18 percent predicted for 1992.[71] The rate of inflation, 19 percent in 1990, had reached 20 percent per month by early 1992.[72] The number of unemployed persons was expected to reach at least 2 million by the end of 1992, with forecasts that ranged as high as 20 million.[73] Shortages of consumer goods became still more widespread; by 1991 drinking water was being rationed.[74] In at least one Soviet city coupons were even being issued for burials.[75] Not that coupons were a solution: They were often counterfeit. The goods that could be purchased with coupons were sometimes unobtainable and, at any rate, did not provide the basis of an adequate diet.[76] According to the polls, people did not believe that the communist authorities, in summer 1991, had a credible program for extracting the country from these difficulties. Only 2 percent of people polled expected a "considerable improvement"; 18 percent thought there would be "some improvement," 27 percent anticipated that the situation would be worse in the future, and 36 percent thought things would get much worse.[77]

In parallel with these developments and in line with the experience of those in Eastern Europe, there was a sharp fall in public support for the regime and its political institutions. During 1990 Gorbachev's approval rating as president and general secretary fell from 60 percent to 12 percent; by the end of 1991, in a poll designed to find the Soviet Union's most popular politician, it had fallen as low as 4 percent.[78] When they were asked to comment in more detail in spring 1991, 28 percent (the largest group) found the Soviet president "hypocritical and two-faced"; 20 percent found him "flexible and able to maneuver." The same proportion, however, found him "weak and lacking in self-confidence"; and 18 percent thought him "indifferent to human suffering." Boris Yeltsin, by contrast, was "open and straightforward" (34 percent), "ambitious" (26 percent), but also "resolute" (24 percent).[79] There was a corresponding decline in public support for the Communist Party, the regime's central support for more than seventy years. In February 1989, 37 percent were prepared to trust the party, but by 1990 only 8 percent were willing to do so, and by September 1991—just after the coup and the party's suspension—its level of support was down to 2.3 percent.[80] The Soviet government, for its part, was "probably held in deeper contempt than any other in the world" by late summer 1991, and support for Marxism/Leninism in general was down to 2 percent of the population at large.[81]

This situation at least appeared to satisfy two of the necessary conditions for transition to a postcommunist order: economic decline and a collapse of regime legitimacy. To establish and maintain a stable, self-sustaining pluralist system, however, there are still further requirements. One of these, according to an older, but still instructive, literature, is an identification with democratic institutions in themselves, quite apart from the material benefits they may provide.[82] Another requirement, according to a newer literature that has itself been heavily influenced by the experience of communist rule in Eastern Europe, is a civil society; in other words, a network of autonomous and self-regulating civic associations of various kinds, from political clubs to sporting societies and church groups.[83] An "alternative society" of this kind allowed Solidarity in Poland the political space in which to sustain its challenge to the communist authorities; and the framework of the Lutheran church in East Germany, similarly, allowed a broadly based coalition of oppositionists to develop into a political movement powerful enough to bring down the regime itself. A civil society helped to undermine totalitarian structures by providing a realm of citizen self-activity that was beyond the reach of government, and the parties and movements that matured within this civil society could then provide the basis of a postcommunist regime.

Viewed from this perspective, there were at least three features of the political system that emerged from the former Soviet Union after the demise of communist rule that suggested a stable pluralist order might still lie some distance in the future. The first of these is the weakness of the party system that emerged in the late 1980s and that was then responsible for providing political leadership in the early 1990s. There was certainly no shortage of political organizations, as such: By summer 1992 more than one thousand parties, movements, or foundations had been registered in Russia alone, including twenty-five officially registered political parties, with a further dozen that had not yet completed the necessary formalities at the Ministry of Justice.[84] Some organizations restored the names of prerevolutionary parties, like the Constitutional Democrats; others took more obvious labels, such as the Social Democratic Party; and still others were more innovative. There was a Humor Party, for instance, formed in Odessa, and an Idiots'

Party of Russia, certain of victory in a "land of fools," whose slogan was "give the people beer and sausage." There was even a "Union of Stalinists."[85] A guide to the newly formed parties and associations published in late 1991 listed over 300 organizations, covering the entire spectrum from the far Left (with 9 separate anarchist parties) to the far Right (with 17 different monarchist groups).[86]

The new parties, however, suffered from a number of serious weaknesses. For a start, they had relatively few members. Some did not keep central records and they, therefore, could not report any figures; others kept their membership lists secret; others exaggerated the numbers; and in all cases there was double-counting. Some organizations were centrally disciplined neo-Bolshevik parties, and others were loose confederations that allowed the formation of fractions, even of communists, within their ranks. Taking these various circumstances into account, it was still clear that by the early 1990s no grouping of parties had emerged that could take the place of the formerly dominant CPSU. The People's Party of Free Russia, led by Russian vice-president Aleksandr Rutskoi, appeared to be the largest of the new parties in the early 1990s, with a claimed membership of at least 100,000 people. Nikolai Travkin's Democratic Party of Russia, with about 50,000 members, was the second largest party; the "Left centrist" Republican Party, with an estimated 20,000 members, was third in size; and Socialist and Christian Democrats each had about 10,000 members. Taken together, the new parties could count upon approximately 300,000 members, or about 30,000 activists.[87] All of them could not compare with the 15 million members the CPSU still commanded in summer 1991 and the 46,000 that were prepared to join it in the first three months of the year.[88]

The new parties, moreover, received the support of a very limited proportion of the total population. Polls in summer 1991 found that about 69 percent of the mass public had no clear party preference at all; but of those that did, the Communist Party still came in first, with 19 percent supporting it. Democratic Russia, a coalition of reformers rather than a party, as such, came in second with 7 percent; the Democratic Party had 2 percent; and then came the Social Democratic, Peasant, and other parties, with 1 percent support or less.[89] When asked how they would vote in an election in summer 1992, 3 percent supported the "patriots," 5 percent the (illegal) Communists, but no more than 14 percent supported the "democrats." A massive 50 percent favored no party at all, but wanted "experienced practical people and industrialists, regardless of party affiliation."[90] This hardly suggested a nascent party system.

In addition to limited support, the new parties were prone to damaging splits (as when Gary Kasparov left the Democratic Party in spring 1991[91]), and they proved incapable of forming stable groups in the Soviet or the Russian parliament. Gorbachev, speaking to U.S. senators in 1990, described the USSR as the "most politicized society in the contemporary world."[92] The elements concerned, however, were still very fluid, and it would clearly be some time before Russia and the other successor states established competing, nationally organized parties that could offer a coherent alternative to the CPSU (in the view of some Western scholars, this process could take seventy years or more[93]).

A second major weakness was the lack of a firmly based rule of law, before or even after the end of communist administration. A rule of law was essential if any boundary was to be drawn and maintained between the state and the civil society, and it was necessary if the "politicization of society," which was a characteristic of totalitarianism, was to be resisted. The attempted coup was at least nominally legal: The State Emergency Committee based their action upon article 127(7) of the Constitution, which stated that if the president of the USSR were unable to perform his duties "for any reason," his functions would automatically pass to the vice-president. (The Constitution was changed in September 1991 to guard against any repetition of these circumstances. Under the new Constitution, if the president were unable to perform his functions for reasons of ill health, a medical commission appointed by the Supreme Soviet would have to confirm the diagnosis and the newly formed State Council would elect a temporary president from its own membership.[94]) The defeat of the coup and the demise of communist rule, for their part, have been followed by a series of actions that give little reason to believe that the new Russian system will be marked by the supremacy of law.

One of the earliest actions was the decree issued by President Yeltsin banning a series of newspapers, for the most part those that the Emergency Committee had allowed to appear. Under the Law on the Press, however, adopted in June 1990, a newspaper may be suspended or banned only if it advocates the forcible overthrow of the government. Whatever their criticisms of the Gorbachev leadership, *Pravda, Sovetskaia Rossiia,* and the other newspapers concerned had hardly been advocating any action of the kind. In any case, the banning or suspension of a newspaper, under the new law, must be the result of a court decision, not a politician's directive, and only after evidence has been produced in support of the charges and, if necessary, contested.

As *Izvestiia* pointed out, there were "quite a few precedents" for actions of this kind in world history, but they had always been associated with seizures of power, never with democratic transformations. "The power of government to decide where information in the press is 'accurate' and where it is 'false,'" the paper argued, "is the first step to dictatorship."[95] The head of Soviet radio and television, Leonid Kravchenko, was similarly dismissed by a Russian presidential decree in the immediate aftermath of the coup. Whatever his shortcomings (and he had, it emerged, given his backing to the coup) this was an action that clearly exceeded the proper powers of that office.[96]

Nor, it appeared, was there an adequate legal basis for the suspension of the Communist Party (the Russian Constitutional Court itself began to examine the issue in summer 1992). As a department head at the Moscow Juridical Institute pointed out, the party could properly be suspended only under a state of emergency. This was no longer in force after the coup had collapsed and after the Emergency Committee's actions had been repudiated. Similarly, the existing law did not allow the nationalization of the property of the CPSU or of any other public organization. Under the Law on Public Associations, adopted in October 1990, the property of liquidated organizations reverted to the state; but the Communist Party had not been liquidated and only the USSR Supreme Court could adopt a decision to that effect.[97] The Russian Parliament went still further in November 1991 when it authorized Yeltsin to suspend elections and referenda until December 1992 and to form local administrations and appoint members to them throughout the Russian Federation. More than this, he was specifically authorized to issue decrees in a limited number of areas, even if these contradicted existing Russian or Soviet laws.[98] Yeltsin, who had suspended the operations of the Communist Party in Russia just after the August coup, banned the party outright in November 1991 on the grounds that the coup had been the "logical outcome" of Communist Party policies; this action was again without judicial foundation.[99]

A lack of respect for legality was not a new phenomenon in Soviet or Russian political practice. During 1990 all the Soviet republics in turn had adopted declarations on sovereignty, insisting that their own laws took precedence over those of the USSR, even though the Soviet Constitution (in article 74) provided exactly the opposite. The Soviet president, Gorbachev, despite his verbal support for a law-based state, had himself issued a decree on economic sabotage in January 1991 that allowed private homes to be entered by the police, despite the constitutional guarantee of the inviolability of the home.[100] Law, in fact, had come to have very little influence of any kind by the early 1990s. As Russian Vice-President Aleksander Rutskoi complained in October 1991, Russia had become a country of "absolute powerlessness ... We approve mountains of laws, but no one carries them out, as there is no mechanism for the management of the state or for ensuring implementation. As a result, anarchy rules."[101] By summer 1992 the Russian Constitutional Court warned that the state was being threatened by a wave of "legal nihilism," organized crime, calls for the violent overthrow of public bodies, military involvement in political disputes, and falling trust in government. For the Constitutional Court, as well as for Rutskoi, the immediate prospect was "anarchy," rather than the rule of law.[102]

It was a final and related weakness of the new pluralist order that it appeared to count upon the limited and qualified support of the mass public. There was certainly substantial support, in the abstract, for a multiparty system and for many of the most familiar democratic freedoms. In USSR-wide surveys conducted in 1990, for instance, 54 percent agreed that the competition of various parties strengthened the political system; more than half believed that "the further democratization of society is impossible without the direct involvement of all citizens in the administration of the country"; and about 40 percent claimed to be "supporters or sympathizers" of the new parties and movements.[103] At the same time, several national polls have found substantial support for a "firm hand," rather than for democracy (about 35 percent took this view in a survey in summer 1991[104]). Though large majorities saw the attempted coup as illegal, there was relatively little support for the call for a national strike to oppose it. Gorbachev himself, speaking with journalists after the coup, concluded that as many as 40 percent of the population had actually supported the conspirators.[105] Polls in Kazakhstan, conducted while the coup was taking place, found that the coup had and, indeed, continued to have a "real social base." At least half of those surveyed supported the coup or took an indifferent attitude toward it; and there was a tendency for this support to increase over time.[106]

The coup was certainly defeated by the crowds that gathered to support the "White House," where the Russian Parliament held its meetings. The evidence, nonetheless, suggests a relatively weak level of attachment to representative institutions. It also suggests a steady fall in support for the new institutions of state as the leaders of these bodies argue about procedure while the standard of living of ordinary citizens continues to fall. The "ratings" of newly elected soviets have steadily declined: In August 1991 in St. Petersburg, for instance, only 13 percent did not trust the city administration, and 6 percent did not trust Mayor Anatolii Sobchak; but by March 1992, 55 percent were distrustful of the administration and 54 percent were distrustful of the mayor; about one-third were indifferent.[107] A relatively small minority (26 percent) were planning to vote for the same candidate in future elections; a larger group, 42 percent, were intending to vote against, and many had no intention of voting at all.[108] Of those who were polled on the 6th Congress of Peoples' Deputies in April 1992, a little more than one-quarter (27.2 percent) took a positive view of its activities; more than one-half (51.4 percent) were disapproving; and almost as many (45.7 percent) thought there would be no improvement in public life as a result of the activities of the Congress. (A further 15.7 percent thought things would get worse, notwithstanding the Congress's actions.[109]) Political power, in any case, seemed to lie elsewhere: either with the party authorities (until the 1991 coup) or with the mafia; in summer 1992 only 7 percent thought it lay with the Russian government.[110] The opinion of the public on matters of this kind appeared to reflect "political alienation." Forty-five percent of people said that the deputies they elect "soon forget about our interests." According to another inquiry, there was a general sense of "pessimism and indifference to politics."[111]

This general decline in support for all soviets, all parties, and all leaders (including Yeltsin) was combined with a relatively low level of attachment to civil rights and a sharply hostile attitude toward minorities. Public attitudes tended to be sharply polarized, much more often "against" than "for," and people were more inclined to denounce rather than compromise. The most characteristic attitudes during 1990, according to the polls, were "hatred and aggression."[112] Levels of interethnic hostility, perhaps surprisingly, appeared to be lower in the USSR than in European countries;[113] ethnic and communal tensions, nonetheless, had led to about one thousand deaths by 1990, and 600,000 people had become refugees within what were then Soviet borders.[114] Attitudes toward other minorities, however, were much more intolerant. According to surveys conducted in

1990, a startling 33.7 percent would "liquidate" all homosexuals; similar proportions would "liquidate" all prostitutes (28.4 percent), drug addicts (28 percent), hippies (21.2 percent), and the congenitally abnormal (22.7 percent).[115] In a separate poll in summer 1991, 30 percent of a national sample repeated the call for homosexuals to be put to death; another 30 percent favored imprisonment; and a further 30 percent approved of compulsory medical treatment. In Central Asia support for the death penalty ran as high as 85 percent.[116]

Postcommunist Russia, accordingly, entered the 1990s with its democratic institutions intact but still insecurely founded. It must be remembered that Russia's historical inheritance is very different from that of most of the East-Central European nations. Russia had no experience of Roman law (with its conceptions of private property and due process); it had a very limited experience of independent party activity and competitive elections (just a decade or so before the revolution); and it lacked the articulated class formations that, in the European countries, had held the monarchy in check and that had helped to establish a representative government in their own interests.[117] Broader theories of modernization failed to take account of this national specificity; and seventy years of Soviet rule had scarcely supplied the experience of democratic rule that earlier centuries had not provided. Yeltsin, in a press interview, spoke of a stage of "early democracy" being successfully completed by the time his term of office expired in 1996.[118] Unless Russia's fledgling democracy is sustained by a corresponding network of attitudes, practices, and institutions, its future might once again be undermined by much longer-standing traditions of firm or even authoritarian government as economic collapse continues and the national territory fragments.

Notes

Thanks are due to Vladimir Brovkin and Carol Saivetz for their comments on an earlier version of this chapter.

1. Stephen White, "Communist Systems and the 'Iron Law of Pluralism'," *British Journal of Political Science* 8, no. 1 (January 1978), p. 104.

2. The standard exposition is Carl J. Friedrich and Zbigniew K. Brzezinski, *Totalitarian Dictatorship and Autocracy,* 2d ed. (Cambridge, MA: Harvard University Press, 1965).

3. See, for instance, Timothy Dunmore, *Soviet Politics, 1945–1953* (London: Macmillan, 1984).

4. For this transition see J. F. Brown, *Surge to Freedom: The End of Communist Rule in Eastern Europe* (Durham, NC: Duke University Press, 1991).

5. See Andrej Korbonski, "Soviet–East European Relations in the 1980s: Continuity and Change," in Marco Carnovale and William C. Potter, eds., *Continuity and Change in Soviet–East European Relations* (Boulder, CO: Westview, 1989), p. 22.

6. Z. K. Brzezinski, *The Grand Failure: The Birth and Death of Communism in the Twentieth Century* (New York: Scribner's, 1989).

7. R. V. Burks, "The Coming Crisis in the Soviet Union," *East European Quarterly* 18 (Spring 1984), pp. 61–71; Richard Pipes, "Can the Soviet Union Reform?" *Foreign Affairs* 63 (Fall 1984), p. 50.

8. Developmental theories are discussed at greater length in Stephen White, *Political Culture and Soviet Politics* (New York: St. Martin's, 1980), ch. 8.

9. This information is based on Talcott Parsons, "Evolutionary Universals in Society," *American Sociological Review* 29, no. 3 (June 1964), pp. 339–57. Parsons argued elsewhere that the communist states would be compelled to evolve in the direction of the restoration—or where it had not existed, the institution—of political democracy; this was the "*only* possible outcome—except for general destruction or Breakdown" ("Communism and the West: The Sociology of the Conflict," in Amitai Etzioni and Eva Etzioni, eds., *Social Change: Sources, Patterns and Consequences* [New York: Basic Books, 1964], pp. 396–8). Parsons accordingly is misconceived as a theorist of convergence, as suggested in Roland Robertson and Bryan S. Turner, eds., *Talcott Parsons: Theorist of Modernity* (London: Sage, 1991), p. 226.

10. Samuel Huntington has included David Easton, David Apter, and Gabriel Almond among those who have developed the Parsonian tradition. See Fred I. Greenstein and Nelson W. Polsby, eds., *Handbook of Political Science,* vol. 3 (Reading, MA: Addison-Wesley, 1975), p. 3.

11. Robert A. Dahl, *Polyarchy* (New Haven and London: Yale University Press, 1971), pp. 64–5, 77–9, 218.

12. Alexander Eckstein, "Economic Development and Political Change in Communist Systems," *World Politics* 22, no. 4 (July 1970), pp. 475–95.

13. Merle Fainsod, "The Dynamics of One-Party Systems," in Oliver Garceau, ed., *Political Research and Political Theory* (Cambridge, MA: Harvard University Press, 1968), pp. 227–9.

14. Samuel Huntington and Clement H. Moore, eds., *Authoritarian Politics in Modern Society* (New York: Basic Books, 1970), pp. 40–1 and 513; Roy Medvedev, *Kniga o sotsialisticheskoi demokratii* (Amsterdam and Paris: Herzen Foundation and Grasset and Fasquelle, 1972), p. 118; Karl W. Deutsch, "Cracks in the Monolith," in Harry Eckstein and David A. Apter, eds., *Comparative Politics: A Reader* (New York: Free Press, 1963), p. 506.

15. Gabriel A. Almond, *Political Development* (Boston: Little, Brown, 1970), pp. 27 and 318–19.

16. For a review of these developments see Karen Dawisha, *Eastern Europe, Gorbachev, and Reform,* 2d ed. (New York: Cambridge University Press, 1990).

17. For the "iron law" see White, "Communist Systems."

18. Moshe Lewin, *Political Undercurrents in Soviet Economic Debates* (Princeton, NJ: Princeton University Press, 1975), pp. 264–7.

19. Moshe Lewin, *The Gorbachev Phenomenon* (Berkeley, CA: University of California Press, 1988), pp. 146–7.

20. Lucian W. Pye, "Political Science and the Crisis of Authoritarianism," *American Political Science Review* 84, no. 1 (March 1990), pp. 6–11.

21. Isaac Deutscher, *The Unfinished Revolution: Russia 1917–1967* (London: Oxford University Press, 1968), pp. 59–60 (slightly adapted).

22. The wider context of reform during the Gorbachev years is considered in Richard Sakwa, *Gorbachev and His Reforms, 1985–1990* (London: Philip Allan, 1990); and Stephen White, *Gorbachev and After,* 3d ed. (New York: Cambridge University Press, 1992).

23. See Stephen White, "Noncompetitive Elections and National Politics: The USSR Supreme Soviet Elections of 1984," *Electoral Studies* 4, no. 3 (1985), p. 222. On electoral

reform in general see Stephen White, "Reforming the Electoral System," in Walter Joyce et al., eds., *Gorbachev and Gorbachevism* (London: Cass, 1989), pp. 1–17.

24. *Pravda*, March 7, 1984, p. 1.

25. Ibid., December 4, 1988, pp. 1–3.

26. See Stephen White, "From Acclamation to Limited Choice: The Soviet Elections of 1989," *Coexistence* 28, no. 4 (December 1991), pp. 77–103.

27. See Darrell Slider, "The Soviet Union," and Rein Taagepera, "The Baltic States," *Electoral Studies* 9, no. 4 (December 1990), pp. 295–302 and pp. 303–11, respectively.

28. *Materialy XIX Vsesoyuznoi konferentsii KPSS* (Moscow: Politizdat, 1988), p. 35.

29. For information on the Supreme Soviet's discussion see Stephen White, "'Democratisation' in the Soviet Union," *Soviet Studies* 42, no. 1 (January 1990), pp. 3–24.

30. *Pravda*, December 3, 1988, pp. 1–2.

31. *Izvestiia*, June 3, 1991, p. 3.

32. Ibid., November 5, 1991, p. 2. For the cost of the old Supreme Soviet see *Soviet Weekly*, August 12, 1989, p. 4.

33. *Materialy XIX Vsesoyuznoi konferentsii*, pp. 70–3.

34. Ibid., pp. 124–8.

35. *Pravda*, February 10, 1987, p. 2.

36. Ibid., October 1, 1988, p. 1; and *Materialy Tsentral'nogo Komiteta KPSS 8–9 oktyabrya 1990* (Moscow: Politizdat, 1990), p. 201.

37. *Izvestiia TsK KPSS*, 1989, no. 1, pp. 81–91.

38. Ibid., 1989, no. 7, p. 113. It turned out that the Communist Party of the Soviet Union had three American members, seven Englishmen, and 125 Eskimos.

39. *Izvestiia*, March 24, 1989, p. 3; and *Pravda*, July 29, 1990, pp. 1–2.

40. *Materialy XXVIII S"ezda KPSS* (Moscow: Politizdat, 1990), pp. 38–9.

41. *Pravda*, February 6, 1990, pp. 1–2.

42. *XXVIII S"ezd Kommunisticheskoi Partii Sovetskogo Soyuza: Stenograficheskii Otchet*, 2 vols. (Moscow: Politizdat, 1991), Vol. 1, p. 90.

43. See Stephen White, "Rethinking the CPSU," *Soviet Studies* 43, no. 3 (1991), pp. 408–11.

44. M. S. Gorbachev, *Izbrannye rechi i stat'i*, 7 vols. (Moscow: Politizdat, 1987–1990), Vol. 2, p. 131.

45. *Sovetskaia kul'tura*, June 16, 1988, p. 2; *Pravda*, June 3, 1991, p. 4.

46. *Izvestiia*, June 20, 1990, p. 3.

47. *Komsomol'skaia pravda*, October 7, 1990, p. 2, and *Izvestiia*, March 14, 1991, p. 1.

48. *Pravda*, April 5, 1991, p. 3.

49. Ibid., October 24, 1988, p. 2.

50. Mikhail Gorbachev, *Perestroika* (London: Collins, 1987), pp. 105–9.

51. *Materialy XIX Vsesoyuznoi konferentsii*, pp. 145–8.

52. *Pravda*, December 3, 1988, pp. 1–2.

53. Ibid., July 16, 1989, p. 2; *Izvestiia*, July 19, 1991, pp. 2–3.

54. *XXVIII S"ezd KPSS*, Vol. 2, pp. 196–7.

55. For the text of the draft program, see *Kommunist*, 1991, no. 12, pp. 3–15; and see Boris Gidaspov, *Pravda*, July 27, 1990, p. 4.

56. Gorbachev, *Izbrannye rechi*, Vol. 5, p. 219.

57. Ibid., p. 300; and *Pravda*, September 30, 1987, p. 1.

58. Gorbachev, *Izbrannye rechi,* Vol. 6, pp. 61, 205, 212.

59. Ibid., pp. 342, 393, 401, 411.

60. Ibid., p. 442.

61. Ibid., Vol. 7, p. 228.

62. Ibid., pp. 588–9, 591.

63. *Kommunist,* 1991, no. 12, p. 10.

64. For this distinction see Judy Batt, "The End of Communist Rule in East-Central Europe," *Government and Opposition* 26, no. 3 (Summer 1991), pp. 368–90.

65. *Rossiiskaia gazeta,* October 23, 1991, p. 1.

66. *Izvestiia,* October 23, 1991, p. 1.

67. See ibid., August 30, 1991, p. 2; the party was banned at the same time in several republics, including Ukraine (*Pravda,* September 2, 1991, p. 3).

68. *Pravda,* September 7, 1991, pp. 1–2.

69. See, for instance, Batt, "End of Communist Rule"; Paul G. Lewis, "Democratization in Eastern Europe," *Coexistence* 27, no. 4 (December 1990), pp. 245–68; and Grzegorz Ekiert, "Democratization Processes in East-Central Europe: A Theoretical Reconsideration," *British Journal of Political Science* 21, no. 4 (October 1991), pp. 285–313.

70. See, for instance, Ferenc Feher, Agnes Heller, and Gyorgy Markus, *Dictatorship over Needs* (Oxford: Blackwell, 1983), pp. 104, 277–9.

71. *Izvestiia,* May 8, 1992, p. 5.

72. Ibid., June 19, 1992, p. 1.

73. Ibid., June 17, 1992, p. 2.

74. In the city of Ufa: *Komsomol'skaia pravda,* March 12, 1991, p. 2.

75. In the city of Kazan': *Izvestiia,* August 1, 1991, p. 1.

76. See White, *Gorbachev and After,* p. 139.

77. *Soviet Weekly,* August 15, 1991, p. 7.

78. Ibid., p. 6; *Argumenty i fakty,* 1991, no. 34, p. 1. (In these polls 74 percent of the people supported Yeltsin).

79. *Nezavisimaia gazeta,* February 28, 1991, p. 1.

80. *Izvestiia,* October 1, 1991, p. 9.

81. *Soviet Weekly,* August 15, 1991, p. 6; *Izvestiia TsK KPSS,* 1990, no. 8, p. 129.

82. See Gabriel Almond and Sidney Verba, *The Civic Culture* (Princeton, NJ: Princeton University Press, 1963). For the continuing discussion see Gabriel Almond and Sidney Verba, eds., *The Civic Culture Revisited* (Boston: Little, Brown, 1980).

83. For a helpful account of a voluminous literature see John Keane, ed., *Civil Society and the State* (London: Verso, 1988); and John Keane, *Democracy and Civil Society* (London: Verso, 1988).

84. *Argumenty i fakty,* 1992, no. 24, p. 8; *Izvestiia,* April 20, 1992, p. 2.

85. For a general overview, see V. N. Berezovsky et al., eds., *Rossiia: partii, assotsiatsii, soiuzy, kluby,* 2 vols. (Moscow: RAU-Press, 1991). For the Humor Party see *Pravda,* March 30, 1991, p. 1; for the Idiots' Party see *Pravda,* October 14, 1991, p. 1; and for the Union of Stalinists see *Izvestiia,* March 4, 1992, p. 1.

86. See Berezovsky et al., *Rossiia.*

87. *Izvestiia,* April 20, 1992, p. 2.

88. *Partiinaia zhizn',* 1991, no. 11, p. 6.

89. *Pravda,* July 2, 1991, p. 3.

90. *Nezavisimaia gazeta,* July 29, 1992, p. 2.

91. *Izvestiia,* April 26, 1991, p. 4.

92. *Pravda,* April 13, 1990, p. 1.

93. See Philip Converse, "Of Time and Partisan Stability," *Comparative Political Studies* 2, no. 2 (July 1969), pp. 139–71.

94. *Vedomosti S"ezda Narodnykh Deputatov i Verkhovnogo Soveta SSSR,* 1991, no. 37, item 1082, art. 4.

95. *Izvestiia,* August 24, 1991, p. 2.

96. *Pravda,* August 23, 1991, p. 3; *Izvestiia,* August 24, 1991, p. 2.

97. *Pravda,* September 10, 1991, p. 2.

98. *Izvestiia,* October 30, 1991, p. 2.

99. Ibid., November 7, 1991, p. 1.

100. *Sovetskoe gosudarstvo i pravo,* 1991, no. 7, p. 5; the decree on economic sabotage was later rescinded; *Pravda,* October 22, 1991, p. 1.

101. *Pravda,* October 10, 1991, p. 1.

102. *Izvestiia,* June 27, 1992, p. 1.

103. *Politicheskie issledovaniia,* 1991, no. 2, p. 22; *Sotsiologicheskie issledovaniia,* 1990, no. 10, pp. 24 and 22. Similar conclusions are drawn by Jeffrey Hahn, "Continuity and Change in Russian Political Culture," *British Journal of Political Science* 21, no. 4 (October 1991), pp. 393–421.

104. *Argumenty i fakty,* 1991, no. 41, p. 1.

105. *Izvestiia,* September 20, 1991, p. 3.

106. Ibid., August 27, 1991, p. 3.

107. Ibid., April 18, 1992, p. 2.

108. *Izvestiia TsK KPSS,* 1991, no. 1, p. 65.

109. *Pravda,* April 23, 1992, p. 1.

110. *Izvestiia,* May 25, 1992, p. 3.

111. A. A. Protashchik, ed., *Cherez ternii* (Moscow: Progress, 1989), p. 777; *Pravda,* May 30, 1992, p. 2.

112. *Dialog,* 1991, no. 5, p. 5.

113. *Times-Mirror* poll reported in the *Guardian* (London), October 4, 1991, pp. 21.

114. *Dialog,* 1990, no. 9, p. 88.

115. *Obshchestvennoe mnenie v tsifrakh,* no. 2, 1990, p. 11.

116. *Argumenty i fakty,* 1991, no. 30, p. 5.

117. Max Weber's reflections on these subjects remain instructive: see *Voprosy filosofii,* 1990, no. 8, pp. 119–30.

118. *Izvestiia,* July 15, 1992, p. 3.

CHAPTER 2

Pluralism and the New Press in Russia

Mervyn Matthews

The Soviet media are a subject that could occupy many volumes, and indeed much has already been written about them. My main objectives here are necessarily narrow: to document important changes in the newspaper world in Russia during a period of social and economic turmoil (approximately from 1986 to spring 1992); to outline the fate of the old, Stalinist-type press; and to discuss the problems faced by new publications. Although my main focus is on newspapers, I shall occasionally refer to magazines and broadcasting when this is needed to complete the picture.[1]

I use the term "Stalinist" with due consideration, as one can easily argue that despite a growth in volume and coverage, the Soviet press changed little in essence between the late 1920s and Mikhail Gorbachev's advent to power. Following a brief review of the Soviet press as it was during this period under Joseph Stalin, Nikita Khrushchev, and Leonid Brezhnev, I shall consider the legal milestones on the path of change through 1990 and 1991. I shall then conclude with an overview of the availability of the larger newspapers, as discernible in early 1992.

My account embraces four distinct themes, namely: legal guarantees of freedom of expression (which must form the basis of any truly pluralistic press); the extent of continuing state involvement in newspaper publishing; the new commercialization of the press; and the current circulations of "old" and "new" (mainly post-1987) newspapers. It is tempting to treat each theme individually, but so intertwined are they that a combined chronological treatment appears to be most convenient.

The Soviet Press Before Perestroika

Most aspects of newspaper publishing in the former USSR are familiar to readers and require no more than a brief listing here. In terms of volume, the Soviet press was quite impressive; by the mid-1980s the USSR was producing, according to official data, 8,427 newspapers and 5,180 magazines. Of the former, about one thousand were central or *oblast'* publications, and 471 came out five or seven times a week. The Soviet press was generally characterized by an enormous gross circulation: a full print-run of all titles together could exceed 190 million copies. This compared with some 9,100 newspapers in the United States and a circulation of about 63 million copies.[2]

The Soviet papers were generally long established and free from economic pressure.[3] The larger ones made profits on the basis of low fixed costs, but many local papers had small, uneconomic print-runs and had to be supported by party or state subsidies. Until the mid-1980s (when policies began to change) advertising was deliberately restricted. If any newspapers closed, it was through administrative order rather than financial failure. Technical control and coordination of publishing generally lay in the hands of the union-republican State Committees for Publishing, Printing, and the Book Trade (Goskomizdat).[4]

As for printing establishments, some were dedicated to a given paper or group of papers (like the *Pravda* house in Moscow); some belonged to so-called social organizations, particularly the trade unions; others to ministries and state committees; and yet another type was owned directly by Goskomizdat.[5] The configuration of ownership and publication was apparently never revealed, but final control undoubtedly lay in one or more departments of the Central Committee of the Communist Party of the Soviet Union (CPSU). Paper was allocated by state order and at low state prices. As for the distribution of newspapers, the larger ones went out mainly to subscribers, but a proportion of all print-runs was sold directly through the Soyuzpechat' network (which operated some 38,000 kiosks in 1985); this was a monopolistic branch of the Ministry of Communications.[6] Newspaper prices were nominal at just a very few kopeks per issue.

Control over the printed word in the USSR has been well explored by outsiders—insofar as exploration has been possible.[7] Officially, freedom of expression and publication was guaranteed, but only "in accordance with the interests of the toilers and with the aim of strengthening the socialist structure," by article 50 of the 1977 USSR Constitution. Such freedom in practice was further limited by a number of well-known instruments. Foremost among them were the infamous articles of the USSR Fundamentals of Criminal Law and the republican criminal codes, covering anti-Soviet propaganda and agitation, slandering the Soviet state, and breaching the rules of state secrecy.[8] On this basis a stringent union-republican system of censorship (*Glavnoe upravlenie po okhrane gosudarstvennykh tain v pechati*) perused all texts before publication and ensured the observance of prohibitions listed in detailed handbooks. The importation of foreign publications was restricted and foreign broadcasts were jammed. Under long-standing rules (somewhat revised in 1958 and 1959) state legislative bodies could, at their own discretion, abstain from publishing acts and decrees, which meant that much of the oppressive legal edifice was invisible to the public. In the arts, the doctrine of socialist realism precluded direct criticism of Soviet reality, as indeed did obligatory adherence to the tenets of Marxism-Leninism.

The result of all this, as is well known, was a cheap but extremely uninformative press, often with multiple printing of identical texts and careful exclusion of almost all that was negative or detrimental to any current leadership. These stringencies provoked, probably from the mid-1950s, a tiny but vigorous "samizdat" (underground literature) movement, mostly comprising individual documents and appeals typed with carbon copies and distributed among friends. The largest and sturdiest of them was probably the *Chronicle of Current Events,* founded in 1967 and still available in the 1980s. The samizdat movement reached its peak in the 1970s, after which it was largely suppressed, being, of course, illegal under Soviet law. The overall output of samizdat was nevertheless politically significant; by the end of the 1980s, for example, the Radio Liberty "Materialy samizdata" series contained some six thousand documents.[9]

The Effects of Perestroika and Glasnost, 1985–1990

The stages in Gorbachev's glasnost campaign have been followed by many observers and need no detailed exposition here.[10] It was apparent soon after the 27th Party Congress (held in February 1986) that significant changes were afoot. First, Gorbachev was prepared to tolerate a degree of political freedom, preferably in the form of mild opposition to the CPSU, which required overt public involvement. Second, though he did not embrace freedom of speech as we understand it, Gorbachev called for "openness," so as to allow the media to reveal, and alleviate, social problems. Third, he favored some limited forms of private enterprise that could be of relevance to newspaper publishing.

These policies were to have profound effects on the Soviet press; although there were at first no significant institutional changes, a trickle of untoward facts in the "traditional" newspapers—references to dissidents, accidents, crime, and social problems—soon suggested that the censors' handbooks were being revised or overridden.[11]

A firm indication that legal relaxation was envisaged came with the publication, in August 1986, of a list of planned legislative acts and government decrees. This list contained an item intriguingly entitled "USSR Law on the Press and Information," to be drafted by the USSR Union of Journalists; the State Committees for Publishing, Printing, and the Book Trade; and the Ministry of Justice. It was due for passage through the legislature in the fourth quarter of 1987.[12] On the one hand, about the same time there was some discussion of a more general law on glasnost, but the draft of this evidently proved too contentious and was suppressed.[13] On the other hand, one or more drafts of the proposed press law were indeed put into internal circulation in 1987 and were referred to in a number of periodicals. They were said, however, to be extremely conservative, and they attracted negative comment. But the matter did move forward, and the end result was a press law that had its first reading in the USSR Supreme Soviet some two years later, on November 27, 1989.[14]

At a more general level, a hesitant step toward freedom of speech was taken on April 8, 1989, in the form of amendments to articles 7 and 11 of the USSR Fundamentals of Criminal Law. These overarched the above-mentioned republican articles on anti-Soviet propaganda and agitation and those on violations of national and racial equality. The USSR articles were now rewritten: Most importantly, the crime of "anti-Soviet agitation and propaganda" was replaced by the more specific one of "public appeal to overthrow or change the Soviet state and social order by anti-constitutional means." The initial penalty was reduced from a maximum of seven years' to three years' imprisonment. The new formulation was by no means liberal, but, nevertheless, it made critical comment rather safer in the media.[15]

The freer attitude toward public expression greatly favored the political opposition that arose with perestroika. The pattern of development may never be fully known, but there is no doubt that things were well under way by 1987. A listing compiled by the bibliographer A. Suetnov relating to late 1989, contains 328 political groups that could be traced through their publishing activities. Clearly, this was only part of the total. Listings produced by the SMOT unofficial trade union information center late in 1990 and in spring 1991 contained about one thousand groups, including 132 in Moscow alone. Some were to vanish, but others survived, and yet others came to form the basis of the new system of politics.[16]

Apart from freedom to operate and sufficient public interest, any newspaper requires a good financial basis. The most relevant changes in this regard were the granting of more managerial freedom (in theory if not in practice) for state productive enterprises and the encouragement of the cooperative movement. The June 1987 USSR Law on State Enterprises, though extremely conservative, required enterprises to make a profit by selling their output; they were encouraged to advertise and to conclude contracts beyond the state plan at mutually agreed prices. Since printing works, like others, were evidently included, this measure opened important avenues for would-be newspaper publishers. In any case, by the time the June law was overridden in the Russian Soviet Federated Socialist Republic (RSFSR) in December 1990, contracts for "unofficial" publishing were common.[17]

As for cooperatives, the USSR law of May 26, 1988, did not include publishing as a permissible cooperative activity, and ministerial opposition was evident; in any case, the capital investment required would have been prohibitive for most aspirants. Yet a more tolerant attitude on the part of the authorities was illustrated by the decree of the USSR Council of Ministers of December 29, 1988. Although the decree banned "publishing activity which produced works of science, literature and art," it permitted cooperatives, with appropriate authorization, "to offer editorial and publishing services to organizations which [already] had publishing rights, particularly ... [for] printing advertisements, forms, labels, menus, [and] instructions."[18]

The New Press

Despite the formal continuance of most of the old Stalinist restrictions on publishing and the virtual suppression of samizdat, glasnost allowed considerably more open public expression. According to the survey mentioned above, before 1987 there were only ten or twelve new papers, but by the end of 1989 the total was over seven hundred. Two of the earliest and best known publications were *Glasnost* (founded in June 1987 by Sergei Grigoriants) and *Ekspress-khronika* (founded in August of the same year by Andrei Podrabinek).[19] Some idea of the pattern of growth is provided by the useful (but evidently partial) listing of papers compiled by the samizdat section of Radio Liberty. The 662 titles acquired up to November 1991 were distributed as follows:[20]

1985 and before:	3
1986	2
1987	24
1988	110
1989	232
1990	291

Bibliographers in several locations made attempts to collect and categorize them, but the absence of organized registration and distribution procedures means that a full count, including provincial publications, will probably never be possible. By 1990 the estimates based on titles actually obtained varied from over one thousand to fifteen hundred publications. Subsequently, a high mortality rate was registered. SMOT counts, for example, which were quite limited, showed a fall from 533 to 311 between December 1990 and April 1991.[21] Since publishing restrictions had by then been eased (a matter I turn to next), other explanations must be sought. These may include financial failure, growing competition among survivors, the appearance of stronger papers with larger print-runs, and a shift in public interest after the initial impact of antigovernment publishing had passed.

Not surprisingly, the groups professionally involved in publishing also began to reorganize themselves. A USSR "Union of Independent Journalists" was founded in April 1988 and thereafter held annual conferences. The initial membership was said to be two hundred, but it subsequently declined. In spring 1991, the USSR Union of Journalists transformed itself into a "self-governing, nongovernmental, politically independent, creative organization" with a confederative structure. The Moscow Journalists' Union set up its own Committee for the Defense of Free Speech and the Rights of Journalists, which proved to be very eloquent on its chosen themes. An independent publishers' association, uniting both "official" and cooperative publishers, made its appearance in July 1990.[22]

The newspapers that were available during this period varied enormously in almost all respects: sponsorship, orientation, frequency, print-run, and quality of production. Thus, in spring 1991 a reader could purchase on the streets of Moscow about one hundred titles, varying from occasional one-page items produced in the provinces to copies of the new independent dailies with print-runs of over 400,000. Arguably, three characteristics unified them: They were all new, largely uncensored, and openly available to the public. Most of the larger newspapers were founded in 1989 and 1990. The three current giants—*Kommersant, Megapolis ekspress,* and *Nezavisimaia gazeta*—first came out in February 1989, May 1989, and January 1990, respectively.

The new press operated with little legal security. Even though small sheets appeared without registration, more substantial ones might enjoy precarious local authorization. Papers not printed at home depended on individual printing contracts, expensive, grey-market paper supplies, and casual (sometimes illegal) street sales. I have found no reference to new printing facilities. The new papers did not carry the traditional censor's number. They operated by seeking sponsors and, at the same time, by endeavoring to be economically self-supporting, which meant that they cost between 30 kopeks and one ruble, that is, perhaps ten times as much as the established CPSU press.

Their existence also depended on a restrained reaction on the part of the local authorities. Given the absence of clear instructions from the center and the continued existence of the instruments of political repression, it is not surprising that many papers suffered greatly. There were numerous reports of journalists being molested, of copies of papers being seized, and of street sales being disrupted. On the whole, as the above figures show, the press resisted. The *Narodno–Trudovoi Soiuz* (NTS) managed to register the newspaper *Tret'ya sila* in a one-room flat in Samara, and it acquired its own printing facilities. Issue number two (a copy of which is in my possession) came out in November 1990, with a printing of 10,000.

So much for the birth of the new press. Emergent pluralism also forced unprecedented changes in the old CPSU-sponsored or government-approved organs. Two main trends can be distinguished. The first concerns content. All publications became more informative, and the editorship of some—primarily *Moskovskie novosti, Ogonek,* and *Argumenty i fakty*—passed into more liberal hands. *Ogonek,* for example, started investigating criminality and published an interview by Oleg Kalugin, the KGB renegade; *Moskovskie novosti* defended the practice of free meeting and discussion on a small area of pavement outside its offices; and the weekly *Argumenty i fakty* transformed itself from a boring propaganda sheet into a riveting source of facts and figures on privilege, poverty, and capitalistic well-being. To a lesser extent *Literaturnaia gazeta* and *Izvestiia* were associated with this trend. Some party papers, led of course by *Pravda,* maintained a muted campaign against perestroika and glasnost.

Second, officials in the Central Committee decided that some institutional restructuring of the party press was now essential. True, they had always tampered with it: Attempts had been made in 1983 and 1984 to activate small provincial papers, so as to improve their financial viability.[23] A resolution of August 6, 1989, established two new periodicals at the Center—*Rabochaia tribuna* and *Dialog,* evidently to ensure CPSU participation in the new newspaper boom. In the same resolution, local party offices were given more freedom to set up their own publications, and although existing sources do not allow one to judge the impact of this change countrywide, new local papers certainly appeared in districts of Moscow.

The August 1990 Decrees

It was in a sense ironic that the birth of the new press should have preceded the very enactments that ensured its existence. Such, however, was the case: The USSR law, "On the Press and Other Mass Information Media," was passed on June 12, 1990, and finally came into operation on August 1, by which time the transformation of the press was well advanced. The press law was accompanied by two other measures hardly of less importance, namely on registration and censorship. It is also noteworthy that in June 1990 the RSFSR government, as a gesture of independence from the USSR administration, declared that the RSFSR was entitled to its own system of public information.[24]

The key element in the long-awaited press law was the explicit prohibition of censorship. Beyond this, however, the law granted groups and individuals a series of truly pluralistic rights: to register new periodicals, at both the all-union and the local levels; to obtain an explanation if the authorities refused registration (any refusal had to rest on certain clear grounds); and to publish papers with print-runs of fewer than one thousand copies without any formal registration at all. The law also provided some protection for editors and journalists who inadvertently published incorrect information, and it gave them the right to maintain foreign contacts. The rules for the registration of periodicals passed by the USSR Council of Ministers on August 2 placed this function in the hands of the Russian news agency, TASS, and of three USSR state committees (for the press; for television and radio; and for cinematography). The fees set were fairly modest, for example, only 2,000 rubles for periodicals.

From the point of view of those who observed decades of stifling state control, the August press law seemed to be aglow with promise. Yet it was criticized by Soviet journalists on several counts. It was said to have been drafted under the influence of conservatives; it granted the state authorities a monopolistic position with too much power; and it did not enunciate the principle that anything could be published unless it was specifically prohibited. In a word, it was still too paternalistic.[25]

The new statute on censorship (August 24, 1990) was temporary, but also strikingly innovative. In fact, it was the first such statute to be published for about sixty years.[26] The USSR Main Administration for the Preservation of State Secrets in the Press and Other Mass Information Media (GUOT) was to retain its union-republican structure and its local offices, but its main function hitherto—ideological control—was not even mentioned. The administration now had to "conduct a unified state policy of defense against the disclosure of information comprising a state secret ... against the overthrow of the existing state and social order by force, propaganda of war, the use of force and cruelty, racist, nationalist, religious exclusivity or intolerance, pornography, and the encouragement of criminal acts."

The GUOT was to establish and publish lists of prohibited information and of decrees and instructions; to exercise a selective perusal of material after issuance; and to offer, for pay, supervision services to editors, so as to help them avoid inadvertent infringement of the law. It was also to provide training and to check publications coming from abroad. Financing for all these activities was to come from the state budget. There was no mention of KGB involvement (which had been written into the 1921 statute), but it is too early to draw firm conclusions from this. (I found a GUOT spokesman at the Moscow office quite forthcoming and unsecretive when I telephoned.)

According to comments made by a newspaper editor in the provinces in spring 1991, the old substantial list of restrictions had indeed been reduced to some eight pages and relations with the local censor's office (staffed by about five women) were "relaxed." Nationally there was a call for the publication of a law on state secrets, and this would presumably make the list public.

It is interesting to observe that the virtual abandonment of central control over content left no vacuum in the matter of control over publishing. Such administrative (as distinct from political) oversight was traditionally in the hands of the union-republican State Committees for Publishing, Printing, and the Book Trade. As a consequence of the RSFSR "separatist" policy, the RSFSR acquired its own Ministry for the Press and Mass Information, which, according to a detailed decree of October 17, 1990, was to ensure "objective, truthful, varied information" and the satisfaction of the public need for the printed word. Although the new body was also directed to encourage private enterprise, to counter monopolization, and to assist in commercial initiatives, its interventionist powers remained considerable. These powers included handling registration procedures, "coordinating" publishing efforts, collecting information on publishing, and closing publishing houses that broke the law. It was also given the right to halt all-union laws that contradicted RSFSR legislation.[27]

Moreover, the local authorities were by no means always benign in their reactions. Even after the August 1990 decree, reports of difficulties—editorial, production, and distributional—were legion. The Moscow city soviet, in its way a beacon of liberalism, had to act to curb the repressive activities of the militia. To quote a decision passed on January 21, 1991:

In the course of 1990 the Moscow militia frequently arrested people distributing *Svobodnoe slovo* [the organ of the Democratic Union Party], the *Vestnik khristiyan-skoi demokratii* [the organ of the Christian-Democratic Union of Russia], and *Kariera* [the organ of the Moscow Union of Journalists]. There were cases of papers being destroyed and income confiscated. This was done ... on the basis of article 150 of the RSFSR Code on Administrative Violations, Personal Trading in Unauthorized Places. Since this contradicted the August 1990 law on the press, [the decision continued] distribution of the mass information media ... is to be unhindered throughout Moscow, provided no sales appliances were used, and that the sales were not on official or private premises.[28]

The Events of 1991: The Coup and Its Aftermath

The political events of the momentous year 1991 have been the subject of much comment; as for the press, the year began badly. In January, on the last day of the fourth session of the USSR Supreme Soviet, Gorbachev announced that the August 1990 press law should be reviewed. The Committee for Glasnost, Citizens' Rights, and Appeals was to examine the text so as to ensure "an objective revelation of events taking place in the country." Obviously, the new freedom of criticism made the political establishment feel uneasy; and a shudder of apprehension passed through the journalistic community.[29]

A debate that followed in the committee a few weeks later allowed conservatives like Mikhail Fedorovich Nenashev, Chairman of the USSR Goskompechat' (State Committee on the Press), to complain that there was in fact no organ responsible for "coordinating" the public media, nor any mechanism for legal inspection. Many editorial offices did just what they wanted to do, were not "overseen" by the state, were too subjective, pursued group interests, and fought among themselves. Leonid Petrovich Kravchenko, head of the new State Television and Radio Company, affirmed that the Soviet people's trust in their media was being destroyed.

A number of voices spoke in favor of the press law, but the committee nevertheless decided to draft a decree on "perfecting and regulating the activities of the mass media" for discussion at the USSR Supreme Soviet. This decision had a sinister ring to it. On August 7, the Novosti Press Agency reported that a new agency was being set up to provide advice on how to avoid divulging state and commercial secrets. In the RSFSR there was indication of a more liberal policy, insofar as criminal and civil law was amended (March 1991) to protect investigative journalists and strengthen the penalties for libelous reporting.[30]

The coup of August 19 affected the press immediately. The conspirators, it will be recalled, laid much of the blame for national problems on the media. Under the terms of their decree no. 2, the publication of all but nine central newspapers (which were to be used to announce official policies) was banned.[31] The RSFSR television and radio network was also closed. These actions were in apparent violation of article 13 of the USSR Press Law, which stated that the cessation of publication was possible by decision of the founder, the official registering body, or a court of law, and also in the event of abuse of freedom of speech as defined in article 5.

The opponents of the coup were not, however, easily cowed. In Moscow, the USSR Ministry of the Press and Information questioned the ruling, and after discussion with the putsch leaders authorized the publication of several dozen papers using the strange formula "as requested by the editor in chief." These editors were subsequently criticized for affording the putsch indirect recognition.[32] Alternately, *Moscow News, Megapolis ekspress, Kuranty,* and *Rossiia* published unauthorized emergency issues, and another eleven papers brought out a joint issue entitled *Obshchaia gazeta.* The Leningrad papers continued to appear (Anatolii Sobchak, the mayor, had of course opposed the coup). Reactions elsewhere have yet to be explored, but there is little doubt that the putsch leaders' control over the media was vigorously opposed in many places.[33]

Yeltsin's own actions, after his return to power, smacked no less of authoritarianism, though with, perhaps, some short-term justification; Gorbachev, it will be recalled, had virtually excluded him from all-union television, and the Russian republican government was engaged in a fierce battle to obtain its own channels. On August 21, Yeltsin annulled the putsch restrictions on press freedom, and the previous press legislation was left in place. Since the USSR machinery of government on which the legislation was based had obviously lost credibility (if not formal power), responsibility for the press was transferred to the RSFSR Ministry for the Press and Mass Information, and to USSR TV, which now came under RSFSR control.[34]

On August 22, Yeltsin issued a decree "temporarily stopping" publication of six of the national papers used by his opponents. These papers were allowed to publish again as registered, independent entities, by a decree dated September 11. Repercussions of the failure of the putsch were not confined to central publications: Forty newspaper editors were said to have been removed, and as a consequence of the seizure of CPSU property, the RSFSR Ministry of the Press acquired a "monopoly position" in the possession of printing facilities, against the 4 percent it had held before.[35]

Despite the apparently happy outcome of events, it soon became apparent that relations between the Russian administration and the media were to remain somewhat tense. There were claims that the RSFSR Ministry of the Press was trying to inhibit critical reporting and was impeding the privatization of the former communist press. A decree of June 21, 1990, had granted the RSFSR Supreme Soviet the right to set up its own newspapers, and *Rossiiskaia gazeta* and *Rossiia* were established on this basis.[36] This caused resentment because as progovernment organs they were favored with facilities and subsidies, in the old CPSU manner. At one point their subscription period was extended beyond that of other papers to give them some commercial advantage.

There were signs of a strengthening of state controls, rather along the lines proposed before the coup. A decree of the RSFSR Council of Ministers of October 25, 1991, established the new State Inspectorate for the Defense of the Freedom of the Press and Mass Information, based at the offices of the GUOT.[37] When questioned about it, Fedotov affirmed that the move was not sudden, but was envisaged before. The problem was that people who hindered journalists were not being prosecuted, as now provided for by law. He described the new inspectorate's carefully defined functions: to see that the press did not call for the forcible overthrow of the state or promote interethnic strife, to protect the press from outside pressures, and to check the observance of basic administrative rules. The principle of state secrecy would be retained, though it was difficult to do so in the absence of a specific secrecy law. The deputy minister concluded that the inspectorate had no prohibitive or punitive powers, neither could it act as an arbitrator. It was to act as a friend, not as an overseer, to journalists. Evidently, time will tell.

Events in winter 1991–1992 included the familiar mixture of threat and reassurance. When the long-promised Russian Federation Law on the Press came before the Supreme Soviet in December 1991, attempts were made to give it a conservative coloring. Ruslan Khasbulatov, the chairman, was well known for his yearning for press constraint, and spoke in favor of it on a number of occasions. Such attempts to control the press, however, were defeated (with Yeltsin's help) and the measure came into force on February 6. It was more liberal than the USSR version in many respects: It gave editors and journalists more protection in matters of confidentiality of their sources, access to information, and appeal; it increased the role of the courts in settling disputes; it made the restriction of distribution and destruction of print-runs more difficult; and it banned the jamming of broadcasts. It was, in fact, a much more detailed and satisfactory document.[38]

Deputies to the 6th Congress of People's Deputies of the Russian Federation, which met in April 1992, expressed concern about what they saw as the overly critical attitude of the press toward their activities. It was proposed on that occasion that the matter be brought up for debate, and Minister Mikhail Poltoranin actually prepared a defense. Fortunately, the debate was canceled with the backing of Yeltsin, who, in his summing up, emphasized his commitment to press freedom. Thus an imminent crisis in newspaper-state relations had been averted.[39]

In conclusion, the old CPSU press inevitably suffered as a consequence of all these developments. The failure of the coup was followed, on August 24, by the transfer of all CPSU publishing in the RSFSR to the jurisdiction of the RSFSR Ministry of Press and Information. All party property was nationalized on the same day. The highly protected status enjoyed by the CPSU press was thus formally ended, though papers like *Pravda* continued to benefit from their excellent premises and established support. (Editorially, *Pravda* also maintained a somewhat pro-CPSU stance.) Indeed, their advantages, as compared with the new press, were a source of some envy and criticism.[40]

Problems of Commercialization

The removal of the long-standing political constraints on Soviet newspapers was followed by the appearance of serious economic constraints. The old, assured allocation of premises, equipment, staff, and material supplies, together with distribution at nominal rates, was largely replaced by difficult market conditions, a

shortage of material supplies and services, high inflation, and a competitive struggle for sales.[41]

Of all the commercial problems facing the industry by the beginning of 1992,
paper supplies, printing costs, and distribution were mentioned most frequently.
Paper has long been a deficit commodity in the USSR—by the late 1980s there
was said to be a shortfall of up to 30 percent of the national requirement. Under
the old system, most newsprint was allocated by state order and at low cost: in
1990, for example, Goskompechat' yielded only 16 to 17 percent of its supply to
outsiders. Yet, by the beginning of 1991, *Pravda* and *Izvestiia* were obliged to pay
up to nearly twice the official rate (set at 800–850 rubles per ton) for their supplies. A few months later, large nonstate publishers were reported to be paying
five to ten times the state price. The complete annulment of the state order system
for paper was promised for January 1992; this, it was said, would be fairer and
would settle the market. Even so, one expert anticipated a price of up to 5,000 rubles per ton, that is, six times the old state price, for 1992.[42]

The introduction of contractual relationships in the sphere of printing was said
to have caused printing costs to rise by a factor of two and one-half over 1991. Under the old system, the Ministry of Communications had provided postage services for subscription deliveries and the network of Soyuzpechat' kiosks in the
streets. By 1990 the ministry itself came under increasing pressure to raise
charges: It faced substantial increases in rail transportation costs, demands for pay
raises from its workers, and increased rents for premises and kiosks belonging to
local soviets. Ironically, a fall in the number of subscribers to the all-union newspapers cut the volume of deliveries.[43] As a consequence, the ministry announced
its intention to raise its distribution charges by two-and-one-half to three times, to
run the kiosks on a commercial basis, and to increase the number of titles they carried, thereby giving purchasers a wider choice.[44]

Price increases in one sector caused chain reactions in others, as the various
suppliers of premises, goods, and services looked to their own interests. In consequence, the price of newspapers rose: *Pravda,* for example, cost 4 kopeks in 1988,
30 kopeks in December 1991, and by February 1992, carried the caption "free
price" (*tsena svobodnaia*). In April 1992, as I can attest, many dailies were selling
on Moscow streets for one or two rubles. In summer 1991, most of the national
papers raised their subscription rates for January 1992 by a factor of two-and-one-
half or three, giving figures of 30 rubles or just under. However, by January 1992,
editors were aware that even these rates were disastrously low, and delivery could
be honored only for a few months.[45]

The new publications, as I have noted, were relatively expensive from the beginning: *Nezavisimaia gazeta,* for example, cost 40 kopeks when it started in January 1991. The "traditional" papers, despite their technical advantages, were less
attuned to function in a commercial world and stood to lose much more from it.
Thus, the selling prices of papers in the two sectors appeared to be converging. It
is also noteworthy that the practice of distributing the bulk of an issue by prepaid
subscription could become a massive financial liability. As 1991 passed, the prob-

lems of economic viability became ever more acute, and there were the inevitable reports of threatened closures.[46] Newspaper prices were rising much faster than inflation (a consequence of artificially low pricing before), and with increasing poverty one would suppose people simply had less to spend on publications. The negative psychological impact of the one-ruble newspaper must also have been significant.[47]

The parlous state of most publications raised the question of possible state subsidy, but this in turn brought the specter of state pressure on editors. The RSFSR legislation on the establishment of *Rossiia* and *Rossiiskaia gazeta* had, of course, specifically allowed for subsidization. This could to some extent be justified, and was even essential, if the government was to have assured access to the media at a time of economic collapse: And local soviets evidently protected local papers, too. The government-supported press was supposed to be independent of its founders, but nevertheless was believed to be less critical. This was, in fact, a curious variant of the pre-perestroika situation, with regard to CPSU publications.[48]

In any event, editors of various hues began to call for virtually every kind of help: donations, tax breaks, the provision of premises, regulation of the paper market, and even limitation of large press runs. Apart from this, they sought assistance elsewhere: Some papers attempted to develop associations with Russian commercial enterprises and foreign businesses, even a British publisher, the late Robert Maxwell, was mentioned in this context. The editors also sought revenue from advertising. But state support was soon regarded as the only serious solution.[49]

By the end of 1991, the situation had reached crisis proportions. Early in February 1992 Yeltsin, at a meeting with chief editors, agreed to intervene. The result was the presidential decree of February 20, 1992, which envisaged control of the supply of newsprint by the large monopoly producers; fixed newsprint prices; a prohibition on the export of newsprint from the Russian Federation; demonopolization of, and state subsidies for, the distribution network; and the allocation of state money for periodicals and "socially significant" literature.[50]

The decree was well received and was important, but the ongoing economic crisis was soon to rob it of much of its value. Publication of certain dailies began to falter. Some (such as *Komsomol'skaia pravda*) switched its publication to three days a week. After unsuccessful appeals to its readers, *Pravda* ceased publication in the middle of March and did not reappear for three weeks. In the following months, the situation continued to deteriorate.[51] The longer-term configuration of the press can scarcely be foreseen, but I append, by way of conclusion, a listing of subscription and publication figures for prominent national papers available early in 1992 (see Tables 2A.1, 2A.2, and 2A.3). Though much less complete than one might wish, it does illustrate the predominance of the three giants (*Argumenty i fakty, Komsomol'skaia pravda,* and *Trud*), the relative weakness of the new press, and the astonishing changes in availability over the last three years. How, indeed, hath the mighty fallen.

Appendix

TABLE 2A.1   The Russian/Soviet Newspaper World: Selected Statistics

"Traditional" Giants	Subscriptions (in millions of copies)				Print Runs (in millions of copies)
	Jan. 1989	Jan. 1990	Jan. 1991	Nov. 1991	Feb. 1992
Argumenty i fakty	20.4	31.5	23.8	22.6	[25.7]
Koms. pravda	17.6	20.4	17.2	12.1	13.4
Trud	19.6	20.0	18.2	12.3	13.5
Izvestiia	10.1	9.5	3.9	2.8	3.8
Pravda	9.7	6.5	2.2	0.9	1.4
Sel'skaia zhizn'	6.6	5.8	3.4	3.6	–
Literaturnaia gazeta	6.2	4.2	1.0	0.3	–
Sem'ia	2.1	4.6	3.4	2.9	–
Ogonek	3.1	4.1	1.7	1.5	–
Novy mir	1.6	2.4	0.9	0.2	–
Kommunist	0.9	0.5	0.1	–	–
"New Giants"					
Megapolis ekspress (May 1990)[a]	–	0.1	0.4		1.7
Rabochaia tribuna (CPSU Jan. 1990)		0.9	0.6	–	0.6
Kommersant (Feb. 1990)	–	–	0.5		0.5
Nezavisimaia gazeta (Jan. 1991)	–	0.15	0.5		0.2
Central State-Subsidized					
Rossiiskaia gazeta (Nov. 1990)	–	0.3	–		1.0
Rossiia (Oct. 1990)	–	0.3	–		–
Rossiiskie vesti (May 1991)	–	–	–		0.2
Krestiianskaia Rossiia (June 1991)	–	–	–		0.1
Pravitel'stvenny vestnik	–	–	–		0.1

[a] The dates in parentheses are dates of first issues.

SOURCES: Subscriptions: *Noskovskie novosti*, No. 47, November 19, 1989; *Pravda*, October 12, 1990; *Nezavisimaia gazeta*, January 5, 1991; *Izvestiia*, November 16, 1991. Print runs: Data taken from individual issues, where they usually appear among editorial details. Russian Republic data: *Narodnoe khoziastvo RSFSR v 1990*, Moscow, 1991, p. 258, *and Narodnoe khoziastvo i kul'tura v RSFSR*, Moscow, 1991, p. 327.

TABLE 2A.2   Total Press Output (Russian Republic)

	1985	1989	1990
Newspapers	4,567	4,772	4,808
Size of print run			
(in millions of copies) [a]	132	162	166
Journals and periodicals	3,869	3,781	3,681

[a] Average print run, without "giants" (1991) was approximately 18,000.
SOURCE: *Narodnoe khozyaistvo RSFSR v 1990, Moscow,* 1991, p. 258.

TABLE 2A.3   Number of Newspapers Published by Administrative Area, 1990

All-Union	43
RSFSR	4
Autonomous regions	89
District regions	188
Town, district	2,139
Organizations, enterprises	2,289
Kolkhozy	56

SOURCE: *Narodnoe obrazovanie i kul'tura v RSFSR,* Moscow, 1991, p. 327.

Notes

1. The research section at Radio Liberty in Munich has followed events for some time. See *Research Bulletin,* RL 66/87 (February 23, 1987); Radio Free Europe/Radio Liberty (hereafter cited as RFE/RL) *Report on the USSR* 1, no. 29, p. 1. Many useful updates were contributed by Vera Tolz.

2. *Sovetskaia pechat' v 1985 godu,* Moscow 1986, p. 106. *Statistical Abstract of the United States, 1989,* U.S. Bureau of the Census (Washington, D.C.: GPO, 1991), tables 913, 914. The U.S. figure quoted here is gross for semiweekly, weekly, and daily. The dailies numbered 1,701 in 1985. I am grateful to Nicholas Daniloff for bringing this discrepancy to my attention; comparison is more complicated than might appear at first sight.

3. N. V. Kuznetsov and E. M. Fingerit, *Gazetnyi mir Sovetskogo Soyuza,* Moscow, 1972; certain regulations for CPSU control of the press since 1930 may be found in Ya. N. Zassurskii, *Rabochaia kniga redaktora raionnoi gazety,* Moscow, 1988.

4. B. V. Alekseev et al., eds., *Slovar'-spravochnik rabotnika knizhnoi torgovlii,* Moscow, 1984, p. 40.

5. *Vsya Moskva, Informatsionno-reklamny ezhegodnik,* Moscow, 1991, p. 161.

6. Alekseev et al., *Slovar'-spravochnik rabotnika knizhnoi torgovlii,* p. 211.

7. See Martin Dewhirst and Robert Farrell, eds., *The Soviet Censorship,* Metuchen, New Jersey, 1973: There is a good bibliography, pp. 153–165.

8. The USSR law "Ob ugolovnoi otvetstvennosti za gosudarstvennykh prestuplenii" was passed on December 25, 1958, with the writer of these lines, alas, sitting in the hall. (He would have preferred not to have been born at that time.) The text is in *Vedomosti Verkhovnogo Soveta SSSR,* no. 1 (1959). The principal article in this law limiting freedom of speech was no. 7: "Agitation or propaganda conducted with the aim of undermining or

weakening Soviet power, or committing certain particularly dangerous state crimes; the distribution, with the same aim, of slanderous fabrications which besmirch the Soviet state and social order; and also the distribution or preparation or holding, with the same aim, of literature of that type—is punished by deprivation of freedom for a period of from six months to seven years and with exile for a period of from two to five years, or without exile, or with exile for a period of from two to five years: the same actions conducted by a person previously sentenced for particularly dangerous state crimes, and also crimes committed in time of war—is punished by deprivation of freedom for a period of from three to ten years and with exile for a period of from two to five years, or by a period of deprivation of freedom for a period of from three to ten years without exile."

A number of other articles in the law were relevant, especially no. 12 on the divulging of state secrets and no. 13 on the loss of documents containing state secrets.

In the Russian Soviet Federated Socialist Republic (RSFSR) Criminal Code, articles 70, 75 were discussed at this time. They may be found in *Ugolovnoe zakonodatel'stvo Soyuza SSR i soyuznykh respublik,* vol. 1, Moscow, 1963, pp. 108, 109. The article on violation of national and racial equality mentioned in my text below is covered by article 74.

9. See also Peter Reddaway, *Uncensored Russia: The Human Rights Movement in the Soviet Union,* Cape, London, 1972.

10. See n. 1, ch. 2. For some party documents see Mervyn Matthews, *Party, State, and Citizen in the Soviet Union,* (New York: M. E. Sharpe, 1989), p. 156.

11. For some examples see Mervyn Matthews, *Patterns of Deprivation in the Soviet Union* (Stanford: Hoover Institution Press, 1989). Of course, the CPSU authorities frequently interfered in newspaper publishing, especially at the local level. This is demonstrated by the list of decrees in K. M. Bogolyubov et al., eds., *KPSS—O sredstvakh massovoi informatsii i propagandy,* Moscow, 1979.

12. Matthews, *Party, State, and Citizen,* p. 31.

13. For the draft and an account of this episode, see *Materialy samizdata,* AS. 6207, no. 21, May 13, 1988.

14. For a review of the criticisms see Vera Tolz, RFE/RL, *Research Bulletin,* no. 547/88 (December 6, 1988).

15. Ukaz Prezidiuma Verkhovnogo Soveta SSSR, 106, *Vedomosti S"ezda narodnykh deputatov SSSR i Verkhovnogo Soveta SSSR,* no. 15, p. 181 (1989). I have not explored changes in the RSFSR Criminal Code here because it is again in the course of revision.

16. Gleb Pavlovski, ed., *Spravochnik periodicheskogo samizdata,* A. Suetnov, Moscow, 1990; *Spravochnik po neformal'nym obshchestvennym organizatsiyam i presse,* IAS, SMOT [Svobodnoe professional'noe ob"edinenie trudiaschikhsia] (undated, but procured in February 1991); Moskva, *Spravochnik* 1 (32) obshchestvennye organizatsii (SMOT, May 1991 issue); for listings of parties see *Sodeistvie* (Vilnius) 10(26), June 1–15, 1990, pp. 4–5 (translation); *Sostoyanie strany, analiticheskie vestniki* (no. 4/5) Informatsionnaia agentstvo PostFaktum, 1991.

17. *Spravochnik partiinogo rabotnika,* Moscow, 1988, p. 318. For an abridged version of some legislation, see Matthews, *Party, State, and Citizen,* pp . 278–297. The RSFSR legislation may be found in *Vedomosti Verkhovnogo Soveta RSFSR,* no. 30, art. 418 (December 28, 1990).

18. V. F. Yakovlev, ed., *Koopertivy segodnya i v budushchem,* Moscow, 89, p. 254ff.

19. *Materialy samizdata,* vypusk 8/91, July 5, 1991.

20. I made this count from *Materialy samizdata*, vypusk 13 (two parts, edited by G. G. Superfin), November 4, 1991. Some of the dates are only probable.

21. *SMOT–Informatsionny byulleten'*, no. 50 (December 20, 1990); no. 59 (April, 1991).

22. *Golos*, no. 31, Moscow (August 1989); *Izvestiia*, July 19, 1990; *Russkaia mysl'*, December 21, 1990; *Zhurnalist*, no. 4, p. 2; no. 8, p. 9 (1991).

23. Ya. N. Zasurski, ed., *Rabochaia kniga redaktora raionnoi gazety*, Moscow, 1988, p. 22.

24. *Vedomosti Verkhovnogo Soveta SSSR*, no. 26, p. 690, art. 492 (1990); *Sobranie postanovlenii pravitel'stva SSSR*, no. 19, p. 426, art. 98; no. 24, p. 539, art. 115 (1990); *Vedomosti Verkhovnogo Soveta RSFSR*, no. 4, p. 78, art. 56.

25. *Golos*, no. 39 (1991), p. 7.

26. For the preceding 1931 version, see Mervyn Matthews, *Soviet Government: A Selection of Documents*, Cape, London, 1974, p. 71.

27. *Sobranie postanovlenii pravitel'stva RSFSR, 1991*, no. 3, art. 32, p. 51.

28. Text provided by a Mossovet official.

29. *Kommersant*, no. 3 (January 14–21, 1992).

30. *Izvestiia*, February 16, 1991; RFE/RL *Research Report*, no. 33 (August 16, 1991). p. 40; "Ugolovny kodeks RSFSR s izmeneniyami i dopolneniyami na 5 maya 1990 i zakon RSFSR ot 21 marta 1991" (Moscow: Maloe predpriyatie "Reprint," 1991), p. 149.

31. Resolution no. 2 in *Pravda*, August 20, 1991, *Izvestiia*, August 20, 1991 (see *Current Digest of the Soviet Press* (hereafter cited as *CDSP*), 43, no. 33, p. 10). Resolution no. 1, article 8, established control over the news media, implementation to be assigned to a "special agency." (See *CDSP*, 43, no. 33, p. 3.)

32. *Golos*, no. 33 (August 26, 1991).

33. A good account of some of these events is to be found in Vera Tolz's cyclostyled paper, "The Role of Journalists and the Media in Changing Soviet Society," Radio Liberty, September 21, 1991.

34. *Vedomosti S"ezda narodnykh deputatov RSFSR*, no. 34, art. 1143, p. 1420 (1991). In November, the USSR authorities declared that their state officials could no longer be paid; according to reports, this burden was taken over by the RSFSR.

35. *Vedomosti S"ezda narodnykh deputatov RSFSR*, no. 37, art. 1199, p. 1462 (1991). *Golos*, no. 35 (September 9, 1991). The papers Yeltsin closed were *Pravda*, *Sovetskaia Rossiia*, *Glasnost*, *Rabochaia tribuna*, *Moskovskaia pravda*, and *Leninskoe znamya*. This action was criticized as obviously illegal, but Mikhail Fedotov, RSFSR deputy minister for the press, somewhat unconvincingly claimed that this was not so, since the law did not actually cover "temporary" closure.

36. For a brief account of these matters see Vera Tolz, "The Plight of the Russian Media," RFE/RL *Research Report*, February 28, 1992. *Vedomosti S"ezda narodnykh deputatov RSFSR*, no. 4, art. 56 (1990).

37. *Moskovskie novosti*, no. 46, November 26, 1991. The establishment of a state inspectorate was stipulated in Yeltsin's decree of September 11, 1991.

38. Cyclostyled version provided by the Ministry for the Press, dated December 27, 1991, no. 2124–1; *Izvestiia*, January 21, 1992; RFE/RL *Research Report* 1, no. 9 (February 28, 1992), p. 56.

39. *Kuranty*, April 23, 1992; *Rossiiskaia gazeta*, nos. 3 and 49 (double issue), April 17, 1992.

40. See, for example, *Golos,* no. 40 (1991); *Nezavisimaia gazeta,* September 24, 1991. The *Pravda* reports on the xxviii Congress of the CPSU in July 1990 were, for example, presented in an entirely traditional manner, as though there was no other significant news. Among the new papers were several small, procommunist, worker-oriented sheets.

41. The assessment of inflation in the USSR was always difficult; but it seems arguable that the rate moved from something like 8 percent in 1988 to 200 percent or more at the end of 1991. Hyperinflation at several hundred percent was anticipated in 1992. (*Argumenty i fakty,* no. 41 (1991); RFE/RL *Research Report* 1, no. 21 (May 22, 1992), p. 24; *Delovye lyudi* [Business USSR] no. 12, [18], December 1991, p. 19.)

42. On these matters, see, for example, *CDSP* 42, no. 20 (1990); no. 35, p. 35; 42, no. 29, p. 30; *Zhurnalist,* no. 8 (1991), pp. 2, 4; *Argumenty i fakty,* no. 48 (1991); *Izvestiia,* February 8, 1991.

43. *CDSP* 42, no. 33, p. 35; *CDSP* 42, no. 41 (1990), p. 31.

44. *Zhurnalist,* no. 4 (1991), p. 4; no. 8, p. 3.

45. Conversation with *Trud* correspondent about comparative subscription rates. In fact, the outstanding exception was *Argumenty i fakty,* which, it would seem, as a result of its huge print-run kept its subscription rate down to 9 rubles and 88 kopeks.

46. *Golos,* no. 8 (February 24–March 1, 1992).

47. I would not wish to imply that the fall in sales, demonstrated in my table, was entirely a result of price rises. It has been plausibly suggested that the public was tired of reading about perestroika and politics, in general. The availability (for the first time in the lives of all the population) of expensive pornography may also have affected the serious market. My personal observations in Moscow would suggest that a great deal of pocket cash was spent on these lurid sheets.

48. *Vedomosti S"ezda narodnykh deputatov RSFSR i Verkhovnogo Soveta RSFSR,* no. 4, art. 56 (June 21), p. 78; no. 26 (November 23, 1990), art. 332, p. 440; *CDSP* 42, no. 37, p. 26. Conversation with *Komsomol'skaia pravda* correspondent.

49. Numerous news items appeared on this theme. See, for example: *Zhurnalist,* no. 3 (1990), p. 25; *Izvestiia,* July 19, 1990; *Nezavisimaia gazeta,* September 24, 1991; *Golos,* no. 8 (February 24–March 1, 1992); *Rabochaya tribuna,* February 18, 1992.

50. *Komsomol'skaia pravda,* February 22, 1992; *Trud,* February 22, 1992.

51. *Pravda,* February 17, 1992; *Independent,* April 8, 1992.

CHAPTER 3

Pluralism and Politics in an Urban Soviet: Donetsk, 1990–1991

Theodore H. Friedgut

On August 20, 1991, *Vechernii Donetsk,* the Donetsk evening newspaper, appeared with its front page containing proclamation no. 1 of the State Emergency Committee (SEC), which had declared its rule in Moscow. Alongside it appeared the text of Ukrainian leader Leonid Kravchuk's cautiously ambivalent speech to the republic's citizens the previous afternoon and the texts of the Donetsk city soviet's appeals to the Supreme Soviet of the Ukraine and to the citizens of Donetsk, adopted on the afternoon of August 19, denouncing the SEC as anticonstitutional. Somewhat later, a local politician surveying the events remarked, "Full-blown pluralism!"[1]

In fact, the disparate array of opinion was less reflective of pluralism than of fragmentation. To establish this statement as a basis for further development of this discussion, I set as my first goal the definition of these two terms and the establishment of the difference between them.

Fragmentation will be taken to mean multiple political activity unregulated by any agreed framework of norms and interests. In Soviet society, under the rule of the Communist Party of the Soviet Union (CPSU), all politics outside the party framework were regarded by the authorities as fragmenting, and, therefore, illegitimate. What in a different political system, would have been a loyal opposition was treated in the Soviet Union as treason and was repressed. In reality, regime goals were often subverted or avoided by particularistic interests of the bureaucracy or other groups, but the facade of party monopoly was maintained as a shield of legitimacy. When the party monopoly on power ended, no alternative constitutional framework enjoyed broad public acceptance. A latent fragmentation of the Soviet political system had existed since the regime's inception. When the Communist Party, the sole unifying factor of the Soviet Union, disintegrated, social and political fragmentation erupted violently. Thus the policy of actively imposing unification carried within itself the seeds of that very disintegration it sought to avoid.[2]

Pluralism, in my usage, will mean the legitimate organization of political activity by groups with differing outlooks, contending or cooperating autonomously within an agreed framework of obligatory norms. In latter-day pluralist theory, both European and U.S., discussion revolves primarily around questions of equitable social and ethnic representation. Since the time of Montesquieu and Tocqueville, the existence of a multitude of political groupings has been taken for granted. In the Soviet context, the problem of pluralizing both government and political institutions must be approached from the more fundamental aspect of establishing an actual and legitimate right for the autonomous organization of contending political ideas. This is so because the Communist Party's claim to control all areas of public life was an attempt to impose a monolithic structure in which all activity was politicized.

Robert Dahl's model of social groups galvanizing themselves into political action when they perceived a threat to their interests had only limited application in Soviet politics. This is because the Communist Party actively maintained its veto rights over all public discourse, and consequently, in all segments of the public there existed an acute consciousness of the fine line between advocacy and pressure. Only after the principle of free consent has been acknowledged as central in society, giving both social life and politics what Harold Laski calls a federalist structure, both spatially and functionally, can the individual feel both direct self-interest and the efficacy of his participation in political life.[3] Pluralism helps keep the power structure honest by enabling small groups faced with injury to remind both society and government of "how the world ought to be."[4] Only when this foundation of citizen competence is in place can we go on to deal with the questions raised by Dahl's critics regarding equitable distribution of actual and potential power among various social groups or sectors.[5]

The task of understanding the nature of any given political system will be complicated by the possibility of both pluralism and fragmentation existing simultaneously. During the August 1991 Moscow putsch attempt, the State Emergency Committee attempted to deck itself in constitutional norms. Its opponents, among them the Donetsk *gorsoviet* (municipal council), rejected this claim unequivocally. Kravchuk, sensitive to the implications of the power struggle in progress, staked out a middle ground, speaking up for constitutional norms but not explicitly denying the legitimacy of the SEC.

The stability of any system will quite naturally depend on the ratio between activity restrained within common accepted norms and that unrestrained by such norms. Happy the state in which all citizens salute the flag cheerfully and all parties swear by the Constitution, however much they may quarrel on daily matters. In a state in transition, such as the Soviet Union in the latter half of 1991, it is no surprise that the level of consensus was low and stability noticeably fragile. At times, almost the only element restraining chaos is the Hobbesian consciousness that the war of all against all can lead to no good result, nor can any victor emerge. Perhaps the historical memory of the horrors of civil war, cultivated so assiduously over the years by the Soviet regime, is the most effective existing barrier to total fragmentation.[6] Yet here we must be careful not to fall into the trap, offered by so many in the Soviet Union and elsewhere, that suggests a strong hand at the helm of government is the only alternative to mass bloodshed. Pierre Joseph Proudhon distinguished clearly between anarchy and chaos. Anarchy is not disorder or lack of principle. It is simply an order that is not imposed from any center, but is built up from society's roots to its crown.[7] The collapse of the partocracy need not mean civil war.

Regarding pluralism, we are entitled to ask at this point, "Norms agreed among whom?" The only definitive answer can be "whoever so wishes!" A richly variegated social pluralism underlies the concept of a flexible equilibrium in which the broadest possible range of interests is satisfied. A pluralism in the elements of pluralism, all of them joined by common values but each jealous of its own particularities, appears to be a hopeful model for democracy. The widespread public possession of economic resources, capital, and property in all their forms would appear to be a safeguard of pluralism and of stability. Such resources may be private, cooperative, public, or even state-owned, provided that none is banned and that none enjoys state-mandated exclusivity or overwhelming preference. The guiding principle must be a real possibility of fair competition, allowing each the resources necessary to realize its own interests.

Stanislaw Ehrlich contrasts such a "refereeing function" to a state in which a single, overwhelmingly dominant power elite determines not only investment priorities but also cultural and political norms, thus controlling the overall direction of social life to the exclusion of large sections of society.[8] Indeed, David Nicholls places the relation between unity and diversity at the head of his list of questions regarding the nature and consequences of pluralism. He stipulates that the voluntary groups that absorb so much of the citizen's time and energy must not emanate from any single source or value, and certainly not entirely from the state.[9] Futhermore, he cites John Dewey to the effect that in a democracy the main domestic role of the state should be protection of the autonomous existence of social groups and adjudication of conflicts among them, rather than the advancing of any particular interest.[10] Reinhardt Bendix, with a consciousness formed by a rather different political and social background, saw autonomous social aggregation as dividing society into relatively isolated segments, held together only by the compulsion of the state.[11] This difference of emphasis between the state's coercive role and its refereeing role is fundamental. In the post-Soviet context, restraint of the state must be central to the unfolding of pluralism.

The necessary condition for pluralism to survive is sufficient social acquiescence to permit the political system to function. Montesquieu, Tocqueville, and the Federalists began from an assumption of pluralist democracy and concerned themselves largely with center-periphery relations necessary to maintain such a state (e.g., the Crown versus the Estates, the federal authorities versus the individual states, or state-initiated establishment of religion). But an analysis of politics in the Soviet context must deal primarily with a more basic political relationship, that of the state versus the citizen and the emergence of civil society in what was a highly integrated totalist state system. A pluralist system must have authority in the sense of freely given respect and obedience—not to any specific ruling group or program, but to the norms by which any group can achieve political dominance. Dictatorship, autocracy, and totalitarian rule may all enjoy a measure of authority at some time, but these by definition are not pluralist, and the source of their power does not lie in such freely offered consent. My interest in a pluralist system stems from an inherent faith that, over the long haul, an open system, providing for free introduction of issues into the public agenda and their free contestation, will be fresher and more effective in identifying and solving new problems than will a closed monocratic system. It will have the means of more sensitive reaction to emerging social stresses and, thus, will be less subject to violent upheaval.

John Kenneth Galbraith once wrote a jewel of an essay entitled "Businesses, Like People, Are Not Forever." In the context of the business world he discussed the "aging of the techno-structure" and the "senescence of the corporation." Written in the closing years of what is now known in the Soviet Union as "the era of stagnation," it fit wonderfully the processes then rampant in the Soviet leadership. One of the minor themes of this essay was the tendency for corporate leadership, at a certain stage of its development, to clone itself by selecting executives on a basis of excellence, with excellence defined as that which most completely resembles the outlook of the selectors. Reinforced by the political monism of its partocracy, this policy made the former USSR the epitome of a closed system. The result of such a process is the victory of Roberto Michels over Wilfrid Pareto; accentuation of all the deleterious effects of the "Iron Law of Oligarchy" and attenuation or even total blockage of the natural circulation of elites that should bring new, ambitious, and hungry leaders to the political problem-solving arena.

But not everything can be blamed on Leonid Brezhnev. The Russian autocracy enjoyed considerable public authority for many years, while working assiduously to prevent any development of political pluralism and establishing a closed political and administrative culture. The mainstream of Russian Marxism, one of whose branches became the eventual successor to the autocracy, was monist in its outlook from the beginning. Vladimir Lenin and Joseph Stalin only reinforced this tendency. Lenin did so in 1921 by imposing as a formal rule the monolithic outlook on the party that had been basic to his politics from the beginnings of Bolshevism. At a later point I will discuss the significance of the end of this rule in February 1990. Stalin's mobilization of the entire society into institutions of support for policy spread monolithic politics throughout the social system, delegitimizing not only political opposition but also any pluralist or fragmentationist phenomena in any sphere of life. Laski points out that the theory of the modern monistic state, elaborated by Jean Bodin, Jeremy Bentham, G.W.F. Hegel, and V. I. Lenin, was conceived in ages of crisis.[12] It might be added that crisis-oriented leaders, after coming to power, often tend to perpetuate crisis-justified policies, treating the whole of political life as a protracted crisis situation. Most certainly much of Soviet life can be so understood.

Nor are monistic values foreign to the city of Donetsk. It was born as Iuzovka, a jealously guarded company town in which no impingement on the New Russia Company's monopoly of power was brooked. The name Iuzovka was succeeded by the name Stalin, and little elaboration is needed here. The city is deeply rooted in a monocratic tradition, as is so much, though by no means all, of the former USSR. Such a historical tradition, reinforced by the political practices of Bolshevism, can only affect the style of leadership as well as the reasoning of the public when confronted with political crises. Laski cites Aristotle to the effect that the essence of citizenship is the individual's capacity to rule, and in turn, to be ruled.[13] David Nicholls adds the necessity of belief in the efficacy of civil peace and the acceptance, even if not the absolute acceptance, of "normal" procedures for the resolution of civic disputes.[14] The rules, therefore, are at least as important as the game itself. The Communist Party of the Soviet Union, nurtured on the philosophy of class war, was never able to accept such a view. Always, in communist politics, winning power was more important than how power was won. I will return to this point when I begin my detailed analysis of political behavior in Donetsk.

Leadership and Parties in a Nascent Pluralism

The next problem is that of identifying elements that promote the growth of authority and stability in a political system. Here, I will analyze two principal elements: the nature of political leadership and the institutionalization of political activity, in particular, political parties. Historically, political parties have evolved from personal cliques to mass representations of an idea, or interest, contending for power. The broader the range of societal interests aggregated and articulated by parties, the more broadly inclusive will citizen participation in politics be, and fragmentation will fade to the margins. Yet the building of a distinct and stable identity for a political party is a gradual process, and a feature of the transitional period is the heightened political awareness and activity of the public. Here the ultimate link of a series of equations proposed by Samuel Huntington comes into play. Huntington proposes that the ratio of political participation to political institutionalization equals the propensity to instability.[15] In a period of agitated participation, weakly institutionalized parties are as apt to lose as to gain a stable identity. In addition, a high level of participation, overloading a small number of weak political institutions, is likely to end up spilling into the streets. Indeed, weak political institutions may reveal a distinct propensity for carrying on their activities in the streets, for want of more appropriate means.

In Donetsk, political parties are as new, weak, and inchoate as they are throughout the former USSR. It should be remembered that though the nuclei of some parties emerged in late 1986 and early 1987 from the "informal associations" that sprang up so plentifully, the formal legitimacy of a multiparty system dates only from March 1990. This is when the Soviet Congress of People's Deputies acquiesced to Mikhail Gorbachev's suggestion, proposed through the Central Committee of the CPSU, that article 6 of the USSR Constitution be rephrased to make the Communist Party only one of the parties and public organizations that shape and direct the state's policies. The time was apparently carefully chosen by Gorbachev. The change came too late to allow a full and free mobilization of new parties for the elections scheduled in March 1990 for both supreme and local soviets throughout the USSR. In essence, it gave the CPSU one last five-year head start in which to shape up in a competitive political system in which it enjoyed a general advantage of incumbency or to be shipped out to the wilderness of opposition in the next elections. Gorbachev at this point was still persistently pushing the CPSU to transform itself from a corrupt and mediocre bureaucracy into a lean and vigorous political contender. It was he who repeatedly raised the challenge of abandoning the "leading role" of the party while attempting to revive its "vanguard" political nature.

At the Donetsk municipal level, the only organized party that appeared for the 1990 elections was the CPSU. A municipal association of voters was formed and gave recommendations regarding individual candidates for the Supreme Soviet of the Ukraine. These candidates were to stand on a detailed platform of democratic norms, but the association eschewed party assessment or identification and made no recommendations for the local soviet. Even so, the association's statement and a list of candidates supporting the association's views was not published in the city's newspaper until the issue was raised in a stormy meeting of the *obkom* (the regional Communist Party Committee).[16] The city strike committee, born of the July 1989 coal strike, organized protest meetings demanding the resignation of the old soviet and the creation of a temporary citizens' committee to oversee the elections. However, it formed nothing that could be said to resemble a list or party of candidates. Four veteran "Afghantsy" (those who fought in Afghanistan) joined together to support the candidacy of one of their comrades.[17] From this amorphous political environment, a soviet of 150 deputies was eventually chosen, though four rounds of voting were necessary before the last 7 representatives won election. When G. I. Onishchuk, first secretary of the *gorkom* (city Communist Party Committee), who had been defeated in his constituency, met with a group of the communist deputies (90 of 143 deputies then elected were communists) to form a party fraction, as had been the mandatory practice in Soviet institutions, the deputies voted against his suggestion. Among those objecting to the formation of a party fraction was the deputy nominated by Onishchuk to chair the group.[18] Thus the dominant and, in effect, sole institutionalized political group in Donetsk began curbing its own organized presence in politics. Yet this was not the only sign of decline in the Donetsk Communist Party. At the start of 1990, the Donetsk city party organization numbered 86,004 members—down 343 from the year before. By January 1991 it had shrunk by 14 percent to 73,709.[19]

Since the elections to the Donetsk city soviet, parties have appeared in the city, though none appears to have organized a fraction in the soviet. All are characterized by internal strife, limited numbers, and an unclarified platform. The Ukrainian Republican Party counted seventy members in 1990, until a "re-registration" produced a split, leaving only twenty.[20] The Popular Front of the Ukraine, Rukh, acts as a movement rather than a party. Forty of its members are registered among the 300 adherents of the Party for Democratic Renaissance of the Ukraine, a group previously known as the Democratic Platform and made up chiefly of former members of the CPSU.[21] Meanwhile, a radical wing of Rukh, calling itself Democratic Rukh, split off. Their critics claim they have only 30 to 40 members, but they are active. During 1990 they organized no fewer than twenty-seven street meetings and demonstrations, some of which ended in violence, stirring up anger and anxiety in the city.[22] Two representatives of the Social Democrats of the Ukraine, Nikolai Valynko, and Sergei Vasiliev, both of the Gorkii coal mine, are active in the city strike committee. The party's newspaper, *Istina,* may be bought at some kiosks in Donetsk. The Social Democrats, however, appear to carry on little or no organized activity in the city.[23]

All in all, a pluralist party system exists only in embryo and is made up of weak and unstable components. In addition to the brevity of the period in which parties have been able to function legitimately, in itself a factor of considerable importance, there are several other factors at work.

In the USSR between 1989 and 1991, parties emerged from ethnic and national ferment. Some, beginning as popular fronts, became national parties contending for power at republic level, usually as coalitions against federal Moscow and local Russian presence. In Donetsk, the national element is poor soil for parties. Though the city is indisputably in the Ukraine, the largest national group in the population is and always has been Russian. The Ukrainian population is Russified, and the city's cultural environment is clearly Russian. This is one reason for the modest membership of Democratic Rukh.[24] At the same time, the Russians in Donetsk, many of them descendants of the city's pioneers, feel no threat to their status, and though a Russian Workers' Front was reported organized in late 1990, no subsequent evidence of its existence has appeared. Similarly, a reported attempt to organize a branch of the Russian nationalist Pamiat' in the university died for lack of response. Ethnic-based political parties are thus almost negligible, though as social and cultural movements, as we shall see, they have established an effective pluralism, feeding into the political system.

Unlike the Congress of People's Deputies, where the interregional group evolved into Democratic Russia, the soviet has been equally infertile soil for new parties. Having been chosen on an individual basis and often intensely occupied in their basic professions, the deputies have not shown the taste for turning into political professionals that is needed for the organization of effective parties. Neither the image nor the reality of the urban deputy as a relatively powerless individual representative of his voters has changed. Evgenii Svetlichnyi, a deputy in the city soviet, focuses particularly on the deputies' lack of experience in pluralist politics and in representational politics as the source of this weakness.[25] On a broader historical backdrop, the chairman of the Supreme Soviet of the Ukraine, Leonid Kravchuk, warned that in previous attempts to establish an independent Ukrainian state disunity and "insufficiency of experience in statecraft" had caused failure.[26]

Some ideological parties have emerged, as they did on the "all-union" level, but here the problem of leadership comes into play. First of all, new and uninstitutionalized bodies have a natural tendency to instability of leadership, as different personalities and outlooks contend to mold them each according to his own image or advantage. Leadership is inexperienced, and knowledge of political philosophies is scanty and unsystematic. Those who were the early protesters and prisoners may not always thrive in the new political conditions of legitimate pluralism. The moral absolutes that were necessary for their survival as dissenters generally are less efficacious as a guide to daily politics. Finally, the scarcity of leadership exists at all levels, with the best and brightest attracted upward to the regional and national level. Donetsk's examples are Iurii Boldyrev, the strike activist from the Gorkii mine, who now devotes more and more of his energies to his duties in Moscow as a member of the coordinating council of Yeltsin's Democratic Russia; and E. L. Zviagil'skii, who must ration his time (free of his duties as director of one of the city's most successful coal mines) between the city soviet and the Supreme Soviet of the Ukraine in which he also serves.

The professional politicians and parliamentarians envisioned in Gorbachev's political reforms are not yet setting the tone in Donetsk politics. Alexander G. Makhmudov, the professor of computer sciences who was elected chairman of the Donetsk city soviet and of its executive committee, might have grown into such a person, but he retired from leadership of the soviet in early 1992. As of today, the city sorely lacks a national-class leader who will devote himself heart and soul to the city's welfare—a Fiorello La Guardia or a Teddy Kollek (mayors of New York and Jerusalem, respectively). Here we must note that Donetsk is far from barren in terms of persons qualified to lead and to represent in politics. If one of the central problems of old Iuzovka was the paucity of intelligentsia and the virtual non-existence of the worker-intelligent, such is not the case today. Donetsk is a city rich in large-scale industrial enterprises, with a large university and a number of higher technical institutes. It enjoys a broad technical and cultural intelligentsia. In addition, it has an educated working class. Of the deputies in the *gorsoviet*, forty-three are workers, and of these, one-half have higher education.[27] With the traditional authority of the CPSU discarded and the entire political system as yet too new and unstable to produce solid leaders by routinized rational-legal procedures, charismatic leadership is necessary for the establishment of authority, and this, as always, is in short supply. Of interest in this context is the fact that G. I. Onishchuk, the former chairman of the Donetsk *gorispolkom* (city executive committee) and former first secretary of the *gorkom,* a youthful, vigorous and effective executive, has left the region and has no more formal connections with its politics. The Donetsk Communist Party organization now has its third leader in the past two years, with the two previous secretaries dismissed for failure and now out of politics, along with a former *obkom* (*oblast'* Party Committee) first secretary.

And what is the view that Soviet citizens in general hold of political pluralism—of the multiparty system? In one national survey carried out in 1989 it was found that 27 percent of those questioned found the multiparty system both natural and necessary. An additional 20 percent expressed the opinion that since the CPSU encompassed various approaches, other parties were unnecessary. Nineteen percent thought that additional parties would simply mean more talk and bureaucracy, and 11 percent claimed that considering the monocratic history of the Russian Empire and the Soviet Union, a multiparty system would be artificial. Close to a quarter of those surveyed expressed no opinion on the subject.[28] It should be remembered that this poll was taken at a time when a multiparty system did not yet exist and was still vigorously opposed by the ruling authorities. It may, however, be taken to represent, at least roughly, the skepticism of Soviet citizens regarding party politics.

It is not only the form of the parliamentary system but its content as well that is in doubt. A discussion of nonattendance at sessions of the soviet by the deputies led to complaints that the soviet, as a whole, was unproductive and to a move to cut the number and size of its standing commissions.[29] These commissions are one of the institutions in which the deputy can carry on effective work in the preparation and improvement of legislation and are also the forum in which supervision of the executive branch is exercised. Cutting them is, therefore, a diminution of power of the representative body and a setback to its development.

The chairman of one of the nine district soviets in Donetsk, B. I. Adamov, himself a nonparty person (his membership application had been rejected by the party), expressed the view that divisions among the parties should be the least important thing in the soviet. Some groups had formed in his soviet, including a fraction of seventy communists—"and if they put forward sensible, relevant proposals, what's wrong with that?" On the whole, however, Adamov shared the same distrust of factionalism that haunted some of the framers of the U.S. Constitution, the fear that it might subvert the common interest and paralyze the work of government.[30] However, Adamov has never had the opportunity to study the contention of James Madison in Federalist Paper 10, that elimination of a faction is a cure worse than the disease; that the proper antidote to the fragmenting evils of factionalism is encouragement of the bonds of common interest; and that the art of politics lies in the control of faction and not its annihilation.

The problem of parliamentary pluralism as a balance against the executive dominance that has so long been a characteristic of Soviet local politics is very real. Here, along with the reflex reactions of the old-time administrators who still dominate the city's various offices and the conservative bent of the central authorities who still largely determine the arena of politics, the economic crisis plays a central role.

The most serious step in this reconcentration of power was the law on local soviets passed by the Supreme Soviet of the Ukraine.[31] The separation of powers and the incipient growth of checks and balances that were the core of Gorbachev's political reforms of 1988–1989 were totally reversed. The chairman of the soviet is now, as in prereform days, also chairman of the soviet's executive committee—the *ispolkom*. Members of the *ispolkom,* salaried executives subordinate to the elected representatives under the reforms, are now once more eligible to be elected as deputies and to sit in the triple capacity of legislator, executive, and auditor—and somewhere, Lenin smiles. It should be noted here that the law on local government passed by the Supreme Soviet of the Ukraine was essentially contradictory to the draft law proposed by the Donetsk soviet. The Donetsk variant emphatically maintained the separation of powers and the representative check over the executive.[32]

Perhaps the preferences of the professional executives and the higher soviets would have less effect in Donetsk were it not for the economic difficulties faced by the city. In mid-1991 there were 20,000 to 25,000 persons unemployed in Donetsk *oblast'* (province), and the number was expected to rise to 80,000 to 100,000 by the year's end.[33] One of the city's coal mines was suddenly closed because of its inability to produce competitively, the first such case in Donetsk. This was the realization of a nightmare that has been haunting the miners since their 1989 strike.[34] In addition, drought in spring and summer 1991 reduced the *oblast'* crop yield by almost 50 percent, and much of what is harvested is being held on the farms with considerable subsequent waste, raising the prospect of winter food shortages.[35]

Squeezed between growing economic demands from the *raisoviety* (district soviet) below and a hostile niggardliness from the *oblast'* soviet, Makhmudov and his staff succumbed to the same tendencies that have appeared in Moscow and in other municipalities. They chose the path of executive prerogative as the way to heighten the effectiveness of municipal government. The consumer supply economy of the city is still controlled by the *gorispolkom,* even when privatized firms produce the goods. No substantial start has been made in moving the control of land or housing out of municipal hands or in broadening private or independent public activity in the city's supply economy. Plans have been discussed, but action seems notably absent.[36] Rationing and attempts to institute a municipal income tax have proven inimical to the creation of confidence between the public and the many components of the Donetsk political system—executives, representatives, and authorities at the municipal and urban district levels.

Although these difficulties have been recognized and weekly consultations go on between *gorsoviet* and *raisoviet* leaders, the evolution of procedures to create a working symbiosis, and from it a more effective government, is slow. Here I must point out that, as is the case in so much of the Soviet Union, the executives controlling the administration of much of the economy and society remain the same people who were the previous elite. They are the experienced cadres. In the crisis conditions prevailing in the economy they command the knowledge and resources to maintain their dominance.[37] In addition, they have considerable support from the *oblast'* and the republic authorities. Until such a time as they agree to adopt the new norms of the elected municipal powers, the progress of reform will be slow and public confidence will remain low.

Pluralism in Donetsk Society

If the growth of an institutionalized political system appears dangerously slow, Donetsk society provides a more encouraging picture. This is as it should be, for the inputs of pluralist politics should come from clearly defined autonomous aggregations of ethnic, professional, or economic interests. If perestroika is to flourish, it must proceed from below, from strong social roots. Here I will examine the growth of professional, ethnic, and economic groupings, as well as the pluralization of communications in Donetsk.

The first element of social pluralism I present is the opening up of the communications of the city. Although this is a late and still-developing phenomenon, it is a necessary condition of successful pluralism. Without multiple sources of information and multiple viewpoints to consider, public opinion cannot develop into a broad spectrum. Like every other Soviet city, Donetsk had a local newspaper that was the joint organ of the *gorsoviet* and the *gorkom,* though naturally dominated by the latter. *Vechernii Donetsk* entered the age of glasnost in the wake of a stormy plenum of the *obkom,* at which the editor's refusal to publish the program of the Municipal Voters' Association was condemned. By October 1990, it was registered as an independent sociopolitical newspaper, run by its workers.[38] With over 150,000 subscriptions and a print-run of one-quarter million copies, it is the most widely distributed newspaper in the *oblast'.* Thus deprived of its press organ, the *gorkom,* together with the city's Voroshilov *raikom* (district) founded *Pervaia liniia*—but with a print-run of only 20,000 copies. In addition, a commercial newspaper, *Donetskie novosti* began to appear. The *gorsoviet* now publishes its own newspaper, *Gorod,* and there are two *oblast'* newspapers, *Sotsialisticheskii Donbass,* whose affiliation to the *obkom* has now been relegated to the back page, and *Zhizn',* published by the *obispolkom* (provincial executive committee). Rounding out this new wealth of communications is the roughly bimonthly appearance of the sixteen-page newspaper *Aleph,* published by the city's Center for Jewish Education and Culture. For a city that until 1917 had no local press whatsoever and has known only a Communist Party press since, this is indeed a luxury. The local television station, since 1989, has asserted its professionalism in offering full and open cooperation to foreign journalists and filmmakers. It has broadcast the emergency meeting in the *gorsoviet* (filmed by a Polish TV crew, as well) that drafted a denunciation of the SEC on the afternoon of August 19. The citizens of Donetsk are thus exposed to a myriad of differing evaluations of current local affairs, along with the broadened spectrum of information and comment on national and world affairs provided by the Soviet and post-Soviet press today.

The earliest effective appearance of civil society in Donetsk was the miners' strike of 1989.[39] It eventually produced not only city and regional strike committees to coordinate the miners' defense of their professional interests but also two national miners' congresses that gave birth to an independent trade union. The evolution of this union as it clarifies its essence is a subject unto itself. Here it is sufficient to note the gradual change from a multifunctional institution toward a predominantly professional identity and the formation of additional professional groups in the city.

The miners' success in institutionalizing their strike evoked emulation. A Union of Toilers of the Donbass (*Soiuz trudiashchikhsia Donbassa*) was formed early in 1990. Its initial program focused on countrywide needs, rather than local or purely professional ones, and it appeared to be more of an incipient political party than a workers' organization.[40] It appears to have evolved into a general human rights movement, devoted to a democratic development of society. By the end of 1990 the Union claimed 2,000 members, including "those belonging to any movements devoted to democratic political development." (But it explicitly excluded members of the CPSU.) The Confederation of Independent Trade Unions of the Ukraine was next to appear, concentrating its attention at first on transport workers but later organizing and acting on behalf of a broad spectrum of workers. The independent miners' union is a member, as are workers of cooperatives and other groups. The confederation focuses on social protection for workers during the transition to a market economy.[41] Even the old Soviet trade union organization, VTsSPS, has renamed itself the General Federation of Labor and has tried to reinvigorate its local activities, clashing with a mine director who closed kindergartens and day-care centers as a measure of pressure against striking miners in spring 1991.

Two new professional associations have been formed and have successfully defended themselves from *apparat* attempts to put them under control. A Society of Ukrainian Law Scholars was formed in Donetsk, with the aims of reviving interest in "the Ukrainian School of Legal Thought"; defending the professional interests of jurists; and spreading public knowledge of the law.[42] A Free Donetsk Medical Association, claiming to represent 7,000 doctors in the city, was also formed. A militant package of economic demands put forward by a representative of the existing Union of Medical Workers attending the founding conference was rejected. The meeting affirmed that its aim was, first and foremost, improvement of the expert status of the medical profession.[43]

The consciousness of the lawyers and doctors in fending off attempted *apparat* control came in the wake of the experience of the miners' city strike committee. The first leaders of the strike committee in summer 1989 had evidently succumbed to co-optation by the establishment and had been ousted from their positions. The strike committee now maintains the custom of having two cochairmen. They are periodically rotated out of power, though they both remain active in the

leadership of the committee. This is an attempt by the committee to prevent cor-
ruption while maintaining effective leadership.[44]

Donetsk prides itself on being a multiethnic city. The advancement of Russian
culture has been taken for granted, while that of the Ukrainian minority has
proven sensitive because of past neglect, despite the long-time existence of a
Ukrainian Language Association, named for the poet Taras Shevchenko, as part of
the Ukrainian Cultural Fund.[45] However, the nonterritorial minorities of Donetsk
have flourished under perestroika. Jews, Germans, and Greeks have all founded
new and active cultural associations and carry on contacts with their conationals
outside the former USSR. These organizations are generally sensitive to their position in today's unstable environment, but on occasion they inject themselves
into the city's political life. In spring 1990, rumors circulated throughout the
USSR that on May 5 there would be massive pogroms against the Jews. As the
date approached, the Jewish Cultural Center, together with Rukh, other ethnic
groups, and the city strike committee, requested a meeting with representatives of
the militia, the KGB, and the Communist Party for a discussion of these rumors.
Along with their having received assurances that there was no evidence of substance behind the rumors, the representatives of the organizations were promised
that there would be augmented presence of law forces wherever necessary and
that any disorders would be promptly stopped. Armed with this reassurance each
of the representatives could return to his constituents to assure them that social
peace would be maintained in Donetsk.

In addition to the activities of ethnic communities, the flowering of social organizations that is so much a feature of today's post-Soviet era has not passed by
Donetsk. A branch of Memorial (an organization dedicated to honoring Stalin's
victims) has been organized, as has an active ecological group and numerous other
groups, including a Pittsburgh-Donetsk Friendship Society. As groups proliferated, a new group *Ednannia* (Unity) appeared to coordinate and unite all social
forces within the framework of the Constitution, economic perestroika, and inter-
nationalism.[46] Apparently this was an attempt by the Communist Party to co-opt
all the new groups, for it included the Soviet Peace Committee, the Red Cross,
and other old-line mass public committees, as well as old-line catchwords. If this
is so, then it would appear that there has been a deep change in public attitudes in
Donetsk, because *Ednannia* is listed as one of the groups that gathered on August
20, 1991, on the premises of the *gorsoviet,* to sign a petition to the Supreme Soviet of the Ukraine condemning the State Emergency Committee as unconstitu-
tional and undeserving of public recognition, despite the clear stand of the local
communist organization against denouncing the coup attempt.[47]

Conclusion

The weakness of political pluralism in Donetsk has many roots. It is a natural, if
unfortunate, phenomenon that will be changed only with much time and effort.

There is a lack of historical precedent as well as a near-total absence of personal experience of legitimate, pluralist politics in Donetsk. Parties are small, undefined, and unstable. Leadership in such conditions is a scarce commodity, further exacerbating the precarious nature of pluralism. Such leadership as does exist often abandons the local scene for the higher spheres of all-union politics, where the unresolved grand issues of political philosophy and power are being battled out. At the same time, the central political bodies are themselves as yet too weak and overburdened to devote resources to the solution of particular municipal problems.

With such a background, the effective pluralizing of the municipal government must be difficult, despite the free elections through which the city administration was formed. The hardships facing the city soviet in its quest for effectiveness are compounded by economic crises. They are also compounded by hostile tendencies in the Donetsk *oblast'* soviet and in the Supreme Soviet of Ukraine, both of which have a greater conservative influence than exists in Donetsk. Essentially, the former USSR today is at all levels a severely fragmented political system. As a result, the growth of pluralist institutions in the city soviet has been obstructed.

In contrast to the slow pluralization of the Donetsk political system, society has shown more organizational resiliency. The explanation may be found in the grouping of society around clearly defined personal, ethnic, professional, or material interests. Insulated by their very nature from political power and from responsibility for the general fate of society, these voluntary associations enjoy a much calmer growth. Their internal crises of leadership and of programmatic priorities are of a much lesser magnitude. They have far more margin for error in the learning of internal democracy. In time, these groups may provide the political systems with leaders who enjoy a measure of local authority and who may gain some political experience.

The growing breadth of the organized social spectrum provides reinforcement of pluralism against fragmentation. As social organizations proliferate, individuals become involved in numerous bodies and find themselves relating to others in a variety of modes, some cooperative, others adversarial or neutral. Russian, Jewish, and Ukrainian doctors, lawyers, or miners, separate, competitive or even conflictual in their ethnic or cultural activities, find themselves joined in a common professional interest, attenuating the former divisions.[48] This "cross-weaving" of interactions and affiliations reinforces pluralism as it decreases the possibility of fragmentation. As noted, Donetsk enjoys a propitious environment for such bonding. This is enhanced by the historically rooted sense of communal achievement, of urban identity, and of civic pride that has been successfully promoted by all the city's governments.

It is necessary that a stable plural political system be rooted in a stable social pluralism. The two are organically related. The society, necessary as it is, cannot, however, guarantee the flourishing of pluralist politics. These politics are further conditioned by other factors in the political system and in its surroundings—external example, local leadership, effective administration, resource availability, and the institutional environment. In all of these, political pluralism in Donetsk still faces formidable obstacles.

Notes

1. I. Zaria, "19–20. A Chronicle of Protest and Faint-Heartedness," *Vechernii Donetsk,* August 30, 1991.

2. For a generalized statement of this proposition, applicable to any political system, see David Nicholls, *The Pluralist State* (London: Macmillan, 1975), p. 121.

3. Harold J. Laski, "The Pluralistic State," Appendix B in David Nicholls, *The Pluralist State* (London: Macmillan, 1975), p. 151. Laski goes beyond the national, regional, or ethnic dimensions of pluralism, and includes the functional, i.e., the structure of industry, trade unions, and professional groupings of every sort.

4. David B. Truman, *The Governmental Process* (New York: Knopf, 1951), p. 348.

5. Robert J. Waste, *Power and Pluralism in American Cities* (Westport, Conn.: Greenwood Press, 1987), presents a concise survey of the evolution of U.S. theories of pluralism from James Madison to the present. For a critique of Robert Dahl, see pp. 84–86.

6. For a striking example of the consciousness of the danger of civic violence see *Vechernii Donetsk,* February 12 and 13, 1990, protocol of the enlarged session of the Donetsk *obkom* (regional Communist Party Committee). Identifiable conservatives, Gorbachev centrists, and radicals all spoke intensely of the need to avoid the type of civil strife that took place in Romania when the Nicolae Ceausescu regime was deposed.

7. See the discussion of the Polish scholar Stanislaw Ehrlich, *Pluralism: On and Off Course* (Oxford: Pergamon Press, 1982), p. 18.

8. Ibid., p. 113. As an example of this, consider Stalin's "revolution from above"—the industrialization and collectivization in the USSR.

9. David Nicholls, *Three Varieties of Pluralism* (London: Macmillan, 1974), pp. 1–2. A similar view will be found in William Kornhauser, *The Politics of Mass Society* (Glencoe, Ill.: Free Press, 1959), pp. 78–80.

10. Nicholls, *Three Varieties of Pluralism,* p. 22.

11. Reinhardt Bendix, *Conflict and the Web of Group Affiliations* (Glencoe, Ill.: Free Press, 1964), cited in David Nicholls, *Three Varieties of Pluralism,* p. 3.

12. Laski, "The Pluralistic State," p. 145.

13. Ibid., p. 150.

14. Nicholls, *The Pluralist State,* p. 123.

15. Samuel P. Huntington, *Political Order in Changing Societies* (New Haven: Yale University Press, 1968), p. 55.

16. See the discussion and publication of the association's statement in *Vechernii Donetsk,* February 13, 1990.

17. Ibid., April 12, 1990.

18. Ibid., May 5, 1990. The vote against forming a party fraction was 25 to 20, indicating that half of the communist deputies did not even attend the meeting.

19. Compare the figures given by G. I. Onishchuk in *Vechernii Donetsk,* March 19, 1990, to those given by his successor, A. A. Bolotov, in *Pervaia liniia* (Donetsk), January 5, 1991.

20. *Sotsialisticheskii Donbass,* August 22, 1990.

21. See the report of the party's formation in *Vechernii Donetsk,* December 11, 1990.

22. For a report on one such incident, see *Vechernii Donetsk,* November 12, 1990. The photograph accompanying the report shows placards, one of which reads "Freedom for the Wild Animals—Jail for Communists."

23. I saw no announcements of meetings on city notice boards during a visit in July 1991; I saw no reports of Social Democrats' activity appearing in any of the city or *oblast'* newspapers. Also, *Istina* carried no reference to Donetsk or to activities in Donetsk.

24. A portion of the support for the mainstream of Rukh was attributed to the desire of both Russian and Ukrainian coal miners to have a strengthened Ukrainian Republic so that control of the mines would be in Kiev rather than in Moscow.

25. See the criticism of Donetsk deputies' performance by Evgenii Svetlichnyi, *Vechernii Donetsk,* June 28, 1991.

26. *Vechernii Donetsk,* August 29, 1991.

27. Ibid., May 12, 1990.

28. N. Popov, "Narod i vlast'," in A. Protashchik, ed., *Cherez ternii* (Moscow: Progress, 1990), p. 779. There were two or three other opinion groups listed, and the author explained that each interviewee was allowed more than one choice; thus, there is a total of more than 100 percent in the statistics.

29. *Vechernii Donetsk,* June 12, 1991.

30. See B. I. Adamov's interview in *Sotsialisticheskii Donbass,* December 31, 1990.

31. For the text of the law on local soviets see *Vechernii Donetsk,* December 15, 1990.

32. For a discussion of the Donetsk variant see ibid., October 30, 1990.

33. Ibid., June 10, 1991.

34. Ibid., August 30, 1991.

35. *Izvestiia,* September 12, 1991.

36. Only about two hundred apartments were sold to residents to mid-1991, and these at prices substantially higher than the norm in Moscow.

37. The *oblast'* Statistical Administration recently surveyed the 2,529 senior executives of the region. Though seniority in office was calculated, the figures were not published and I have not yet succeeded in getting them. The executives are 95 percent male; recently they appeared to have been a stable group (the average age grew by one full year); the number of those of pensionable age grew from 105 to 149; 44.2 percent were 50 years old or more. Figures on party membership, nationality, and seniority in office were not published. See *Shakhtar'ska slava,* June 4, 1991.

38. See the announcement concerning the miners' strike in *Vechernii Donetsk,* October 19, 1990.

39. For a detailed examination of the miners' strike and its effect on the institutions of Donetsk see Theodore H. Friedgut and Lewis H. Siegelbaum, *The Soviet Miners' Strike, July 1989: Perestroika From Below* (Pittsburgh: University of Pittsburgh Center for Russian and East European Studies, Carl Beck Papers, no. 804, March 1990). The film "Perestroika from Below" (New York: Past Time Productions, 1990) gives a vivid documentation of the miners' civic consciousness.

40. For the program of the organization see *Vechernii Donbass,* October 30, 1990.

41. See *Pravda Ukrainy,* August 17, 1991.

42. See the notice of the association's founding and its declaration of independence from existing associations in *Vechernii Donetsk,* June 11, 1991.

43. See ibid., August 29, 1990

44. Note the clarification in *Vechernii Donetsk,* December 17, 1990, emphasizing that the replacement of the cochairmen was routine procedure and that they remain active in the strike committee's executive department. For accounts of *apparat* success in dominating emerging pluralism in Magnitogorsk, see Stephen Kotkin, *Steeltown, USSR* (Berkeley and Los Angeles: University of California Press, 1991).

45. Only 3 percent of the city's children of Ukrainian descent have hitherto received education in the Ukrainian language.

46. *Vechernii Donetsk,* April 14, 1990.

47. Ibid., August 21, 1991. Alongside this resolution, Memorial published its own resolution calling for the immediate dissolution of the SEC, stating: "We want no more fear and lies, not for ourselves, not for our children and grandchildren, not for anyone."

48. This model of stability for democratic society was first derived by Stein Rokkan from his investigations of Norwegian society. See, for instance, Stein Rokkan, "Norway: Numerical Democracy and Corporate Pluralism," in Robert A. Dahl, ed., *Political Oppositions in Western Democracies* (New Haven: Yale University Press, 1966), pp. 70–72.

CHAPTER 4

How Democratic
Are Local Russian Deputies?

Jeffrey W. Hahn

The system of local government that existed in the former Soviet Union before 1988 provided scant opportunity for popular control over those who governed, surely an essential feature of representative democracy.[1] At best, locally elected officials, called deputies, could sometimes act as "ombudsmen" in the communication of citizen preferences to those who governed.[2] In his speech to the 19th Party Conference of June 1988, however, General Secretary Mikhail Gorbachev outlined his dramatic proposals to "democratize" the Soviet political system, including local government. Among other things, these proposals called for competitive elections, a division of executive and legislative powers, an end to the interference of the Communist Party of the Soviet Union (CPSU) in local governance (called *podmena*), and greater local decision-making authority.[3] The reforms were introduced in the Russian republic in 1990. Did they have their intended effect? Have they contributed to the emergence of democratic pluralism in Russian politics? The purpose of this chapter is to contribute to the answer to this question by looking at how the role of the deputies elected to Russian local government changed in the first year or so after the implementation of the reforms.

Any answer to this question presupposes a clear statement of what is meant by democratic pluralism and of the criteria by which the development of democratic pluralism is to be measured. Moreover, because the requirements of democratic pluralism encompass more than the issue of representative government, the relationship between the two must also be clarified. This chapter will employ the U.S. rather than the British usage of the term pluralism[4] and accept the conceptualization by Robert Dahl that essentially it refers to: "organizational pluralism, that is, to the existence of a plurality of relatively autonomous (independent) organizations (subsystems) within the domain of the state."[5]

But what does pluralism have to do with democracy? For Dahl, not all pluralist systems are necessarily democratic. They become so only if they exist within the conditions of what he calls "polyarchy," the two central dimensions of which are public contestation and participatory inclusiveness.[6] His criteria for ideal democracy (voting equality, equal participatory opportunity, "enlightened understanding," control over agenda, and inclusion of all adults) can be fully realized only in small-scale regimes; large-scale democracies require mechanisms of representation. Among these, a fair electoral process for choosing the few who will make rules for the many is certainly critical if representation is to be democratic. "Perhaps no institution is more critical to the differentiation between polyarchies and non-polyarchies than competitive elections."[7] Yet since a single vote in a large country can only have the slightest impact on government, representation must also be achieved through associational organizations such as parties and interest groups. It is in this sense that he concludes: "All democratic *countries* are pluralist democracies."[8]

In his study of community power, Robert Presthus adopts a similar usage of the term pluralism, defining it as "a system in which political power is fragmented among the branches of government; it is, moreover, shared between the state and a multitude of private groups and individuals."[9] For Presthus, the antithesis of pluralism is elitism or "monism," which connotes the concentration of political power or rule by one or few. Just as Dahl ranges actual systems relative to the opposing ideal types of democracy and autocracy, Presthus places any given community on a continuum between being comparatively pluralist or elitist.[10] He proposes that five conditions be met for a community to be located near the pluralist end of the spectrum. Since they offer a set of norms against which to measure progress toward democratic pluralism in other countries, including Russia, they are worth noting here:

1. Competing centers and bases of power and influence exist within a political community;
2. There is opportunity for individual and organizational access into the political system;
3. Individuals actively participate in and make their will felt through organizations of many kinds;
4. Elections are a viable instrument of mass participation in political decisions, including those on specific issues;
5. A consensus exists on what may be called the "democratic creed."[11]

In the conceptions of both Dahl and Presthus, pluralism is an essential ingredient of a democratic polity because of its importance in linking the public with those who make decisions. That is, in a representative democracy, if the popular will is to be expressed, if popular control is to be exercised, the elected representative must be cognizant of the public will and take it into consideration. There must be what Austin Ranney calls "popular consultation."[12] Empirical research has tended to conceptualize the problem in terms of "constituency influence" and to focus on analyses of congressional voting behavior.[13] In their book *Public Opinion and Responsible Democracy,* Dennis Ippolito, Thomas Walker, and Kenneth Kolson hypothesize three basic paths of public influence: direct influence (voting, petitioning, demonstrating); group influence (parties, interest groups); and indirect influence (representatives reflect the public will through attitudinal congruence).[14] Such linkages are possible only under conditions of political pluralism.

At this point it is possible to return to the problem identified at the outset of this paper: Is Russian local government becoming more democratic? From the theoretical overview presented here, at least three criteria suggest themselves. These can be expressed as continuums. First, it seems clear that democratic pluralism requires a dispersion of power. If power remains centralized or monopolized by one or even a few groups, then progress toward pluralist democracy would be minimal. Second, a relatively high degree of contestation would be expected. The absence of legitimate opposition, openly expressed, must also be regarded as a deficiency from the standpoint of democratic pluralism. Finally, a public role in local governance is required. There must be mechanisms for the communication of citizen preferences and evidence that these preferences are taken into account in making decisions. The lack of same would indicate the absence of real popular consultation. In short, the emergence of democratic pluralism will vary with the relative absence or presence of dispersed power, political contestation, and popular consultation.

The task of this chapter is to determine what evidence there is that these indicators of democratic pluralism are becoming characteristic of Russian local politics. How do I propose to do this? The evidence I offer here is drawn from a single case study of the city government of Yaroslavl' during the first year or so (1990–1991) of the implementation of the local government reforms initially proposed by Gorbachev.[15] More specifically, I will focus on the role of locally elected deputies to the city soviet. To understand how their role has changed and to assess whether they have become more democratic, in this chapter I will first examine the election of the deputies in March 1990. Then I will describe how the new soviet works, including first-hand observations of a session of the city soviet held in June 1991. Finally, I will explore the relationship between the deputies and those who elected them. To do so, I will rely in part on in-depth interviews with some of the deputies that I conducted in June 1991 and on the results of systematic survey questionnaires that the Yaroslavl' city soviet's own Center for the Study of Public Opinion administered in May 1991.[16]

The advantage of the case study approach proposed here is that it can provide a picture of the democratization process that is rich in detail and "thickly descriptive."[17] The obvious disadvantage is that there is no way of confirming the generalizability of conclusions based on only one case. Though there is no apparent a priori reason to suggest that Yaroslavl' is so far out of the Russian political mainstream that it constitutes a unique case, it should be emphasized that my purpose is not to offer definitive answers about whether Russian local politics is becoming more democratic by looking at what is happening in Yaroslavl', but to generate hypotheses that may be tested in other communities of that vast land.[18]

How Local Russian Deputies Are Elected

Competitive elections are surely the cornerstone for the development of democratic pluralism. They are the locus of popular control in representative government, for those in elected office who choose to ignore their constituents' concerns are periodically subject to removal by them. Few students of democratic theory would disagree with H. B. Mayo when he writes: "The one institutional embodiment of the principle universally regarded as indispensable in modern democracies is that of choosing the policy-makers (representatives) at elections held at more or less regular intervals."[19] At the same time, it is clear that not all elections are equally democratic. According to Gerald Pomper, at least six requirements need to be met before an election can be regarded as truly free: meaningful choices; the freedom to know and discuss the choices; a manageable number of clear choices; the equal weighting of votes; free registration of choices (a secret ballot); and accurate registration, counting, and reporting.[20]

By these standards, elections in the Soviet Union before 1989 can hardly be considered democratic despite the persistent claims of Soviet scholars of that time to the contrary. Reports of nearly universal turnout, public financing, demographic representativeness, and universal suffrage could not alter the simple fact: There was no choice of candidates. Until 1989 the Communist Party and only the party determined who would be elected, by virtue of its control over the nomination process. For the sake of establishing a baseline for comparison, it is worth describing, briefly, how the old system worked.[21]

Nominations to various legislative councils (known as the soviets) were conducted in the workplace. Although there was no legal requirement that only one candidate be nominated for each seat in the soviets at various levels, in order to ensure an artificial representation of different demographic groups (by gender, age, education, occupation, party membership, etc.), the corresponding party secretary at each level of government would inform the Party Committee at the place of work as to the number and composition of the deputies it should nominate. After discussions with leaders of the Komsomol (Communist Youth Organization) and trade union committees at the workplace, a list of willing candidates would be drawn up, confirmed, and presented at a general meeting, for what usually was unanimous nomination. On election day, voters were mobilized by local "agitators" into dropping ballots listing a single candidate for each office into a ballot box. Since the outcome was foreordained and the poll workers wanted to get home early to enjoy the holiday, voting irregularities were apparently widespread and tolerated.[22] About the only requirement of a free election that was met was the equal weighting of votes: All votes were equally unimportant.

The introduction of a competitive element in the electoral process was originally called for by Gorbachev in a speech to the CPSU Central Committee in January 1987. Subsequently, an experiment in competitive elections was proposed and carried out in less than 5 percent of the seats at stake in the June 1987 local

elections.[23] The results proved disastrous for many of the old party and state officials whom Gorbachev had come to regard as a "brake" on his economic reforms.
In hopes of undermining his opposition further he proposed to the 19th Party Conference in June 1988 that competitive elections become the norm in national elections to be held in 1989 and in local elections thereafter.

Although it provided a legal basis for the freest elections in Soviet history, the
Law on Elections adopted on December 1, 1988, for elections to the Congress of
People's Deputies in spring 1989 contained a number of defects. It set aside one-
third of the seats for public organizations, most of which went to the CPSU or
party-dominated bodies. It required preelection meetings, which could be (and
were) used to discourage candidates who were critical of the party's political monopoly. The law allowed the possibility that seats could go uncontested (400 out
of 1,500 seats were uncontested). And since the new Parliament was to be elected
indirectly, Gorbachev was assured a majority of votes even before it met. In fact,
it can be argued that the election rules were arranged to produce just this result.[24]

Unhappiness on the part of many reformers, including Andrei Sakharov, with
the 1988 electoral law resulted in significant changes in the laws adopted on October 27, 1989, for Russian republic and local elections.[25] The Law on Local Elections provided for direct elections to all local soviets on the basis of equal and universal adult suffrage and by secret ballot. No seats were to be assigned to public
organizations, and the requirement that candidates be approved at preelection
meetings of district election commissions was abolished. Candidates could be
nominated at the workplace, as before, or by officially registered public organizations, or at places of residence. The number of candidates per single-member district was "unlimited" (again making uncontested districts possible). To be
elected, a candidate had to receive more than 50 percent of the votes cast, with no
fewer than 50 percent of the eligible electorate turning out to vote. Since it was
clearly possible that no one would emerge victorious in a district with several candidates, provisions had to be made for runoffs (*povtornye golosovanie*) and for repeat elections (*povtornye vybory*). Runoffs occurred in districts in which three or
more candidates were running and none got 50 percent. Repeat elections (including new nominations and time for campaigning) were held in districts in which
there were one or two candidates running and none got 50 percent.

The point to be made here is that the election law of 1989 is cumbersome, to
say the least. By not allowing the winner to take all and by requiring that 50 percent of those eligible vote, it creates the possibility for virtually endless elections;
from the standpoint of the average voter, the process is unnecessarily complicated.
A simple majority without a required level of turnout would be equally democratic. Despite its many shortcomings, however, the law provided a legal basis for
comparatively democratic elections.

The first round of elections was held in Yaroslavl' (as in the rest of the Russian
republic) on March 4, 1990. Runoff elections were held two weeks later on March
18, and repeat elections were held on April 22. Did they meet the requirements of

a free election? The first of these requirements, meaningful choice, has both a quantitative and a qualitative dimension. Quantitatively, there must be at least two candidates for each position. Generally speaking this was the case in Yaroslavl'. There were 565 candidates registered for the 200 seats in the city soviet, an average of 2.8 candidates per seat, although 52 of these withdrew before election day. There was considerable variance from the mean, however. Twenty districts had from 5 to 7 candidates, but in 47 districts there was only one. It is noteworthy, however, that running unopposed did not guarantee election. In 7 of the 47 such cases, more than 50 percent of those voting defeated a candidate by crossing his name off the ballot; among the defeated were the first and second secretaries of the city Party Committee (*gorkom*).

As this last point suggests, the local elections in Yaroslavl' provided some degree of meaningful choice in a qualitative sense, as well. On the one hand, voters could voice their opinions on the old party-state apparatus by voting these candidates out of office. Approximately 65 members of the *apparat* were on the ballot on March 4; only 27 of the 179 seated for the first organizational session of the city soviet that met on May 10 were from this group. On the other hand, the Yaroslavl' Popular Front (YPF) represented an alternative for which people could vote. The YPF originated as a protest movement against the election of former *oblast'* Party Committee (*obkom*) first secretary, Fedor Ivanovich Loshenkov (often referred to locally as "Tsar Fedor"), to the 19th Party Conference in summer 1988.[26] Although the movement was initiated mostly by those in the party committed to Gorbachev's policies of perestroika, it became radicalized over time. By the time of the local elections, it was openly campaigning against the local party establishment, even though four of its five cochairs were party members.[27] Although splintered by the emergence of a more radical group called the Movement for Popular Rule, the YPF had managed to elect Boris Shamshev to the USSR Congress of People's Deputies and had become broadly affiliated with the Inter-Regional Group of Deputies (of which Shamshev was a member) and the national democratic movement, "Democraticheskaia Rossiia."

The YPF supported 67 candidates in the March elections, winning 22 seats to the first session of the soviet, which was convened on May 10, 1990. Although this does not, at first glance, compare favorably with the ratio of winners to losers among the *apparat,* appearances are deceiving. In fact, enough of the remaining deputies were sufficiently sympathetic to the YPF that they formed a voting bloc of 44 deputies called "Democratic Yaroslavl'," which, in coalition with two other reform-minded deputy groups, easily controlled the election of the chair and vicechair of the city soviet.[28]

Moreover, despite its limited resources, the YPF acted like a protoparty. Not only did it recruit and support candidates it also organized mass demonstrations on February 25 and on March 17. It disseminated information to the public by maintaining a kiosk in the center of town next to the city bus terminal. The leadership provided a measure of internal discipline, although not always efficiently. At an organizational meeting that I attended on the eve of the March 4 elections, much of the discussion turned on getting out the vote, giving out telephone contact numbers, going over the mechanics of voting, reading telegrams of support from Boris Yeltsin and Gavrill Popov—in short, the sort of precinct politics that I was familiar with from eight years of elective office in city government in suburban Philadelphia.

However, there were also important differences from the U.S. experience of local politics. These differences may help to account for the fact that the YPF did not do better than it did and must be acknowledged in any assessment of meaningful choice. Pomper's model, cited earlier, specifies that choices should be manageable and that voters must have the opportunity to know and discuss these choices. It is hard to conclude that these requirements were met. The first reason has to do with the law, or more accurately, with the lack of one, for registering political parties.[29] Candidates could not run on a party label. The only hint of partisan identification was whether the candidate was a member of the CPSU. If not, they were identified as nonparty (*bezpartiinyi*). Since 70 percent of the candidates were Communist Party members, including many supported by the YPF, these labels had little meaning. The absence of legislation by which alternative parties could register and identify their candidates meant that voters had to rely on word of mouth and on other forms of mass communication to know which candidates stood for what.

It is in connection with this last point that the second problem arises. At the time the elections were held, the local party officials had an overwhelming advantage in resources: They commanded a fleet of cars, telephones, finances, and the main means of mass communication, including access to radio, television, and the press. They had offices and an infrastructure—in short, an effective organization. The YPF had none of these advantages. How were they to make their case known to the voter? Demonstrations, word of mouth, and a kiosk were hardly sufficient to ensure that YPF-supported candidates could publicize their names and policy positions so that voters could make an informed choice. In retrospect, it is surprising that the YPF did as well as they did.

The other three requirements for a free election identified by Pomper—equal weighting of votes; free registration of choices; and accurate registration, counting, and reporting of ballots—appear to have been largely fulfilled in Yaroslavl'. With respect to equal weighting of votes, the average number of voters registered in each district was 2,312. Though the range varied from a low of 1,299 voters in district 163 to a high of 3,455 voters in district 154 (a clear violation of the principle of one man—one vote), the standard deviation from the mean was only 295, indicating that in two-thirds of the districts the actual number of eligible voters was less than 13 percent larger or smaller than the norm.

The critical condition for the free registration of choices is a secret ballot. In contrast to previous practice, Russian voters were now required to take their paper ballots into a curtained booth to be marked. Personal observation at several precincts randomly chosen during both the March 4 and March 18 elections gave the impression that this procedure was routinely followed, although a few older voters tried to go directly to the red ballot boxes on the other side of the booths to deposit their unmarked ballots, as in the old days, and had to be gently reminded that things were different now.

The same may be said about registration, counting and reporting procedures. In the precincts that I visited, voters went first to a table, where 10 to 15 members of the election commission sat, and had their names verified on a voter list. They were then given five differently colored ballots, one for each level of government in which seats were to be filled: borough, city, *oblast',* and Russian Soviet Federated Socialist Republic (RSFSR) national and territorial. The polls were open from 7 A.M. to 8 P.M., during which 283,691 voters cast their ballots (a 62 percent turnout). The percentage voting in elections for representatives to the Russian Republic Parliament and in rural districts was higher, in some cases substantially so.[30] After the polls closed, the ballot boxes were sealed by the chair of the election commission, unused ballots were destroyed, and counting began.

I received permission to be present on March 18 when the votes were counted for precinct 9/174, which was located in the ship-building area of the Frunze borough (*raion v gorode*). Sixty-three percent of the eligible electorate had voted, down from about 70 percent who came out on March 4. The work had to be done by hand in the absence of voting machines, and all results were confirmed independently by at least two counters. Although it was legally possible for someone from the YPF to be present, the only observer there, except for a colleague and me, was the secretary of the factory Party Committee. He did not, however, interfere in any way with the proceedings. At the end, the chair read the results and asked for objections. After hearing none, the chair signed the protocols and sent the results to the city's Central Election Commission.

From the standpoint of election mechanics, were the elections honest? Clearly there were opportunities for fraud and manipulation. I myself witnessed a number of minor violations. Numerous complaints of election irregularities were made at a post-election meeting of the YPF on March 20. However, a fully representative survey of voter opinion that I conducted in Yaroslavl' showed that nearly 70 percent of the electorate felt that the March 4 elections had been fair; only 16 percent of those surveyed thought they had not been.

How Local Russian Deputies Behave as Legislators

The organization of local government in the Soviet Union before 1989 reflected V. I. Lenin's conceptualization, following Karl Marx, that the soviets should be "a working, not a parliamentary, body."[31] Representatives of the working class, elected by universal suffrage and subject to recall, should be directly involved not only in making local decisions but in carrying them out. The soviets were to be a "school for the masses" in self-administration. One consequence of this conception was that the number of elected deputies was large, as many as 500 in some cities and up to 1,000 at one point in Moscow. In 1985 more than 2.3 million deputies were elected to 52,041 local governments.[32] Since the turnover at each two-and-one-half year term was about 50 percent, an enormous number of people held public office at one time or another.

Partly because the soviets were too large to conduct the daily business of government and partly because of Lenin's proscription against separating legislative and executive authority, the deputies at their first session would elect from among their members an executive committee, known as an *ispolkom,* consisting of perhaps fifteen members. In addition to a chair, a vice-chair and a secretary, the *ispolkom* included the heads of the major administrative departments of government. Though the deputies met four times a year, usually for a few hours, the members of the *ispolkom* were full-time professionals. The chairman of the *ispolkom* functioned more or less like a U.S. mayor and was responsible for governing the city. The one other structure intended to ensure a continued legislative presence was the system of standing committees, which ostensibly oversaw the work of the executive departments for whom they were responsible.

Although, in theory, the soviets embodied the principles of direct democracy in which the people exercised control over their government through their participation as elected representatives, in practice, they were anything but. Because the soviets were large bodies and met infrequently, deputies could have, at best, a marginal impact on local governance. The brevity of the deputies' tenure in office and the fact that they held full-time jobs elsewhere further diminished their impact. They possessed neither the expertise to govern nor the time to acquire it. As a result, by 1985, the running of local government in the old Soviet system was left to the members of the *ispolkom,* who operated virtually without regard to popular control; the people's elected representatives provided little more than token approval for decisions already made elsewhere.

The real explanation for the absence of democratic pluralism in Soviet local government during this time, however, must be found in the role of the CPSU. In the Leninist conception, the Communist Party, and only the party, could define the interests of society and was, therefore, entitled to a monopoly of political power. The party exercised its complete control over the soviets in several ways. As we have seen, the first secretary of the city's Party Committee controlled the outcome of single-candidate elections by controlling the nomination process at the workplace. Although a majority of the elected deputies were not party members, no one unwilling to accept the party line would be nominated. Furthermore, the *gorkom* first secretary commanded the loyalty of those deputies who were party members and who constituted a caucus called the "party group" among the deputies. Through them, party first secretaries controlled the nomination and unanimous election of a single slate of members to the *ispolkom,* normally including themselves. Finally, in order to ensure the implementation of the party's policies, the local party structure duplicated the administrative departments of the *ispolkom.* The Russian word for this complete usurpation by the Party of the authority of the state was *"podmena,"* and although it was officially condemned, it was universally practiced.[33] In sum, the legislative branch of government was completely dominated by the executive branch, but the executive branch was entirely the creature of the Communist Party. It was the antithesis of pluralism; it approached a perfect monist system.

It is clear from the foregoing that local political power under the old system was not dispersed, but concentrated; it was not divided among many, but belonged to a few. In Yaroslavl', during "Tsar Fedor" Loshenkov's tenure as *obkom* first secretary, local political power had really belonged to one. Gorbachev's proposals to the 19th Party Conference in June 1988, as implemented at the local level in 1990, aimed at fundamentally altering the old system in two ways: Legislatures were to be given greater control over the executive branch, and the role of the party in governmental affairs was to be diminished.

To implement the first of these goals, members of the *ispolkom,* except for the chair, could no longer be deputies at the same time.[34] Instead, they would be elected by (and subsequently accountable to) the deputies at their first, or organizational, session. To ensure continuous legislative oversight, the deputies would also choose from among themselves a 15- to 20-member presidium, which would consist of the heads of the standing committees as well as the chair and vice-chair of the soviet. The presidium, and not the *ispolkom,* would organize the work of the deputies at their sessions and make sure that the executive branch was carrying out the decisions of the legislature. As to diminishing the role of the party, its control over the composition of the soviet had already been significantly reduced by the introduction of competitive elections. Among other things, the local party leadership would now be exposed for the first time to the voter's judgment. Internally, the structure of the Party was reorganized and the duplication of administrative departments was ended.[35]

How were these reforms put into practice? Did they bring about a greater dispersion of political power? In Yaroslavl', the new system of local government was introduced at the inaugural session of the city soviet. The soviet began its work on May 10, 1990, and continued for about a week. By then, 179 of the 200 seats in the city soviet had been duly filled, enough seats to constitute a quorum.[36] The first order of business facing the deputies, after a temporary organizational committee had been chosen to run the meeting, was the election of someone to chair the soviet. The deputies rejected an attempt to use a list of candidates prepared in advance by the *ispolkom* on the basis of a written deputy survey and proposed nominees from the floor instead. Fourteen candidates were nominated in this fashion. After ten of these withdrew their candidacies, the remainder presented their platforms. Among the four, L. L. Kruglikov, a law professor at Yaroslavl' State University, was favored by the YPF. His main rival was L. L. Karnakov, the *gorkom* first secretary, who had managed to get elected from another district in a repeat election, after losing an uncontested seat in the first round. When it became clear that Karnakov had no chance of winning, he withdrew rather than face certain defeat. On a secret ballot, Kruglikov won easily with 132 votes.[37]

Although the YPF had not actively supported Kruglikov in the March elections, its support of him as chair of the soviet was crucial to his election.[38] This first step established the political character of the new soviet in an important way: Both the contested vote and the defeat of the *gorkom* first secretary made it clear that from then on the political life of the city would be different. The support given to Kruglikov was sustained for the next two items on the agenda: the election of V. N. Bakaev as vice-chair and V. V. Volonchunas as chair of the *ispolkom*. The second of these is particularly noteworthy because Volonchunas had been the *ispolkom* chair under in the previous soviet and, as such, was criticized by the YPF as a member of the old *apparat*. Volonchunas was one of five candidates originally nominated and one of three left in the final balloting. He was finally elected, receiving 125 votes, but only after Kruglikov had personally endorsed him on the basis of his competence and his experience. "Not all apparatchiks are bad," Kruglikov told the deputies. "They should be judged first of all by their performance."[39]

The remainder of the session was taken up with the formation of legislative and executive bodies. On the legislative side, this included the appointment of the legislative standing committees and commissions (of which there are 16), the election of the chair of the city's People's Control Committee (a legislative oversight committee with 3 permanent staff), and the formation of the legislative presidium, consisting of the officers of the soviet and the chairs of the standing committees (21 members in all, with a permanent staff of 5). On the executive side, the remaining members of the *ispolkom* were elected by the deputies by secret ballot. The deputies then decided what other administrative departments they wished to form. Nominees to head these other offices were then proposed by the *ispolkom* chair, subject to confirmation by the deputies.

What are the relations between the city soviet and its *ispolkom* like under the new system? Legally, at least until late in 1991, their relations were governed by the regulations (*reglamenty*) of the city soviet, adopted at its third session in September 1990.[40] According to article 84 of these regulations, the subordination of the executive branch to the decisions of the legislature was clear: "ARTICLE 84. All officials of the *ispolkom* are obligated to implement all decisions of the Soviet and its Presidium. The soviet has the right to revoke any decision of the executive committee. Decisions of the Presidium have priority over those of the *ispolkom*."

Among the decisions belonging to the soviet was approval of the budget prepared by the *ispolkom* and any changes proposed in it. The *ispolkom* could not make discretionary expenditures over a certain amount without the approval of the presidium. To ensure that the executive branch does not exceed its authority, a People's Control Committee was established to oversee the work of the administrative departments. In addition, the deputies and their committees were granted an impressive list of ways to obtain information about executive activities.[41] Finally, the *ispolkom* had to report at least once a year on its activities to the soviet as a whole, and its departments could be required to do so at any time.[42]

The reality of executive-legislative relations is a good deal more complicated than the foregoing legal description would suggest and tends to favor the continued dominance of the executive branch. The reason for this has little to do with shortcomings in the law, nor is it necessarily due to any malevolent power ambitions on the part of the administrators. The fact of the matter is that, as Kruglikov had recognized, these are the professionals. They alone knew how to run a government and they were indispensable. Not only did they know how the government worked but, because they were all a product of the old *nomenklatura* system, they also knew the people who made things work, an "old *nomenklatura*-boy network," if you will. (The *nomenklatura* is a list of positions that can be filled only with Communist Party approval.)

During in-depth interviews with about fifteen of the deputies in June 1991 I asked them directly: Who has more influence over the city's affairs, the chair of the soviet or of the *ispolkom?* Invariably, the deputies named the latter, although some noted the growing influence of the legislative branch and its chair. This impression was confirmed by an in-house poll taken of 90 percent of the deputies in May 1991 by T. P. Rumiantseva, who heads the city's Center for the Study of Public Opinion. When she asked which of the branches of local government had more real power, 53 percent of the deputies named the *ispolkom;* only 12 percent named the soviet.

With respect to the role of the party in local politics, it was clear that even before the failure of the attempted coup of August 1991, the party's fortunes were on the wane, although it continued to retain some influence, especially on the provincial (*oblast'*) level.[43] Its weakness in the city soviet was obvious. Despite the fact that 67 percent of the deputies were party members, the deputy group calling themselves "Kommunisty," which was registered at the organizational session, could muster only seventeen members. The *gorkom* first secretary Karnakov avoided a humiliating defeat in his effort to be elected chair of the soviet only by withdrawing his candidacy at the last minute.

Not only was the party's influence in the soviet evaporating but the party itself was. In the course of the year 1990–1991, membership in the party fell by nearly one-fourth, and the number of *obkom* officials fell by nearly two-thirds. When I asked about the influence of the party in the city soviet, almost all of the deputies I had interviewed in June 1991 agreed that it was negligible or nonexistent. During my interview with him, even the *obkom* first secretary agreed with this assessment at the city level. Whatever remained of the party's presence as a political organization had disappeared, of course, after the failed coup. Yeltsin's decree seizing party property was implemented by the city soviet at its seventh session, held on September 2, 1991. His decree of November 6, 1991, banning the party's activities in Russia, was merely the coup de grace.

A final way to look at how the role of the deputies has changed is to describe their behavior in council sessions. In 1984 I attended a session of a city soviet operating in the old style.[44] It quickly became clear that the entire proceedings were carefully scripted in advance by the organizational-instructional committee of the *ispolkom*. They drew up the agenda, determined who would present reports and on what subject, who would comment on them, and how many minutes each speaker would be allowed. In many cases, they even prepared the texts. The meeting of the 250 deputies lasted the allotted three hours, during which a number of votes were taken, all unanimously. Participation was thus extremely limited and opposition was nonexistent. It is worth recalling this formalistic exercise because it was typical of soviet sessions throughout the USSR, Yaroslavl' included, before 1985. It serves as a benchmark against which to measure change.

The sixth session of the Yaroslavl' city soviet, which began its work on June 26, 1991, stood in stark contrast to previous practice and provides a measure of how far the deputy's role has evolved. Although a detailed description of the session is beyond the scope of this chapter, I can summarize the differences between the two sessions. For one thing, this meeting lasted three days, not three hours. For another, the agenda had been prepared by the presidium of the soviet, not by the *ispolkom* (see Appendix).[45] Although the *ispolkom* could, and did, propose items for inclusion, the presidium arranged the proceedings. No time limits on debate were imposed.

Most significantly, perhaps, the opportunity to participate in these proceedings was open to any and all deputies, and they took full advantage of it. Participation was frequent and often severely critical of those who sat on either the *ispolkom* or the presidium.[46] The deputies openly expressed disagreement among themselves and cast negative votes on virtually every issue. On some matters of importance (for example, they discussed a bill on how to implement privatization) the deputies defeated proposals by the presidium or the *ispolkom*. On at least three occasions, draft legislation was remanded to ad hoc committees and later presented to the deputies as a whole, who then voted on changes introduced—in a manner not unlike a committee "mark-up" session in Congress. In these respects, the deputies demonstrated the characteristics of contestation that mark the emergence of democratic pluralism.

Clearly, this session of the Yaroslavl' city council was far more democratic than the one that I observed in 1984. At the same time, the conduct of this meeting also revealed a number of rather serious shortcomings from the standpoint of democratic development. In the first place, although there was a lot of participation, much of it was not very good: Speakers frequently and freely introduced subjects that were trivial or irrelevant to the matter at hand; debates degenerated into shouting matches; and matters related essentially to constituency service were put up for votes by the body as a whole (a good thirty minutes were spent discussing a bus rerouting that was necessary to service one district). Moreover, the participation was uneven: 136 deputies came to the session, meaning roughly one-third were missing. Among those present, perhaps 30 deputies took an active part in the proceedings. Many of the others seemed unprepared, or even uninterested, in doing so.

Voting was haphazard in the sense that personal whim rather than group affiliation or constituency representation seemed to guide the deputies' choices. The relatively disciplined voting that had characterized the organizational session a year earlier and had resulted in Kruglikov's election as chair had disappeared. The four deputy groups that had been registered at that time also played no apparent role in this session. Although the chair, Kruglikov, was a lawyer by profession, at times it seemed as if procedure was being made as the meeting went along.[47] By the end of the session it seemed as if discipline had all but broken down, as deputies argued about whether to end the session or to continue it on the next day. To this observer at least, chaos, rather than calm deliberation, seemed to characterize much of the work of the June 1991 session.

In his analysis of the first two years of the USSR Supreme Soviet, Robert T. Huber measured the emergence of pluralism as a function of whether legislative institutionalization had taken place.[48] Using Michael J. Mezey's five categories, Huber concluded that the Supreme Soviet should be considered a "marginal legislature," in the sense that despite substantial formal authority and high expectations from both the public and administrators, the members of such a legislature don't deal very effectively with the demands placed on them. Such a conclusion would not seem out of place applied to the mini-Parliament that is the Yaroslavl' city soviet. There are simply too many deputies, with too little political experience and too little organizational discipline, to deal effectively with the numerous complex and urgent problems that face their city today.

How Deputies Consult with Their Constituents

At the beginning of this chapter I argued that democratic pluralism presupposed the possibility of public participation, singly or in groups, in the political life of the community. Such participation is essential if public preferences are to be communicated to those who govern. In a democracy, it is assumed that these preferences will be taken into consideration; representatives who ignore them may be held accountable at periodic elections, thus ensuring popular control. But elections are only one way by which popular preferences can be ascertained, and they are not necessarily the most effective. Political participation can take many other forms: People work in campaigns, for political parties, through interest groups; they contact their representatives directly; they sign petitions, respond to opinion surveys, and demonstrate. Whatever form participation takes, some mechanisms for popular consultation are vital if we are to conclude that democratic pluralism is emerging in Russia. Moreover, there must be some evidence that the people are being heard.

It seems clear from my earlier discussion of pluralist societies that competition for political influence is open to people acting on their own or through groups. In Dahl's view, large-scale democracies are chiefly distinguished by having a number of autonomous groups contending for influence, and Presthus finds the participation of individuals equally significant when the level of analysis is community politics. In assessing the degree to which popular participation is characteristic of political life in Yaroslavl', in this section I will examine, first, what forms of participation (other than voting) are possible for individuals acting on their own. I will then consider group participation. Finally, I will take up the question of whether anyone is listening.

Even before 1985, Soviet law provided for a number of ways by which voters could contact those they elected in order to express personal or community concerns. These methods included the use of voters' mandates (*nakazy izbiratelei*), which were approved at campaign meetings and which specified certain actions that deputies were pledged to fulfill if they were elected. Deputies were also required to meet with their constituents at least four times a year (twice in their districts and twice at the workplace that nominated them) and to hold regular reception hours, called a *priyom,* during which citizens could raise local and personal problems that deputies were expected to address. In addition, the electorate could make its wishes known orally or in writing through a procedure known as "complaints, proposals, and declarations" (*zhaloby, zaiavlenii, i predlozhenii*), which required a response from the deputy. Finally, deputies had the right to make formal inquiries (*zaprosy*) on behalf of their constituents to executive departments responsible for implementing policies in their districts. In short, the institutional basis for the expression of citizen preferences was substantial. Furthermore, there is some evidence that it was used, albeit infrequently.[49]

It is noteworthy that all of these ways of communicating citizen preferences to those who govern appear to have survived the reform process intact, although in Yaroslavl', at least, shortcomings in implementation are candidly acknowledged. The city council was supposed to adopt measures to fulfill the voter mandates at its third session in September 1990, but it ran out of time and didn't do so until its fifth session, six months later. At that time, a plan for implementing 130 mandates was developed. This, however, represented fewer than half of the mandates proposed by voters, because "the candidates for deputy, through their inexperience, did not give sufficiently serious attention to the form and contents of the mandates at the time of the meetings."[50] There also were 476 written and oral complaints and proposals from the voters received by the deputies (206 of them during reception hours). Of these, 235 resulted in on-site inspections by members of the soviet or its committees. The overwhelming majority of these problems (65 percent), as in the old days, concerned housing.

The use of the deputies' right of inquiry (*zapros*) seemed to have greater potential for focusing the deputies' attention on issues with a more widespread community impact. During the sixth session of the city soviet, which I attended in June

1991, the deputies spent considerable time discussing various deputy inquiries. In some cases, they engendered sharp debate, and action was defeated or modified. In the end, action was voted on fourteen items, each sponsored by a different deputy. Many of these were purely parochial in nature, hardly meriting the attention of the soviet as a whole (e.g., roof repairs, bus routes, telephone service, closing a beer hall), but not all were. Among the topics discussed was the provision of housing for refugees from the fighting in Baku, the construction of a new school in one of the microregions, and the conduct of an independent soil test for pollution in the Frunze district.

Though opportunities for citizens, individually, to express their concerns to decision makers are numerous and appear to be heeded, on those relatively infrequent occasions when invoked, the same cannot be said about participation through groups, although this may be changing. As already noted, despite the active role played by the Yaroslavl' Popular Front in the 1990 elections and the formation of quasi-partisan deputy groups at the organizational session that elected the city's leaders, these groups have not maintained their cohesion over time. Partly, this is because, by the nature of its business, municipal governance doesn't tend to foster ideological divisions. But, in Yaroslavl' as elsewhere in Russia, it is also because the deputies didn't run on a partisan platform and don't owe their election to any party organization.

In a different way, the same thing is true for interest groups. The influence of private interest groups in the United States, for example, is derived in no small part from their ability to give or withhold campaign donations. In the Russian elections of 1990, however, there were strict limits on campaign expenditures.[51] The city paid for virtually all of the permissible campaign literature precisely to ensure that candidates would not have an "unfair" advantage by outspending their opponents. To the extent that private or "corporate" interests are expressed, it is probably the result of the fact that the overwhelming majority of deputies were nominated at their place of work and can therefore be "pressured," if you will, into supporting decisions favorable to their employers. Whereas deputies may not feel that they owe their election to private interest groups in general, they do seem to be aware of the views of the work collective that nominated them.

Public interest groups (sometimes called *neformalny*) are another matter. There are a number of such groups in Yaroslavl', including an ecological group called the "Green Bud," a branch of Memorial, the national organization concerned with the victims of Stalinism, and a charitable organization called the "Miloserdtsy." There is also the Russian Orthodox church, which has been lobbying vigorously and with considerable success for the return of some of Yaroslavl's many ancient churches to use for worship. The limits on the influence of groups such as these derive not only from a lack of material means but also, with the exception of the Russian Orthodox Church, from a lack of organizational and political experience; they are political amateurs.[52] Nevertheless, these groups can, on occasion, make their presence felt.[53] In the end, however, although these groups can (and did) call on their members to support candidates in the 1990 elections, they lack the material or organizational resources to make much of a difference. It is doubtful if any of the deputies feel that they are dependent on the support of such groups for their election.

Finally, what about the public? Are they ready to participate politically? Do they feel that their views are taken into consideration by those they elect? Do they find that the new form of government is more responsive than the old? A systematic survey of public opinion on these and related questions was conducted in May 1991 by Tatiana Rumiantseva, the head of the Center for the Study of Public Opinion, which carries out sociological research for the city government.[54] The sample size was more than six hundred people. The results shed some light on the degree to which deputies are likely to be influenced by those they represent (see Table 4.1).

For public opinion to have an impact on decision makers, it is generally assumed that citizens should be interested in what government does, should know something of its policies and personnel, and should be prepared to communicate their views.[55] It seems clear from the results of the survey that a gap exists between the expectations of democratic theory and the reality of local politics in Yaroslavl'. Only 12 percent claimed to know the deputy from their district, and barely 25 percent had even fragmentary knowledge of what the presidium was (65 percent knew nothing). Only 2 percent had directed questions or complaints to the presidium in 1990–1991, and the level of satisfaction with deputy reception hours and written proposals was very low. As to the voter mandates, the largest percentages of respondents (39 percent) felt that "practically none was implemented, only promises."

It can be fairly argued, however, that low levels of knowledge, participation, political information, and trust are found in other democratic systems. Certainly similar results in U.S. cities would hardly be surprising. More disturbing in the Yaroslavl' survey is that most respondents saw little change from the previous system. The results are presented in Table 4.1. Only on the dimension of "democraticness" (*demokratichnost'*) did the respondents see an appreciable increase in the work of local government. On the question of contact with the electorate, few perceived any improvement over the past practice. The one ray of hope may be that so many people responded "hard to say," suggesting that they had not as yet made up their minds. As for the remainder of those responding, the public seems decidedly unimpressed with what they have seen so far of local government reform.

In conclusion, what can be said about how well city politics in Yaroslavl' meets the criteria for democratic pluralism of popular consultation? What struck me in the course of my attendance at the session of the city soviet and during my interviews with the deputies was that they seemed to be voting quite independently of any public input, except perhaps that which they received at their place of work, where they were nominated.

TABLE 4.1
Q. Do you think there have been any changes in the activities of local government today as compared with the previous one?

	Increased	Decreased	No Change	Hard to Say
Organizationally	7.0 [a]	11.7	32.5	46.6
Deputies' professionalism	7.0	7.7	33.4	47.2
Democraticness	27.5	4.0	31.0	31.6
Interest in results	11.9	8.6	32.3	41.3
Bureaucratism	9.4	7.3	37.1	23.8
Contact with voters	8.2	5.3	42.8	36.3
Trust in the city soviet	12.1	11.2	40.9	28.1
Trust in the city ispolkom	4.8	17.8	44.0	29.9
Trust in your deputy	3.3	14.3	43.1	36.0

[a] Responses are given in percentages
SOURCE: Yaroslavl' Center for the Study of Public Opinion (May 1991) Director: T.P. Rumiantseva.

They demonstrated little evidence of any public influence, not from their constituents, not by any partisan allegiance, not from interest groups, or even by ideological predilection. Instead, their choices seemed to be informed by little more than their personal opinions of the moment. In reflecting on why this should be so, it is possible to hypothesize that since the deputies relied largely on personal qualifications to get elected, there is so far little reason for them to think that they are dependent on anything other than their own personal characteristics to get reelected. As a result, from the standpoint of organizational participation in politics associated with democratic pluralism, community politics in Yaroslavl' is still in an early stage of development.

A Mixed Assessment

Are we seeing the emergence of democratic pluralism in Russian politics? The purpose of this chapter was to contribute to the answer to this intriguing question by looking at how the role of locally elected officials has changed since reforms were introduced in 1990 to promote democracy. The standards of measurement were defined as the degree to which a dispersion of power, political contestation, and popular consultation are characteristic of contemporary local Russian politics. Certainly, the practice of local government in Russia and the rest of the Soviet Union before the reforms of perestroika was deficient by these standards: Power was highly centralized; legitimized political opposition was nonexistent; and popular consultation was largely confined to ritual. Has the situation improved? How democratic are local Russian deputies?

On the basis of the evidence presented here, the short answer to this question is that although democratic pluralism is far more characteristic of local Russian politics than it used to be, there is a great deal of room for improvement. Admittedly, the evidence is from only one Russian city, Yaroslavl', but the following conclusions may offer a starting point for understanding what is happening elsewhere.

On the positive side, power is clearly more widely dispersed than it had been under the old system. The Communist Party no longer controls who gets elected to the soviet, nor does it play any role in the formation of the government. Executive and legislative authority are no longer joined, but divided; executive accountability before the legislature is established not only in law but also in fact. Free and competitive elections provide at least the possibility that ultimate accountability will rest with the people. Political contestation is manifest not only in competitive elections but also in the behavior of the deputies in council. What Thomas Remington has referred to as the "mobilization of discontent" is visible in the formation of voting blocs in council and in the open opposition of deputies to policies of government leaders with which they do not agree.[56] Finally, there is some evidence to suggest that, however slowly, the public has become involved in the process by which decisions are made, and not only through voting but through individual and group action.

At the same time, the development of democratic pluralism in local Russian politics, at least as practiced in Yaroslavl', has been limited by a number of factors. Of these, probably none is more significant than the 1990 elections, the administration of which did not fully satisfy the requirements of either political contestation or popular consultation. Voters were simply faced with too many candidates, running for too many offices, in too many elections. Without partisan affiliation to give them political identity, voters relied on candidates' personal qualifications, making their choices less meaningful than they should have been as an indicator of the public's policy preferences. Although there was organized opposition in the form of the Yaroslavl' Popular Front, it was unable to get its message out to the electorate because it lacked the resources, experience, or organization to do so. For this reason, instead of dispersing power, the 1990 elections probably enabled older elites to retain more power than they otherwise would have. To some extent, this is also true in the relations between the soviet and its *ispolkom.* Despite the new separation of powers, the executive branch retained a preponderance of influence, partly by virtue of its expertise and partly through its connections to the old *nomenklatura.* Finally, although the channels for citizen involvement are more open than before, there is little evidence to suggest that they are widely used, or even perceived as particularly fruitful.

For all of these reasons, the prognosis for the further evolution of Russian local politics in the direction of greater democratic pluralism is uncertain. Much will depend on when and how the next elections of local officials take place. As the political theorists of democracy cited earlier almost unanimously concede, no other institution is so central for insuring that the criteria of democratic pluralism are met. Much will also depend on whether the Russians can improve their lot economically. Failure to do so invites demagoguery and authoritarian solutions. Such alternatives are unpalatable, to say the least.

Appendix

Agenda of the Sixth Session
of the Yaroslavl' City Soviet, June 26, 1991.

The following agenda of the day's session was confirmed:

1. Report on the work of the presidium of the city soviet of People's Deputies (speaker: L. L. Kruglikov—chairman of the city soviet).
2. Report on the work of the Executive Committee of the city soviet of People's Deputies (speaker: V. V. Volonchunas—chairman of the Executive Committee).
3. Refining the city budget for 1991 (speaker: V. V. Istomina—director of the Financial Department of the Executive Committee).
4. Estimating the rate for taxes on profits (same speaker as above).
5. On measures for ensuring legal regulation for using Yaroslavl's land resources (speaker: A. P. Bobovich—head of the Executive Committee's Senior Administration of Architecture and Town Planning).
6. On measures for preparing for the privatization of municipal property (speaker: A. V. Suchkov—deputy from electoral district 56; chairman of the Commission on Provisions, Trade, Public Catering, and Public Services; head of the "Paris Commune" industrial complex).
7. On the procedures for material incentives for deputies of the city soviet (speaker: V. N. Bakaev—deputy chairman of the city soviet).
8. On converting the Ad Hoc Commission on Land into a standing committee (speaker: V. M. Kuzmin—deputy from electoral district 19; deputy chairman of the Ad Hoc Commission; assistant chief of the KGB in the Yaroslavl' region).
9. On the petition submitted by the commander of Military Division 40890 (same speaker as above).
10. On the apportionment of space in the department of preschool institutions (speaker: V. V. Volonchunas—chairman of the Executive Committee).
11. On delegating the legislation of final decisions concerning land (V. N. Bakaev—deputy chairman of the city soviet).
12. Organizational questions.
13. Other business.

Notes

The author wishes to thank the Carnegie Corporation of New York and the International Research and Exchanges Board (IREX) for financial support in conducting the field research on which this chapter is based and the National Council for Soviet and East European Research for a grant to support his salary in spring and summer 1992 so that he could write. None of these organizations necessarily shares the views of the author.

1. H. B. Mayo, *An Introduction to Democratic Theory* (New York: Oxford University Press, 1960) p. 60.

2. Jeffrey W. Hahn, *Soviet Grassroots: Citizen Participation in Local Soviet Government* (Princeton: Princeton University Press, 1988), pp. 194–198.

3. Jeffrey W. Hahn, "More Power to Soviets?" *Problems of Communism* 2 (1989) 1:34–46.

4. Austin Ranney and Willmoore Kendall, *Democracy and the American Party System* (New York: Harcourt, Brace & Co., 1965), p. 24; Susan Gross Solomon, "Pluralism in Political Science: The Odyssey of a Concept," in Susan Gross Solomon, ed., *Pluralism in the Soviet Union* (New York: St. Martin's Press, 1983), pp. 8–20.

5. Robert A. Dahl, *Dilemmas of Pluralist Democracy* (New Haven: Yale University Press, 1982), p. 5.

6. Robert A. Dahl, *Polyarchy: Participation and Opposition* (New Haven: Yale University Press, 1971), pp. 3–4.

7. Robert A. Dahl, *Democracy in the United States,* 2d ed. (New York: Rand McNally, 1972), p. 44.

8. Dahl, *Dilemmas of Pluralist Democracy,* pp. 5, 12–16, 29; emphasis added.

9. Robert Presthus, *Men at the Top* (New York: Oxford University Press, 1964), p. 10.

10. Dahl, *Democracy in the United States,* p. 37.

11. Presthus, *Men at the Top,* pp. 22–24.

12. Ranney and Kendall, *Democracy and the American Party System,* pp. 56–81.

13. Heinz Eulau, et al., "The Role of the Representative," *American Political Science Review* (1959) 52:742–756; Warren E. Miller and Donald E. Stokes, "Constituency Influence in Congress," *American Political Science Review* (1963) 57:45–56; John Kingdon, *Congressmen's Voting Decisions,* 2d ed. (New York: Harper and Row, 1989).

14. Dennis S. Ippolito, Thomas G. Walker, and Kenneth L. Kolson, *Public Opinion and Responsible Democracy* (Englewood Cliffs: Prentice-Hall, 1976), pp. 3–13.

15. The city of Yaroslavl' is the administrative center and capital of Yaroslavl' *oblast'* and is located about 200 miles northeast of Moscow. Although it is part of the "Golden Ring" of ancient Russian cities that surround Moscow, most of the work force is employed in industry. The population of over 630,000 is overwhelmingly Russian (over 90 percent). Although Yaroslavl' was one of the first cities to have an active popular front movement, it was by no means the only one. From February 1990 to February 1992, I made five research trips to Yaroslavl'.

16. It may be objected that this study is time bound because it relies on information gathered before the attempted coup of August 1991 and the dramatic changes that followed. In fact, the coup had relatively little impact on the politics of Yaroslavl' other than to end the direct influence of an already diminished Communist party organization. During a brief visit in January of 1992, I found that the legislative institutions and political elites described here continued to function in ways only marginally modified from what was in place in summer 1991. What modifications did occur do not appear to invalidate the conclusions offered here.

17. Clifford Geertz, "Thick Description: Towards an Interpretive Theory of Culture," in Clifford Geertz, ed., *The Interpretation of Cultures* (New York: Basic Books, 1973).

18. This approach has been fruitfully employed in numerous studies of community power in the United States and elsewhere. In fact, the approach used here may be particularly appropriate to analyzing the emergence of pluralism in Russia precisely because of the greater opportunities local government offers for public participation. As Robert Presthus notes in *Men at the Top,* "in sum, field studies of the political process at the community level are needed to test pluralist assumptions, for it is here that widespread participation has the best chance to occur. One would expect to find the closest approximation between pluralist ideals and the realities of social and political organizations"(p. 32).

19. Mayo, *An Introduction to Democratic Theory,* p. 61.

20. Gerald M. Pomper, *Elections in America* (New York: Dodd, Mead, and Co., 1968), pp. 263–266.

21. Hahn, *Soviet Grassroots,* pp. 92–107.

22. Victor Zaslavsky and Robert J. Brym, "The Functions of Elections in the USSR," *Soviet Studies* (1978) 30: 362–371.

23. Jeffrey W. Hahn, "An Experiment in Competition: The 1987 Elections to the Local Soviets," *Slavic Review* (1988) 47: 434–447.

24. Jeffrey W. Hahn, "Boss Gorbachev Confronts His New Congress," *Orbis* (1990) 34: 163–178.

25. Zakon RSFSR, "O vyborakh narodnykh deputatov mestnykh sovetov RSFSR" (Moscow: Sovetskaia Rossiia, 1989); Dawn Mann, "The RSFSR Elections: The Congress of People's Deputies," Radio Free Europe/Radio Liberty (hereafter cited as RFE/RL) *Report on the USSR,* April 13, 1990, pp. 11–14.

26. *Izvestiia,* June 18, 1988.

27. *Izvestiia,* January 10, 1990.

28. Jeffrey W. Hahn, "Local Politics and Political Power in Russia: The Case of Yaroslavl'," *Soviet Economy,* no. 7 (1991), p. 329.

29. Such legislation was eventually adopted by the USSR Supreme Soviet on October 9, 1990, entitled "The Law on Public Organizations" (see *Izvestiia,* October 10, 1990). Accordingly, we may expect that in future elections, candidates will affiliate themselves with one or another party.

30. Hahn, "Local Politics and Political Power," p. 328.

31. V. I. Lenin, "State and Revolution," (1917) in *The Lenin Anthology,* ed. Robert C. Tucker (New York: W. W. Norton, 1975).

32. Hahn, *Soviet Grassroots,* p. 86.

33. Ronald J. Hill, "The CPSU: From Monolith to Pluralist," *Soviet Studies* (1991) 43: 217–235.

34. Zakon, article 12.

35. The legislative basis for the changes that affected the structure of the Soviet state system can be found in the amendments to the USSR and RSFSR Constitutions adopted during winter 1989–1990.

36. The composition of the 179 deputies who had been elected by May 10, 1990, include 29 women (16 percent), 30 workers (16 percent), 18 candidates under the age of thirty (10 percent), and 27 party and state officials (15 percent). In each case, their numbers were far fewer than in the previous soviet. The percent of party and Komsomol members (70 percent) and deputies holding office for the first time (85 percent) was significantly higher.

37. All information comes from the city weekly newspaper, *Gorodskie novosti* (hereafter cited as *GN*), through documentary materials made available to me by the Yaroslavl'

city soviet, or through personal interviews. Information about the organizational session of the city soviet was published in *GN* from May 8–22, 1990, including three special issues. Kruglikov's election was reported in the special issue of May 15.

38. Kruglikov acknowledged as much during my interview with him in June 1990.

39. *GN*, May 16, 1990, p. 2.

40. These regulations remained in force at least until November 1991. A decision was taken at the 8th session of the soviet on October 21, 1991, to replace the presidium with a "small soviet" (*malyi sovet*), consisting of 15 members elected by the deputies as a whole plus the chairman ex officio. This was done in accordance with the Russian republic legislation adopted on July 6, 1991. So too, was the nomination of a mayor (referred to in the law as the *glava administratsii*. This nomination took place at the 9th session of the city soviet on November 18, 1991. The names of three candidates voted on at that meeting were submitted to President Yeltsin, including the former *ispolkom* chair, Victor Volonchunas, who had received the most votes and who ultimately was appointed mayor.

41. Zakon, articles 89–100.

42. Ibid., article 86.

43. Hahn, "Local Politics," pp. 332–334.

44. Hahn, *Soviet Grassroots*, pp. 197–207.

45. The agenda can be found in the Appendix.

46. To mention one example, Iurii I. Verbitskii, the representative of the 13th district, accused the *ispolkom* chair, Volonchunas, of violating a law on historic preservation by building a disinfection station in the middle of a historic cemetery. Verbitskii, who is the head of the city soviet's Standing Committee on Culture, Heritage, and Religion, pursued this cause further at a meeting of the presidium on June 28, 1991, and threatened to take the issue to court if there was no compensation.

47. For example, the deputy from the district 166, Anatolii Samusev, was elected as a vice-chair of the *ispolkom* that is in charge of the city's administrative department for planning and the economy, apparently in direct contradiction to article 12 of the RSFSR Law on Elections, which prohibits deputies from holding administrative appointments. This decision, which was adopted on June 25, 1991, was later corrected at the 7th session of the city soviet on September 2, 1990, when Samusev's deputy status was revoked.

48. Robert T. Huber, "Soviet Defense and Foreign Policy in the Supreme Soviet," in *Perestroika-Era Politics,* ed. Robert T. Huber and Donald R. Kelley (Armonk, N.Y.: M. E. Sharpe, 1991).

49. Hahn, *Soviet Grassroots*, pp. 133–198.

50. The data and this quote comes from a report by city soviet chairman, L. L. Kruglikov, to the 6th session of the soviet, meeting June 25, 1991, entitled "O rabote s nakazami i pros'bami izbirate'lei."

51. Timothy J. Colton, "The Politics of Democratization: The Moscow Election of 1990," *Soviet Economy,* no. 6 (1990), p. 293; Zakon, art. 13.

52. I attended a meeting of the Green Bud on March 22, 1990, as it was choosing candidates for the second round of voting. I was as impressed with their almost total disregard for procedure as I was by the obvious sincerity of their conviction and civic-mindedness.

53. I attended a meeting of the city soviet's presidium, called on June 28, 1991, to discuss charges raised at the general session regarding violations of the law on historic preservation. Considerable pressure was brought to bear by representatives of several of these groups, including Memorial, to reverse an earlier decision of the *ispolkom* about the loca-

tion of a city facility in a historic cemetery. The presidium voted to investigate the charges and report back to the deputies at the next session.

54. The existence of this center is itself a sign of the increased attention being paid to what the public thinks and to what the deputies think. Other surveys undertaken by the center include assessments of proposed changes in the structure of city government, surveys on the city's attempt to reform alcohol sales, and polls concerning who the people favored for election as president of Russia in March 1991.

55. Alan D. Monroe, *Public Opinion in America* (New York: Dodd, Mead, and Co., 1975), p. 11.

56. Thomas F. Remington, "Regime Transition in Communist Systems: The Soviet Case," *Soviet Economy,* no. 6 (1990), p. 185.

CHAPTER 5

Prospects for Political Pluralism in Central Asia

Peter Clement

The collapse of the USSR in 1991 marked the end of but one era in the long, complex history of Central Asia. For the purposes of this chapter, the states of Central Asia include Kazakhstan, Tajikistan, Turkmenistan, Uzbekistan, and Kyrgyzstan. This era dates back to the nineteenth century, when Russia undertook systematic efforts to bring this region under its sway. In the Soviet period, efforts to ensure Moscow's control intensified through the creation of Soviet-style administrations and the implementation of central planning. These political and economic legacies of the Soviet era create serious hardships for the current leaders of the newly independent Central Asian states. At the same time, recent events indicate, that more than one hundred years of Russian and Soviet rule could not erase the regional, ethnic, tribal, and religious forces that have traditionally been the wellspring of Central Asia's political life. In fact, Central Asia's first year of independence illustrates the potency of these so-called traditional forces at a time when Central Asian leaders are trying to eliminate the vestiges of the Soviet legacy and to create new states. Indeed, it is the combination of the Soviet legacies and these traditional forces that seem to work against the creation of both political stability and the emergence of pluralism in Central Asia. Ultimately, the Central Asian experience since the demise of the USSR raises serious questions about the interrelationship of the problems of political development and the emergence of democratic pluralism.

Joseph Rothschild, in his study of ethnopolitics, lists the following as criteria of ethnicity: race, kinship (blood, clan, tribal ties), religion, language, mode of livelihood, regionalism, and a people's political experience.[1] As we look at the political processes unfolding in Central Asia, it would seem that the salience of any one of these factors could be magnified by several of the others. In fact, Ernest Gellner, for example, views ethnicity "as a function of the unevenness of

The author is an analyst in the Office of Slavic and Eurasian Affairs at the Central Intelligence Agency. The views expressed in this chapter are his and do not necessarily reflect the official view of the U.S. government or the Central Intelligence Agency.

industrialization."[2] This may be seen in events in Tajikistan, where a civil war raged for much of 1992.

In this chapter I begin with an assessment of the Russian/Soviet legacy and then go on to describe briefly the political trends in each of the Central Asian states. The bulk of the chapter is devoted to a case study of Tajikistan, because that country's events provide a useful basis for thinking about how the prospects for political pluralism in Central Asia can be shaped by important ethnic, regional, and religious factors. I will conclude by looking at some of the models of political development employed in analyses of other emerging societies and how they may help us to think about possible outcomes in Central Asia.

The Overall Environment: The Soviet Legacy

In my discussion of the Central Asian republics as independent states, the dominant reality is the immense burden or legacy of both Russian and Soviet imperial rule. There are virtually no facets of Central Asian life that have not been seriously affected by the experience of colonial domination. One noted analyst quite correctly calls this region a "tragic experiment" in Soviet rule.[3] The most obvious bequests of the Soviet era are in the political, security, economic, and environmental areas. All affect the processes of building new governmental institutions and viable and stable economies in the post-Soviet era. The legacies from the time of Soviet rule include: a Soviet party bureaucracy and government structure; Russian-dominated security and military organs whose main allegiance was to Moscow rather than to the republics in which they were based; distorted local economies created to fulfill the requirements of a much bigger master plan and command economy directed by Moscow; borders intentionally drawn to create heterogeneous states—frequently to discharge a sense of nation; the use of Russian as the official language; and numerous ecological nightmares (the destruction of the Aral Sea, for example, or the effects of a cotton monoeconomy) that have a direct impact on the daily lives of many Central Asians. Of course, each state in the region has its own unique mix of these factors, although some elements are fairly constant throughout.

The Soviet legacy creates much of the "ground reality" and political environment with which old and emerging political forces must contend; indeed, this reality and environment are often the basis of the defining issues of the political agendas evolving in the Central Asian states. Most of the components are inextricably bound, thus adding to the complexity of the politics. Moreover, dealing with any of these problems may also provoke the underlying indigenous and traditional forces. For example, for a country to create a new national identity, it is required to deal carefully with the several ethnic groups, including Russians, that live within its borders; or a country's attempts to restructure its economy might challenge traditional tribal or clan claims on resources. The following section explores how the influences of indigenous tradition and Soviet rule are played out in current Central Asian politics.

Redefining Relations with Russia

Given the numerous economic dependencies of many Central Asian states on Russia and the related question of security linkages, ties to Moscow will generate debate among the emerging political forces for many years to come. These major dependencies are not lost on the current Central Asian leaders. In the aftermath of the August 1991 coup, for example, the Central Asian republics were the only ones that genuinely supported a continued "union" of republics, making their declarations of independence after the coup somewhat pro forma. Even after the Soviet Union gave way to the Commonwealth of Independent States (CIS) on December 25, it was clear that it was the Central Asians who were most supportive of maintaining closer interrepublican economic and security linkages. At the May 15, 1992, CIS meeting in Tashkent, Uzbekistan, it was largely the Central Asians who signed onto an umbrella security agreement; several of the Central Asian states, including Kazakhstan, Uzbekistan, and Turkmenistan, also signed separate bilateral military accords with Russia. The Kazakh agreement was touted by President Nursultan Nazarbayev as bringing Kazakhstan "under Moscow's nuclear umbrella."[4] At subsequent meetings with Russian officials in November, the Kazakhs and Kyrgyz continued to push for closer CIS ties and other coordinating structures—presumably because of growing concerns about the instability and fragmentation in Tajikistan.

Managing Domestic Ethnic Issues

A major element of the issue of redefining relations with Russia is the question of how to manage ethnic relations within the several Central Asian states. The population of Central Asia numbers some 50 million, of which 12 million (nearly 25 percent) are European; of the 12 million Europeans, over 9 million are ethnic Russians. This striking fact of political demography is all the more significant when we look at the geographic distribution of these Europeans: They generally constitute two-thirds of the population in those areas where they reside, and in the Central Asian capital cities they generally represent more than 50 percent of the population. These demographics are seen most clearly in Kazakhstan, where ethnic Kazakhs number 40 percent of the population, compared to the 51.2 percent represented by the numbers of the combined Europeans, led by the ethnic Russians (38 percent). Moreover, the overwhelming majority of Russians inhabit the more industrialized and resource-rich northern tier of Kazakhstan, where they represent over two-thirds of the local populace. Inasmuch as this area was attached to the expanded Kazakh "republic" when the USSR was formally founded in 1924, Kazakh leaders are extremely sensitive to any references to "reexamining borders," particularly when these concerns are raised by traditionalist politicians in

Russia, such as Vice President Aleksandr Rutskoi. Foreshadowings of these ethnic-related tensions in Kazakhstan and other areas were already evident in the Mikhail Gorbachev era: There were riots in Alma-Ata, Kazakhstan, following the replacement of local party chief Dinmukhamed Kunayev by an ethnic Russian, Gennadi Kolbin, in December 1986; and in September 1989 ethnic Russians voiced their displeasure with President Nunsultan Nazarbayev after he declared Kazakh to be the state language.

These demographic factors work in other ways as well. The ethnic Russians often play critical managerial and technical roles in the local work force; thus, even in republics where Russians are greatly outnumbered by the titular ethnic group, their importance often outweighs their numbers. This dependence is one that strong Central Asian nationalist leaders will have to consider carefully as they chart a new course for their states. The former president of Tajikistan, Rakhmon Nabiyev, explicitly noted this concern in a March 1992 interview on Russian television: "No one should leave us. It was the events of February 1990 [Dushanbe ethnic riots] that was the grounds for all this. Many people left, including high-class specialists, and *Tajikistan feels this loss, because it does not have its own cadres.*"[5] Nabiyev's ouster six months later helped to fuel another emigration of ethnic Russians, who feared that growing civil conflict in Tajikistan could lead to further attacks on their ethnic group.

Indeed, the existence of myriad potential ethnic-related problems in the Central Asian republics is not unthinkable: As previously disadvantaged titular ethnics assert their newly found political dominance, racial violence could occur; there could be intense debates about the utility of retaining old structures or reshaping institutions and laws; there could be increased instability, which stems from laws that reflect the new political realities; for example, the language laws that require knowledge of the native language to obtain or retain certain jobs; large-scale migration of ethnic Russians could result from the political and racial tensions described above; and, of course, there could be the potential for strained, possibly confrontational, relations with Russia itself should ethnic Russians in Central Asia be perceived as unfairly treated or under threat.

The Burden of Genuine Sovereignty:
The Exercise of Power and Building of Constituencies

The former communist bosses in the Central Asian republics now find themselves in a very novel position: As sovereign rulers they have nearly full responsibility for the direction and functioning of their states, except for monetary policy. They must thus make decisions on such fundamental issues as economic policy, national security, and relations with neighboring foreign states, not to mention on the several vexing domestic ethnic issues listed above. Although this sounds fairly normal, it is important to note that these Central Asian rulers, with few exceptions, were primarily executors of overall policy directives emanating from Moscow. They had little real voice in key policy decisions. They did have the benefit of Moscow's tools, the party, the military, and the security apparatus to back them as they went about implementing Moscow's directives. Although many of these bosses still have their own local security and police units, they nonetheless recognize that they must quickly develop real national constituencies that can provide them with political legitimacy. In the new political atmosphere, these leaders must find effective ways to deal with would-be political rivals. The legacy of perestroika and the 1991 coup cannot be erased from public consciousness. Although none of the republics has a well-developed tradition of political toleration, it seems clear that opposition voices will not be easily silenced in the future, be it through legally registered parties or through informal political or religious groups.

The Emergence of Religion as a Potential Political Force

Seventy percent of Central Asians are Muslim, and religion has always been a factor in the political calculations of the ruling elites. Islam, intrinsic to the identity of most Central Asians, will inevitably assume a greater role in the political life of the Central Asian republics. The legalization of religion has spawned a palpable resurgence of "religiosity" in the region, manifested in increasing attendance at Friday prayer services and an increasing demand for copies of the *Quran*. As a result of Gorbachev's perestroika, politically active religious groups emerged in the republics of Central Asia in the late 1980s, notably the Islamic Renaissance parties of Uzbekistan and Tajikistan. (It should be noted that such parties are banned in Kazakhstan, Uzbekistan, and Turkmenistan.) And in Tajikistan radical elements of the Islamic Renaissance Party (IRP) are calling for changes and new laws that would create a more theocratic state structure.

Outside actors have also complicated the politics of Islam in Central Asia. Iranian fundamentalists' entreaties to local Muslims to become more observant, for example, have elicited strong concern from many Central Asian leaders. Iran's religious activities in Central Asia have also contributed to a well-publicized competition among several Muslim states, including Iran, Turkey, Saudi Arabia, Egypt, and Pakistan, for influence in this region. This competition, in turn, has made foreign policy an increasingly important component of each leader's domestic political calculus.

Political Life in the Central Asian Republics

The events of August 1991 and the subsequent collapse of the USSR presented all the leaders of Central Asia with difficult decisions regarding their political identities and their futures. Once it became apparent that the coup would fail, they all burnished their nationalist credentials. After the creation of the CIS they quickly adapted to the changed realities of the post-Soviet era. As noted above, their first tasks were to establish their own legitimacy and to create post-Soviet political institutions. As many observers of developing states have pointed out, these tasks are particularly difficult in multiethnic societies. In *Political Order in Changing Societies,* Samuel P. Huntington argues that institutionalization must keep pace with demands for participation from all quarters of society, in order to ensure stability.[6] Though Huntington is primarily concerned with stability, it would seem that these widening demands for participation may ultimately facilitate the development of democratic pluralism in Central Asia. Yet, as the following brief review of political trends suggests, these states, with the exception of Kyrgyzstan, retain largely authoritarian characters.[7]

Uzbekistan

Party leader and Uzbekistan republic president, Islam Karimov, generally "went with the flow" as the 1991 coup unfolded. The morning of the coup, he told the Uzbek Parliament, "We have always been supporters of firm order and discipline ... a leadership that abandons order and discipline can never return to power." As Karimov banned political meetings and demonstrations and formed an emergency committee, local KGB officials arrested main opposition leaders. Once the coup had failed, however, Uzbek courts declared the arrests illegal. Having sensed the magnitude of the sea change wrought by the failed coup—such as Ukraine's declaration of independence on August 24—Karimov declared Uzbekistan independent on August 31, 1991. This move drew mixed reactions. One leader from Birlik (Unity), the main opposition group, noted that "the government decided the best way to save itself was to declare independence."[8] Karimov's subsequent comment that his republic was not ready for democracy and a market economy (he preferred the Chinese communist model) reflected his concern over the democratization process emanating from a Boris Yeltsin-influenced, restored "center" in Moscow.[9]

Karimov took a number of steps to strengthen his political base and concurrently to delink his fortunes from those of the former Communist Party of the Soviet Union (CPSU). First, he highlighted his nationalist credentials by renaming the local Communist Party the Popular Democratic Party of Uzbekistan. More important, he moved to legitimize his personal position as president by convening presidential elections in December 1991. (In part, he may have felt both encouraged and pressured by the October election in nearby Kyrgyzstan, where an incumbent won the vote.) There appeared to be little risk, given Karimov's control of the former communist state machinery and local administration; indeed, he won 86 percent of the vote. Muhammed Salikh, the candidate of Erk—the only party permitted to run a candidate—took 12.3 percent. According to one observer, had the nationalist party Birlik been allowed to participate, it is possible that Karimov might have faced a run-off election.[10]

Since the election, Karimov has kept a tight rein on political life in Uzbekistan. There are four main political groups, but only two have been allowed to register as parties: Karimov's party, which is the People's (or National) Democratic Party of Uzbekistan (NDP), and Erk. According to a Western researcher who spent six months in Uzbekistan in 1992, estimates on NDP's membership range from 500,000 to 750,000 people.[11] Erk, in contrast, is a small "intellectual's party," headed by poet and writer Mohammed Salikh. He is well known for his writings during the 1970s on the greater "Turkestan."[12] Erk was formed in 1989, largely by Birlik defectors who had personality clashes and differences over strategy with top Birlik leaders. Estimates on Erk membership vary from some 5,000 people to Salikh's own figure of over 40,000.[13] Erk has focused on democratic reform; until mid-1992 it had eschewed the more activist approach of its parent organization, Birlik.[14]

The largest and most active political group in Uzbekistan is Birlik, a grassroots nationalist umbrella group founded in 1988. It includes students, intellectuals, and some workers. Estimates on its size vary from 100,000 to 600,000 members.[15] The principal Birlik leader is Abdurakhim Pulatov, a scholar from Tashkent's Institute of Cybernetics.[16] (Pulatov's energetic courting of the media, particularly Western media, has made Birlik the "most recognized opposition group" in Uzbekistan. Some Western scholars view Erk, in contrast, as a more serious, professional political party.[17]) Apart from its efforts to focus on Uzbek language and culture, Birlik's general platform calls for "restoration of Central Asians' true history" and the creation of a secular state along the Turkish model.[18] Since its initial activities in 1988, Birlik has been hounded by the government, which has forbidden demonstrations and meetings, and individuals having Birlik connections have been discriminated against or fired. Following its declaration of "political party status" at a congress in October 1991, Birlik filed a registation application with the Justice Ministry on November 11, 1991.[19] Despite this application, Birlik has yet to be formally recognized by the government. Ironically, the government claimed that permitting Birlik to be registered as a party would "confuse the people," since Birlik is both a "movement" and a "party." According to a Western researcher who interviewed Pulatov in November 1991, the goals of Birlick (the movement) included "teaching people political consciousness and action" while Birlik (the party) saw "the struggle for power" as its main concern.[20]

In addition to the secular groups discussed above, there are at least two Islamic organizations that should be noted. Unlike the other groups in Uzbekistan, the Islamic Renaissance Party, or IRP, has been outlawed since February 1991, when Karimov declared that religious groups cannot form the basis of political parties. IRP officials in Moscow asserted that Karimov's moves reflected a fear of the party's potential influence in Uzbek politics.[21] Another Islamic-based opposition group, Adalat, stresses more direct and militant strategies for returning to an Islam-based society. Adalat has had some local success, especially in Namangan, where it created neighborhood watch groups to insure the public safety and to make "citizen's arrests."[22]

These opposition groups have had limited impact on Uzbekistan's political life because Karimov has maintained strict control over the media and a tight grip on the opposition. The main newspaper remains *Pravda vostoka;* it is independent, but eschews criticism of the government and focuses largely on the activities of Karimov's NDP. The government has reportedly restrained the opposition's access to newsprint.[23]

Karimov appeared to come down even harder on the opposition during 1992, in part because of efforts by Erk and Birlik to coordinate some of their political activities and to encourage mass political rallies in spring. In late June, for example, following questioning by local procurators, Birlik's leader, Pulatov, was beaten by unidentified hoodlums; he was attacked again in late October.[24] And in December 1992, Uzbek agents abducted Pulatov's brother while he was attending a human rights conference in Bishkek, Kyrgyzstan; he was transported back to Tashkent and reportedly was under investigation for "possibly dishonoring President Karimov."[25] Karimov's willingness to risk possible Western opprobrium from Uzbekistan's human rights abuses almost certainly is tied to his growing concern about the potential spillover of instability and ethnic conflict from neighboring Tajikistan. Karimov's fears may be well-founded; there have been media reports suggesting that Uzbek opposition groups were in contact with their Tajik counterparts and were drawing important lessons from events there.

Kazakhstan

Kazakhstan's political life has been strongly influenced by its geographical vastness and ethnic composition—Kazakhs (6.5 million) barely outnumber ethnic Russians (6.2 million). The rest of the population includes Germans, Ukrainians, and a diverse collection of Uzbeks, Tatars, and other minorities.[26] Consequently, there are few truly republicwide political groups, and many are narrow one-issue associations. Environmental concerns have served as a focal point for activists, spawning numerous groups, such as the well-known antinuclear group, Nevada-Semipalatinsk movement.

In 1991, as glasnost and perestroika emboldened groups across the USSR, the Nevada-Semipalatinsk group stepped up its efforts and pressed for the complete cessation of nuclear testing activities in Semipalatinsk. This growing movement was a source of increasing concern for Nazarbayev, who faced pressure from Moscow to carry out scheduled tests in August. The movement had scheduled a major demonstration for late August, but it was rendered unnecessary by the failed coup in Moscow. Absent the pressures from Moscow, Nazarbayev seized the opportunity to prove his nationalism, and he preempted further action by the Nevada-Semipalatinsk group by announcing the closure of the test site in October.

In order to insure against the revival of the local Communist Party (banned, but reincarnated as the still-influential Socialist Party), the Nevada-Semipalatinsk movement transformed itself in early October into a formal political party, the People's Congress or National Congress Party. Nazarbayev gave his approval to the party and dominated the proceedings of its first congress. The attendees were mostly Kazakhs, with a few ethnic Russians and Europeans.[27] The National Congress cochairman declared that the main mission of the new party was to be the prevention of totalitarian rule under Socialist Party auspices. The National Party Congress will actively run lists of candidates in legislative elections now set for 1994; candidates will be allowed to represent any factions that develop in the National Congress Party.[28]

Although the Kazakh government exhibits some degree of political toleration, important legal constraints against political parties still exist. Specifically, the Justice Ministry's "Rules of Registration" require that lists of all party members be submitted and stamped. Despite this, the authorities assert there are some 120 political parties and movements.[29] Apart from the National Congress cited above, other important forces have emerged. Zheltoqsan (National Democratic Party), a Kazakh nationalist organization founded in May 1989, seeks to cooperate with other nationalist groups like Azat (see below) as a "democratic bloc" to oppose dictatorial practices. It tried to put up a presidential candidate, party leader Hasan Kozakhmetov, against Nazarbayev in the December 1991 elections, but failed to amass the requisite 100,000 signatures. Zheltoqsan supporters have accused the government of stealing important signature petition lists.

Another nationalist group is Azat. It formed in June 1990 and is largely dominated by Kazakh intellectuals. Its primary goal was to gain Kazakh independence, but it now advocates a moderate democratic program, and has sought to attract non-Kazakhs to its fold. Azat joined the National Congress Party and the Socialist Party in voting for Nazarbayev in the December 1 presidential elections.

A more radical group is Alash, a Kazakh Islamic party that seeks to use Islam as the basis for reform. Alash is an unregistered party; it supported Kazakh independence and now favors a Central Asian confederation. Moreover, it backed Zheltoqsan's bid to run an opposition candidate in the December presidential elections. Nazarbayev's feelings about this religious-based party were explicitly acknowledged at the October session of the National Congress; according to a Western scholar present at the congress, Nazarbayev described Alash as "fascist."[30]

Data and trends evident in the polls administered by the Republican Center for the Study of Public Opinion on Social and Economic Questions suggest the fluidity of political life at this early stage of Kazakh independence. This fluidity is likely to continue as new issues emerge and as political and umbrella groups coalesce. Perhaps the greatest difficulty will be to establish a genuine republicwide party that enjoys broad-based interethnic support. The polling data noted above strongly suggest that the organizations most frequently cited as influential have not been playing the "consolidating role" that was previously played by the Communist Party.[31]

Kyrgyzstan

Since his election as president of Kyrgyzstan in October 1990 in the wake of the Osh riots, Askar Akayev has set out a liberal, reformist direction for Kyrgyzstan, which in turn has shaped a generally open political atmosphere. Before Akayev's political ascendancy in fall 1990, political activists channeled their energies into "improvement groups" that emerged in late 1989–1990. Examples of such groups include Ashar (a society of builders in Frunze seeking to ease the housing shortage) and Osh Aimagy (a group seeking land to build homes for ethnic Kyrgyz in Osh).[32] The controversy surrounding Osh Aimagy's alleged role in sparking the June 1990 ethnic riots in Osh exacerbated political differences within Kyrgyz elites and within the Communist Party. Party reformers attributed much of the blame for the riots to former Communist Party boss Absamat Masaliyev's poor handling of events, and thus became more assertive in challenging party traditionalists. Meanwhile, liberal critics of the old communist regime coalesced into the Kyrgyzstan Democratic Movement. Many in this group were to become strong backers of Akayev.[33]

Under Akayev's stewardship since October 1990, opposition groups have been able to operate openly and legally. Unlike the old Communist Party, the other main parties are generally proreform and prodemocracy. These prodemocracy parties include the Kyrgyzstan Democratic Movement, whose base is largely ethnic Kyrgyz; the National Unity Party, which seeks to promote a multiethnic party; and the reformed Communist Party. When the Moscow coup attempt collapsed, Akayev moved to divest the old Kyrgyz Communist Party of key buildings and property and subsequently launched an investigation of the party leadership. This latter move prompted the resignation of many party leaders, though the reform wing of the party is still dominant in the government.[34]

Turkmenistan

Turkmenistan is perhaps the most politically quiescent of the Central Asian republics, largely because it remains under the strong grip of Saparmurad Niyazov, its Communist Party chief since 1985 and republic president since 1990. His views about political pluralism are perhaps best summed up in a response he gave to a question in 1990 about when democracy would come to Turkmenistan; Niyazov reportedly answered, "I am democracy."[35] Niyazov claims to practice "multi-party democracy." He has formally permitted Communist Party veterans to form a new communist party (the old one has been renamed the Democratic Party); obkom (provincial) and raion (district) secretaries can now form a peasant party; and others are free to join his "democratic party." Obviously, these three options are thinly disguised manifestations of the old Communist Party machinery.[36]

The state of political life in Turkmenistan can be gauged by the local events surrounding the abortive August 1991 coup in Moscow and the February 1992 visit to Ashgabat of U.S. Secretary of State James Baker III. During the Moscow coup, Niyazov took a wait and see approach, offering few comments, save one on August 19 that "the USSR is sliding into chaos and order needs to be restored."[37]

The local media did publish an appeal for support from the the junta but did not publish other junta directives.[38] Several members of the opposition criticized Niyazov's equivocal stance and prepared a declaration condemning the coup. They were subsequently arrested.[39] On the eve of Baker's visit to Turkmenistan, key leaders of Agzybirlik, the Democratic Party of Turkmenistan, writers, and journalists were advised to stay at home or were invited for "talks" at the Ministry of the Interior.[40]

In general, some political groups have emerged since 1989, but they are small and relatively few; none is registered. Moreover, such groups have little access to the general public because the regime has maintained total control of all media. Radio broadcasts from the West and the Russian media are the primary vehicles for information about these fledgling groups.

Perhaps the most prominent political group in Turkmenistan is Agzybirlik. It was formed in 1989 by several hundred intellectuals, journalists, and workers. It has moved from its initial cultural-linguistic agenda to a more openly political one. According to one Agzybirlik member, the group calls for glasnost in Turkmenistan and for radical economic reform to "break the cycle of poverty and colonization of … [their] resources."[41] One of its founding members, Mukhamed Velsapar, gained notoriety for writing a short article in *Moscow News* on the high infant mortality rate in Turkmenistan. The April 1990 piece carried a photograph of an emaciated two-year-old.[42] The article was never published by the Turkmen media, but it elicited numerous denunciations; many described it as a libelous attack and as a public humiliation of the republic. When one reformer spoke positively about the Velsapar article during a Supreme Soviet session, he was shouted down and jeered by the other deputies. In the aftermath of this scandal, the government did step up efforts to attack the health problem. At the same time, it clamped down on Agzybirlik writers and film directors, banning a film on child malnutrition and denying the publication of books by Agzybirlik authors.[43]

Of the other new political groups, less well-known is the Democratic Party of Turkmenistan, which was formed in December 1990 during a conference convened in Ashgabat. According to a *Moscow News* correspondent, the party has some 1,200 members. It is headed by three cochairmen: Durdymurad Khodzha-Mukhamad, a senior instructor at the local polytechnical institute; Khandurdy Khangel'dyev, a geophysicist; and Nazarly Shchakhberdyev, a jurist.[44] By mid-1992, the party had changed its name to the "Party for Democratic Development" because Niyazov had appropriated the name "Democratic Party" for the reconstituted Communist Party.

Turkmenistan adopted a new Constitution in mid-May 1992. It effectively insured continued political domination by Niyazov and his entrenched ruling elite. This was underscored in the presidential elections held in mid-June 1992; Niyazov ran unopposed and garnered some 99 percent of the vote—an outcome reminiscent of old Soviet-style elections. Overall, prospects for political reform or any semblance of political pluralism appear slim. If anything, the increasing signs of a new personality cult—the growth of sycophantic literature and the re-naming of a main street to "Saparmurad the Turkmen Leader"—suggest political life in Turkmenistan will continue to be dominated by one individual.

A Case Study: Tajikistan

In order to analyze the dramatic changes in Central Asia in a broader conceptual framework, this case study of Tajikistan will provide a more detailed account of developments there, with an eye toward identifying the particular historical, cultural, ethnic, and regional forces that are driving politics there, and, more broadly, in Central Asia. I will then examine these forces within several theoretical and conceptual frameworks that have been utilized in studies of other emerging Third World societies.

Tajik politics have been in flux since the August 1991 coup. A tug-of-war developed between would-be reformers and entrenched Communist Party legislators and bureaucrats. The hard-line communist regime, headed by Kakhar Makhkamov, was naturally predisposed to support the coup. After noting the "benefits" of the coup on August 19, Makhkamov reversed his opinion on August 21 as the coup plot collapsed; he described the action as a "tragedy" that could have prompted a civil war.[45] He subsequently tried to distance the Tajik Communist Party from the CPSU by condemning the latter for not having opposed the coup. Makhkamov's ill-disguised political opportunism and, perhaps, the realization that the August coup had radically transformed the USSR's political life, seemed to embolden Tajik opposition groups. Indeed, several political opposition groups subsequently came to the fore to challenge Communist Party rule in Tajikistan.

The Tajikistan Democratic Party led by Chairman Shodmon Yusupov, promotes a secular, democratic path for Tajikistan. It specifically ruled out any cooperation with the communists, whom it described as "responsible for 70 years of genocide against the Tajik people."[46] Rastokhez (Tajik National Front), under the current leadership of Tohir Abdur-Jabar, had been active since 1989 in advancing the cause of Tajik independence. Finally, the Islamic Renaissance Party is a branch chapter of a national IRP (with other centers in North Caucasus and Uzbekistan). In March 1991, according to *Moskovskie novosti,* the party's press secretary asserted a national membership of 10,000, with cells in most of the USSR's European cities. Former president Makhkamov rejected the party's request to hold an organizing conference for a local Tajik branch in fall 1990; a conference was held, nonetheless, outside of Dushanbe, and TASS reported some three hundred attendees. Concern about the IRP's activities led the Supreme Soviet to outlaw it formally in December 1990.[47] Of Tajikistan's three emerging political groups, only the IRP was outlawed, and this further signaled the regime's concern about this religion-based party.

In the days after the abortive Moscow coup, the Democratic Party of Tajikistan organized a demonstration in Dushanbe calling for the government and Supreme Soviet to resign and for the republic to hold multiparty elections. On August 29, Makhkamov stepped down in the wake of large demonstrations and in the face of opposition charges that he had backed the Moscow coup. He was replaced by an interim president, Kadriddin Aslonov, who was to serve until elections were held. On September 21, Aslonov banned the Communist Party and confiscated party property. These moves led to anti-communist celebrations, culminating in the destruction of a large Lenin statue in Dushanbe's central square. Two days later, however, the communist-dominated Supreme Soviet responded by forcing Aslonov's resignation and by arresting the mayor of Dushanbe, Maksud Ikramov, for his support of anti-communist demonstrations. The Supreme Soviet installed Rakhmon Nabiyev as the new president and scheduled a new presidential election for October 27. Nabiyev, it should be noted, had been removed as party general secretary in 1985.

The traditionalists' crackdown only served to strengthen links among the disparate opposition groups who shared a common antipathy toward the communists. Large, but peaceful, demonstrations in Dushanbe in fall 1991 prompted Nabiyev to reinstate the ban on the Communist Party; to postpone the election from October 27 to November 24, so as to give the opposition more time to prepare and campaign, and to legalize the IRP. Nabiyev won the election, amid charges from the other presidential candidate, cinematographer Davlat Khudonazarov, that it was rigged. However, the three main opposition groups together voted for Khudonazarov, and he received more than 30 percent of the total vote.

Events between February and May 1992 highlighted the fluidity of the Tajik political scene and the growing influence of the Islamic Renaissance Party. In late February–early March, the Nabiyev government instituted charges against numerous opposition figures: among them the Rastokhez leader (at that time, Mirbobo Mirakhimov), for slander of a government official; proreform Dushanbe mayor Ikramov, for bribery; and Democratic Party head Shodmon Yusupov, for insulting the president.[48] These opposition figures asserted that the timing of these moves—immediately following the visit of U.S. Secretary of State Baker in late February—indicated that a deal had been struck between Baker and Nabiyev. Specifically, they claim that the United States agreed to sanction moves against the democratic opposition in return for assurances from Nabiyev that Tajikistan would eschew an Iranian-style path of development. (Ironically, Yusupov viewed this trend as abetting the cause of the IRP, in that the crackdown on legitimate democratic forces would leave the political field largely open to that group.[49])

Further complicating the situation was the dismissal from the government of Interior Affairs Minister Mamadfayez Navzhuvanov, the highest-ranking of the ethnic Pamirs. His ouster in late March 1992 on charges of exceeding his authority prompted demonstrations in Dushanbe, which culminated in May with the creation of a coalition government that included all opposition parties. According to Russian media accounts, what had begun as a largely Pamir rally of some 500 to 600 people on March 26 grew into a crowd of about 3,000 by the next day; the gathering reportedly was organized by Rastokhez and the Democratic Party of Tajikistan.[50] The people's key demands were the resignation of the Supreme Soviet chairman and the Parliament and the release of Mayor Ikramov.[51] On March 28, *Interfax* reported that members of the local Shi'a community had joined the demonstrations and were organizing an around-the-clock rally on behalf of the ousted interior minister.[52]

The demonstrations continued for approximately eight weeks and, by early May, posed a clear challenge to the rule of President Nabiyev. Progovernment demonstrations began in late April, and it appeared that major violence was inevitable. After several small incidents and several deaths, Nabiyev chose to avert confrontation; on May 11, he announced the formation of a reconciliation government, in effect a power-sharing arrangement with the opposition forces. The opposition was given eight of twenty-four cabinet posts, including Defense, Interior, Foreign Affairs, Education, and Radio and Television. The Supreme Soviet chairman Safarili Kenzhayev resigned his position, as did the vice-president. A national assembly was to be formed, to comprise eighty representatives—forty from the former Supreme Soviet and forty from the opposition groups.[53] The ethnic Pamir interior minister, Navzhuvanov, was reappointed, and Rastokhez leader Mirakhimov was named chairman of Radio and Television.[54] Perhaps most important, IRP deputy chairman Davlyat Usmon was named deputy prime minister—a clear sign of the IRP's growing political activism and influence.

The rise of the Islamic Renaissance Party has raised questions about whether Tajikistan will become a fundamentalist state, and, if so, whether it will emulate Iran. Indeed, some IRP coalition partners, including the Democratic Party and Rastokhez, have voiced doubts about whether the IRP could pave the way toward a more radical, theocratic political culture in Tajikistan. And the revived Tajik Communist Party has made opposition to Islamic fundamentalism a key tenet of its new platform. In one interview, the party chief lamented the rape of Tajikistan by the old "center" in the USSR and how it had left the country "one-on-one with Islamic fundamentalism, debts, and a catastrophically poor people ... the communists never will support the idea of creating an Islamic state."[55]

As President Nabiyev struggled with his new coalition partners through summer 1992, politics in Dushanbe became driven increasingly by ethnic, regional, religious, and urban-rural cleavages. Shortly after the coalition was formed in May, sporadic fighting developed in key regions of the country, notably in the south, in Kulyab and Kurgan-Tyube. In addition, the local government in Leninabad grew increasingly suspicious of the coalition government, which, in its view, was becoming dominated by radical Islamic elements. When President Nabiyev made additional concessions to his opponents in June—granting one-third of the government's ministerial portfolios to reform democrats and

Islamicists—Kulyab refused to cooperate with the Dushanbe government, and fighting throughout the countryside intensified. Tensions were especially bloody in the divided *oblast'* of Kurgan-Tyube, where procoalition administrators came under attack by local groups loyal to Nabiyev.

Nabiyev's coalition partners were frustrated by his seeming unwillingness to facilitate negotiations in the countryside and may have concluded that Nabiyev saw these conflicts as a means of strengthening his own position in the coalition. In retrospect, the decisive event that triggered the move against Nabiyev was the visit of CIS military commander Evgenni Shaposhnikov in late August–early September. His visit spawned rumors of an alliance between Nabiyev and the CIS/Russian military, presumably aimed at strengthening Nabiyev's hand against his domestic adversaries. In early September, Nabiyev's coalition partners moved against him, prompting him to bolt for his home province of Leninabad. However, he was captured en route to Dushanbe airport. Faced by his opponents and a large demonstration, Nabiyev went on television to announce his "voluntary" retirement.

With Nabiyev out, the Supreme Soviet presidium announced that new legislative, and possibly presidential, elections would be held in December; presidential powers would temporarily be assumed by the presidium and the Council of Ministers. The presidium chairman, Akbarsho Iskandarov, was named acting president of the new government. He quickly sought to assuage domestic and foreign audiences by stating that Tajikistan would not become an "Iranian-style" Islamic state.

Nabiyev's subsequent release from Dushanbe later in September ushered in a new phase of the conflict in Tajikistan, essentially, a civil war. Regional and ethnic divisions were involved (the heavily Uzbek-populated, industrialized Khojand region and the poorer, agricultural Kulyab province led the charge against reformers based in Dushanbe), as were differences over Tajikistan's political orientation (reformers versus conservatives versus Islamicists). The collapse of Tajikistan was highlighted in letters from acting-president Iskandarov to the United Nations and to CIS heads of state on September 30, requesting assistance in "making peace" in Tajikistan and in saving "the constitutional regime."[56] Throughout October, units from Russia's 201st Division based in Tajikistan found themselves in a military and political cross fire, particularly in Kurgan-Tyube and Dushanbe. As fighting intensified, anticoalition forces from the Hissar Valley and Kulyab converged on Dushanbe and gained control of much of the capital on October 26; however, by the next day, procoalition militias had pushed these forces out. According to Western press accounts, Russian forces in Dushanbe helped to prevent new pro-Nabiyev forces from reentering the capital, and Tajik officials conceded that they were dependent upon Russian forces to resist new takeover attempts.[57]

The anarchy in Dushanbe triggered alarm bells throughout Central Asia and Russia; according to local press accounts, the leaders of the Central Asian states and Russia met to discuss the Tajik situation on November 4. Russian foreign minister Andrei Kozyrev subsequently traveled to Dushanbe, where he told members of the 201st Division that "Russian servicemen would not interfere in the internal political conflict" but would "guarantee the safety of the Tajik peaceful population, as well as guard important economic facilities."[58] Nonetheless, the fighting continued, and by mid-December, the anticoalition forces had installed a new government and had recaptured control of Dushanbe.

The new chairman of the Supreme Soviet, Imomali Rakhmonov, is an old ally of Nabiyev. Rakhmonov, however, faces numerous challenges, as highlighted by his interior minister in a December 18 interview with *Interfax*. Specifically, the minister cited military attacks by antigovernment forces. He added that the new Tajik government has requested assistance from other signatories to the CIS security accord.[59] Equally revealing of Tajikistan's plight is Rakhmonov's public plea on Dushanbe Radio for foreigners—Russians, Uzbeks, Kyrgyz, Kazakh, Turkmen, and Tatars—not to leave Tajikistan because their departure may "paralyze vitally important institutions."[60]

Viewing Tajikistan in a Broader Framework

This brief overview of recent events in Tajikistan suggests that it is the broader regional, ethnic, tribal, and religious factors that are driving the politics there and, more generally, in Central Asia. All of these factors figure heavily in Tajik political life. Before assessing how the factors noted by Rothschild fit into theories and models of ethnopolitics and modernization, it is worth noting the demographics of Tajikistan. The primary ethnic groups include Tajiks, Uzbeks, Pamirs, and Russians. Tajikistan can be broken down roughly into five regions: (1) Dushanbe and its eastern environs (Garn), (2) Leninabad (Khojand Province), (3) Kulyab, (4) Kurgan-Tyube, and (5) Badakhshan (ethnic Pamirs). Of the overall population of 5.1 million, ethnic Tajiks represent 62 percent, Uzbeks 24 percent, and Russians 8 percent.[61] The Tajiks are largely Sunni Muslims, with some important pockets of Shi'a Muslims in Dushanbe, Leninabad, and Badakhshan (indeed, the dominant Pamirs in Badakhshan are Shi'as).[62] The Tajik language is the sole non-Turkic language in Central Asia; it belongs to the southwest group of Iranian languages. Within this Persian-speaking state, there are four major dialects, used in the north, east, central, and southeastern regions.[63]

The rapid reemergence of ethnic and regional tensions in the post–August 1991 period highlights one of the major flaws in traditional liberal theories of development, namely, that modernization eliminates the salience of ethnicity as a political force. This flaw is noted in many studies of ethnic politics in emerging African societies. Scholars, for example, have demonstrated the enduring vitality of ethnic and regional factors in discussing the "double consciousness" or dual identity of members of the elite. By retaining concurrent membership in both ethnic community *and* "modern society," individuals mitigate the insecurity of the urban setting by maintaining links and land in their rural regions.[64] Stated another way, urban elites and leaders have a "fallback position" when the urban environment turns hostile.[65] These linkages can be seen in the revival of provincial and regional politics once the delicate political balance in Dushanbe had crumbled in 1992. The situation of the Pamirs offers a good example of this phenomenon. It will be recalled that the incident that prompted the demonstrations of March 1992 and that culminated in Nabiyev's acceptance of a coalition in May was the dismissal of Pamir interior affairs minister Navzhuvanov. Moscow had been adept at playing on Pamir-Tajik differences during the Soviet era. The Pamir region of Badakhshan was granted autonomous status within the republic of Tajikistan, and ethnic Pamirs were prime candidates for the Ministry of Interior police forces.

The relevance of other theories of ethnopolitics is also evident when we examine regional distinctions in Tajikistan based on economic development. As Gellner argues, when uneven industrial development overlaps with ethnic geographic regions, natural discrepancies and the potential for conflicts emerge.[66] Moreover, this is especially true when the central government of an emerging state is the primary allocator of economic resources. Clearly this is directly applicable to Tajikistan. During the Soviet period, Dushanbe, under Russian guidance, focused key investment in the development of the mineral-rich northern province of Khojand; this, in part, helps to explain the strong reaction of Leninabad *oblast'* to the fall of Nabiyev, a native son. Quite apart from their concern over a fundamentalist regime emerging in Dushanbe, those in Leninabad probably feared that the new coalition would seek to redirect political influence and economic resources toward the other, less developed regions of Tajikistan. Not surprisingly, then, Leninabad authorities have highlighted their economic advantages—more developed industrial infrastructure and transport systems—as a means of reminding the new government of the consequences of ignoring Leninabad. Some conservatives have raised the specter of fragmentation—with Khojand leaving Tajikistan to unite its heavily Uzbek population with Uzbekistan. This convergence of ethnic, regional, and economic factors make Khojand a prime example of the vitality of ethnopolitics.

The rise of Islam as an influential political force comes as no surprise in the political calculus of Tajikistan. Soviet ideologists failed to appreciate the extent to which Islam is inherent in the identity of most Central Asians. Thus, despite seventy years of Soviet atheist propaganda and antireligion policies, Islam has remained a key element in the national identity of most Tajiks.[67] Moreover, free of Moscow's grip, religious activists are entering the mainstream of Tajik political life. Indeed, the more radical elements of the heretofore outlawed IRP seek to shape Tajik politics in ways that not only will insure religious freedoms but also will advance some of the tenets of Islamic life into civil law. However, the IRP itself is not monolithic: It too has moderates and other factions. What remains unclear is the degree to which Iranian influence will shape the politics of Tajikistan's Islamicists and how this, in turn, will alter domestic politics, as well as Tajikistan's relations with its other Central Asian neighbors. In any event, Islam will continue to be an important part of Tajik political life.

When viewed in the broader context of writings on the modernization process in emerging Third World states, recent events in Tajikistan are in keeping with the findings of Samuel P. Huntington. In his paradigm, significant changes wrought by the modernization process—increased literacy and education, urbanization, industrialization, and the growth of a political consciousness—serve to undermine the traditional bases of political power and authority in emerging societies. In Tajikistan, Russian-Soviet policies aimed at "modernizing" Tajikistan did undermine, or at least co-opt, those traditional sources of power—but only temporarily. As soon as the Soviet glue of stability evaporated, those traditional forces (regionalism, ethnic and tribal ties, and religion) quickly reemerged to fill the vacuum. There is some irony in Huntington's astute assessment of why the communists enjoyed greater success in their Third World competition with the West during the 1960s: Whereas Western policymakers focused on economic development as a means to promote a pluralistic political culture, Moscow chose to focus on "the political gap" and the need for stability. Indeed, Huntington even cites James Madison in one of the *Federalist Papers* to underscore the critical point of the necessity of "public order" in new states. "The great difficulty lies in this: you must first enable the government to control the governed; and in the next place oblige it to control itself."[68]

The recent events in Tajikistan could be a harbinger of complex interstate political turmoil related to underlying ethnic-religious-territorial problems in the region. Inasmuch as some 3.5 million Tajiks reside in Afghanistan—roughly equivalent to the population in Tajikistan itself—continued Tajik political instability could prompt the entry of Afghan-Tajiks into the political scene and could possibly lead to the creation of a greater Tajikistan. On the northern border, the sizable Uzbek minority could use new instability to argue, like Gorno-Badakhshan, for greater autonomy, if not outright annexation to Uzbekistan. (Tashkent probably would prefer to avoid such a "redistricting," because this could call into question other historical territorial matters relating to Samarkand and Bukhara, which many Tajiks see as "their cities.") Certain Tajik provinces, both in the north and the south (Khojand and Kulyab) took up arms in support of Nabiyev after the power-sharing arrangement was reached, and this shows the continung role of clans and regionalism in Tajik political life. Islamic leaders will also be increasingly important, but they too must carefully assess their role to avoid provoking a backlash against "radical fundamentalism." It is noteworthy, for example, that the main reason Nabiyev was allowed to retain the presidency for so long was that the opposition was concerned that his ouster would pull Tajikistan asunder: According to ITAR-TASS, the Kazi Akbar Turajonzoda (the chief Muslim leader of "official Islam") openly stated that "Nabiyev represents old thinking, but his departure might cause the disintegration of the country."[69]

This brief analysis of the operative political forces in Central Asia, and specifically in Tajikistan, indicates the existence of numerous obstacles to the emergence of democratic pluralism there. If anything, the experiences of Central Asia thus far highlight the obstacles far more than they emphasize the movement toward pluralism.

The term pluralism has been variously defined; it implies a diffusion of power and the participation of individuals and groups in the political process. In the five Central Asian republics, nascent political groupings do exist. As we have seen, some are organized around specific political agendas and others are based on ethnic, religious, or clan ties. These groupings cannot be compared to political parties or even interest groups, in the Western sense of these terms. In most cases they have been denied access to the decision-making process by the former communist leaders of the Central Asian states. Ironically, the leaders are themselves vulnerable. Despite their having stood for popular election, true "contestation" in Dahl's term was limited at best. Certain candidates were forbidden to run, and even where there was more than one candidate, elections were probably rigged.

However they were elected, the Central Asian presidents currently risk being overwhelmed by age-old tribal, ethnic, regional, and religious forces, coupled with the pressing economic and political problems of the post-Soviet era. As the study of Tajikistan indicates, the emergence of democratic pluralism is clearly related to the problems of political development. For example, the Tajik experience strongly suggests that clan ties, coupled with regionalism, will weigh heavily on the politics of the other Central Asian states. These clan networks, in the aftermath of the collapse of Soviet rule, actually have been strengthened by virtue of their long experience in exercising authority and making things run. To the extent that these clan and family networks can address the basic economic needs of society, they may be able to minimize popular support for emerging political parties, which many view as "elitist" or as only reflecting the political goals of a small intelligentsia or middle class.

In Uzbekistan, for example, President Karimov may be dependent on traditional clan or familial links because the country is the most populous of the Central Asian republics and possesses only a modicum of natural resources: Recent research indicates that Karimov is dependent on a fragile alliance of influential Ferghana Valley families, including relatives of the former Communist Party secretary Sharaf Rashidov. Thus it is not surprising that Rashidov's name and reputation is currently enjoying a renaissance of sorts; streets and squares are being named in his honor.[70] The key task for Karimov is to insure that major families do not join forces against him: In January 1992, he reportedly was successful in fending off the challenge of a competing coalition of families, headed by a long-time rival, Abdi Mir-Saidov.[71]

In contrast, Turkmenistan has many of the clan or familial linkages common to the other states, but its relatively smaller population and its abundance of valuable resources—natural gas and oil—may enable President Niyazov, or a successor, to resist or limit political reform by literally "buying off" the populace. Indeed, Niyazov has already publicly stated his desire to make Turkmenistan "the Kuwait of Central Asia."

If Karimov has thus far succeeded in using clan alliances to maintain power and if Niyazov thus far has not needed to use the networks, the same cannot be said of Nabiyev in Tajikistan. There, clan politics reinforced by economic dispari-ties, religious concerns, and regionalism had led to a civil war that could cause the disintegration of the state. Ultimately, these problems, loosely labeled "develop-mental," must be solved before questions related to pluralism can be addressed.

Notes

The author thanks Professor Stephen Burg of Brandeis University for comments on an early draft of this chapter presented during an April 1992 seminar at the Russian Research Center, Harvard University. The author also expresses his thanks to the following individu-als for sharing their knowledge and insight into the history, politics, and culture of Central Asia: Reef Altoma, Rick Grimes, Malvin Helgesen, Pauline Jones, David Knuti, Eve Lebo, Doug Mathews, Renee Pruneau, and Mary Jo Roos.

1. Joseph Rothschild, *Ethnopolitics: A Conceptual Framework* (New York: Columbia University Press, 1981), pp. 86–94.

2. Ernest Gellner, ed., *Thought and Change* (London: Weidenfeld and Nicolson, 1964), pp. 171–172, as cited in John A. A. Ayoade, "Ethnic Politics in Nigeria," in Dennis L. Thompson and Dov Ronen, eds., *Ethnicity, Politics and Development* (Boulder, CO: Lynne Rienner, 1986), pp. 107–108.

3. Stimulating, if depressing, overviews of Central Asia are presented by Boris Rumer, *Soviet Central Asia: A Tragic Experiment* (Boston: Unwin Hyman, 1989), and by William Fierman in *Soviet Central Asia: The Failed Transformation* (Boulder: Westview, 1991).

4. For details on the May 15 CIS Security Pact, see *Moscow Interfax,* May 15, 1992, as cited in *FBIS Daily Report–Central Eurasia,* May 21, 1992, p. 22.

5. Emphasis added. For text of interview, see Moscow Ostankino Television First Pro-gram, as translated in *FBIS Daily Report–Central Eurasia* (FBIS-SOV 92–061), March 30, 1992, pp. 40–43.

6. See the discussion in Samuel P. Huntington, *Political Order in Changing Societies* (New Haven: Yale University Press, 1986).

7. For an excellent discussion of the politics in all the former Soviet republics from Le-nin to early 1990 under Gorbachev, see chapters on the individual republics by various spe-cialists in Graham Smith, ed., *The Nationalities Question in the Soviet Union* (London: Longman, 1990).

8. Edward Gargan, "The Soviet Transition: Some Changes in Central Asia, but the Style is Still the Same," *New York Times,* September 18, 1991, p. 1.

9. For a thoughtful and detailed assessment of Karimov's policies and the potential for reform in Uzbekistan, see Renee Pruneau, "Democratization in Uzbekistan," *AACAR Bul-letin* (Association for the Advancement of Central Asian Research), ed. H. B. Paksoy, vol. 5, no. 1 (spring 1992), pp. 19–21.

10. See, for example, the analysis provided by Bess Brown, "The Presidential Election in Uzbekistan," in Radio Free Europe/Radio Liberty (hereafter RFE/RL) *RFE/RL Research Report* 1, no. 4 (January 24, 1992), pp. 23–25.

11. Roger Kangas (University of Mississippi) provides many valuable details on emerging political life in Uzbekistan in "The Role of Political Parties in Post-Soviet Uzbekistan," a paper presented to the American Association for the Advancement of Slavic Studies at their November 1992 convention in Phoenix, Arizona. For data on NDP membership, see p. 4.

12. Donald Carlisle, "Uzbekistan and the Uzbeks," *Problems of Communism* 40, no. 5 (September–October 1991), p. 43.

13. Ibid.

14. See ibid., p. 43, and Hedrick Smith, *The New Russians*, (New York: Avon Press, 1991), p. 320.

15. Smith, *New Russians*, pp. 317–318.

16. Ibid. Smith offers many insightful observations on Uzbek political life and society, see pp. 297–323.

17. See Kangas, "The Role of Political Parties in Post-Soviet Uzbekistan," pp. 5–7.

18. Moscow Central Television, November 16, 1991, as cited in Pruneau, "Democratization in Uzbekistan," p. 20.

19. See the lengthy editorial by Abdurakhim Pulatov published in *RFE/RL Daily Report*, no. 63, March 31, 1992.

20. Pauline Jones, "'Stunning Elections' in Reverse: Understanding Electoral Outcome in Uzbekistan," unpublished manuscript, Harvard University, Cambridge, Massachusetts, April 1992, p. 6. This is an excellent detailed account of the emerging political parties in Uzbekistan, especially Birlik and Erk.

21. See Bess Brown's informative assessment of the Uzbek IRP for more details, "The Islamic Renaissance Party in Central Asia," *RFE/RL Report on the USSR* 3, no. 19 (May 10, 1991), pp. 12–14.

22. See Kangas, "The Role of Political Parties in Post-Soviet Uzbekistan," p. 8.

23. See Bess Brown, "Media In Central Asia," *RFE/RL Research Report*, no. 39, October 2, 1992, p. 25, for a good review of the status of media in the region.

24. Bess Brown, "Another Attack on Birlik leader," *RFE/RL Daily Report*, October 20, 1992.

25. See Steve LeVine, "Ex-Leaders Rebound in Central Asia," *Washington Post*, December 26, 1992, p. A25.

26. For a good historical overview of ethnic relations between Russians and Kazakhs, see James Critchlow, "Kazakhstan: The Outlook for Ethnic Relations," *RFE/RL Research Report*, January 31, 1992, pp. 34–39.

27. For a detailed account of the meeting of the People's Congress, see James Critchlow, "Kazakhstan and Nazarbayev: Political Prospects," *RFE/RL Research Report*, January 17, 1992, pp. 31–34.

28. Ibid.

29. Ibid., based on Critchlow's interview with government officials on October 4, 1991.

30. Ibid.

31. Ibid.

32. For additional details on the role of these improvement groups, see Bess Brown, "The Fall of Masaliev: Kyrgyzstan's 'Silk Evolution' Advances," *RFE/RL Report on the USSR* 3, no. 16 (April 19, 1991), pp. 12–15.

33. Ibid., pp. 13–14.

34. For a detailed chronology of events in Bishkek during the August coup, see Bess Brown, "Central Asia: Mixed Reactions," *RFE/RL Report on the USSR* 3, no. 36 (September 6, 1991), pp. 44–45.

35. David Remnick, "In Central Asia, Death Stalks the Children," *Washington Post,* May 22, 1990, p. 1.

36. Bess Brown, "Central Asia Emerges on the World Stage," *RFE/RL Research Report* 1, no. 1 (January 3, 1992), p. 53.

37. Brown, "Central Asia: Mixed Reactions," p. 46.

38. Ibid., p. 44.

39. Ibid.

40. Remnick, "In Central Asia." In this case, "talks" is a euphemism for reprimands.

41. Ibid., p. 1.

42. Official Soviet statistics from 1989 indicated that Turkmenistan had the highest infant mortality rate in the USSR—54.2 per 1,000 births. In the poorer regions of the republics, some reports state a rate of 111 infant deaths per 1,000 births. Remnick, ibid., p. 12.

43. Ibid.

44. See *Moskovskie novosti,* January 13, 1991; and February 23, 1992, p. 9. My thanks to Rick Grimes for referring me to the January 1991 article.

45. For a more detailed account of politics in Tajikistan during the coup, see Brown, "Central Asia: Mixed Reactions," pp. 46–47.

46. *Moscow Postfactum,* February 4, 1992, cited in *FBIS–Daily Report* (FBIS-SOV 92–049), March 12, 1992, p. 63.

47. For a good overview of the origins and development of the Islamic Renaissance Party, see Brown, "The Islamic Renaissance Party in Central Asia," pp. 12–14.

48. *Postfactum,* March 7, 1992, in *FBIS Daily Report–Central Eurasia* (FBIS-SOV 92–047), March 10, 1992, pp. 39–40.

49. Ibid.

50. *Nezavisimaia gazeta,* March 28 1992, p. 1.

51. Ibid.

52. *Interfax,* as cited in *FBIS Daily Report–Central Eurasia* (FBIS-SOV 92–061), March 30, 1992, p. 40.

53. *Moscow Postfactum,* May 13, 1992, as cited in *FBIS Daily Report–Central Eurasia,* May 14, 1992, pp. 55–56.

54. For details on the various cabinet appointments, see Dushanbe Radio May 11, 1992, as cited in *FBIS Daily Report–Central Eurasia* (FBIS-SOV 92–092), May 12, 1992, pp. 57–59.

55. Text of interview with Communist Party Chairman Shodi Shabdolov is in *Rossiiskie vesti,* reported in *FBIS Daily Report–Central Eurasia* (FBIS-SOV 92–047), March 10, 1992, pp. 45–46.

56. Russian media, as cited in *RFE-RL Daily Report,* no. 189, October 1, 1992.

57. Steve LeVine, "Tajiks Turn to Moscow For Help," *Washington Post,* November 3, 1992, p. 17.

58. ITAR-TASS, November 6, 1992.

59. See *Interfax,* December 18, 1992, as cited in *FBIS Daily Report–Central Eurasia* (FBIS-SOV 92–245), December 21, 1992, pp. 68–69.

60. For text of Rakhmonov's radio address, see ibid., pp. 67–68.

61. See the 1989 Soviet census data cited in *Natsional'nii sostav naseleniia SSSR,* Moscow 1991, p. 130.

62. For a detailed discussion of Islam in Tajikistan, see Alexandre Bennigsen and S. Enders Wimbush, *Muslims of the Soviet Empire: A Guide* (Bloomington: Indiana University Press, 1986), pp. 85–93.

63. The ethnic and linguistic groups in Tajikistan are discussed in Shirin Akiner, *Islamic Peoples of the Soviet Union,* rev. ed. (New York: KPI Ltd., 1986), pp. 302–313 and 374–379.

64. John A. A. Ayoade, "Ethnic Politics in Nigeria," pp. 107–108.

65. Ibid., p. 112.

66. Gellner, *Thought and Change.*

67. See Muriel Atkin, "The Survival of Islam in Soviet Tajikistan," *Middle East Studies* 43, no. 4 (Autumn 1989), pp. 605–618, for a good overview of Tajik religious practices.

68. Huntington, *Political Order,* pp. 5–8

69. ITAR-TASS, *SOVSET Daily Report,* no. 91, May 13, 1992.

70. See Kangas, "The Role of Political Parties in Post-Soviet Uzbekistan," pp. 10–11.

71. Ibid.

CHAPTER 6

Pluralism Versus Corporatism: Government, Labor, and Business in the Russian Federation

Elizabeth Teague

It was often said of Mikhail Gorbachev's Soviet Union that political liberalization was launched more readily than economic reform. Nowadays the point is frequently made that political liberalization in Boris Yeltsin's Russia remains a fragile process and that its prospects are highly uncertain. It seems to me that both these observations are correct and that the apparent ease with which the old, authoritarian, communist system broke down has not yet been followed in Russia (or, for that matter, elsewhere in the Commonwealth of Independent States [CIS]) by the kinds of social developments that would definitively establish a new, open, and plural political order.

Of the difficult economic situation now facing the postcommunist societies, for example, David Dyker writes: "One thing has become abundantly clear. It is easy enough to abolish central planning. That has now been accomplished in the Soviet Union, as elsewhere in Eastern Europe. It is quite another matter to put something in its place."[1] Of the chaotic political situation in the former USSR, Vera Tolz observes: "It seems that founding political groups independent of the CPSU [Communist Party of the Soviet Union], a process that was well under way by the end of 1988, was relatively easy; what is more difficult to achieve is the transformation of these groups into full-fledged political parties."[2]

In this chapter I describe some of the sources of that difficulty by examining relations among workers, government, and employers. The discussion is ordered around the distinction between pluralist and corporatist frameworks for the articulation of the interests of labor and business.

Pluralism Versus Corporatism

Pluralism describes a political system in which there is no single source of authority. Social forces and interests, and the groups and associations that represent them, are recognized as being independent of the state and as having equal and legitimate claims upon it.[3] In an often quoted definition, Philippe Schmitter describes pluralism as

> a system of interest intermediation in which the constituent units are organized into an unspecified number of multiple, voluntary, competitive, nonhierarchically ordered, and self-determined (as to type or scope or interest) categories that are not specifically licensed, recognized, subsidized, created, or otherwise controlled in leadership selection or interest articulation by the state and that do not exercise a monopoly of representational activity within their respective categories.[4]

Pluralism is frequently contrasted with the concept of corporatism. Corporatism has been defined by Schmitter, who is its leading exponent, as

> a system of interest representation in which the constituent units are organized into a limited number of singular, compulsory, non-competitive, hierarchically ordered, and functionally differentiated categories recognized and licensed (if not created) by the state and granted a deliberate representational monopoly within their respective categories in exchange for observing certain controls on their selection of leaders and articulation of demands and supports.[5]

Corporatism has a bad name with many political thinkers because of its connections with unashamedly undemocratic regimes such as those of Benito Mussolini in Italy and Juan Perón in Argentina. Under systems such as these, individuals were viewed less as free and equal citizens than as members of functional categories such as workers, soldiers, entrepreneurs, mothers, and so on. Social groups and organizations were deemed subordinate to and dependent on the state, and representative political institutions were declared to be superfluous.[6] The applicability of the concept of corporatism to the political system in the USSR during the Leonid Brezhnev era has also been cogently argued.[7]

However, Schmitter has identified two distinct types of corporatism. The first, which he calls authoritarian or "state" corporatism, describes the kind of system established in countries such as Fascist Italy and, arguably, Brezhnev's USSR. Under the second category, which Schmitter calls liberal or "societal" corporatism, fall a number of today's major industrialized democracies—the Federal Republic of Germany, Austria, and the Scandinavian countries, among others.[8] Used in this sense, liberal corporatism (also known as "neocorporatism," "social partnership," "tripartism," or "consociationalism") is clearly not incompatible with an open society.

The keynotes in a liberal corporatist system are the maintenance of social stability and the avoidance of conflict. National economic and social policies are elaborated in the course of close, institutionalized cooperation between the government and organizations representing the main producer interests (trade unions and employers' associations). Decisions are adopted only if there is consensus since each interest group (government, business, and labor) possesses a veto. Typ-

ically, government and business seek moderation in wage settlements from organized labor in return for policies favoring full employment and generous spending
on social welfare.[9]

Accordingly, corporatism entails privileged access to government for certain
interest groups and, inevitably, some degree of exclusion for other groups; the
role of Parliament tends to be diminished. And, if liberal corporatism is to prove
viable without recourse to repression, a high level of national consensus is presupposed; "social partnership" is unlikely to take root in countries whose popula-
tions are deeply divided or strongly diversified socially, ideologically, or ethnically.

The Government/Labor/Business Triad

The differences between pluralism and liberal corporatism can be seen in the
varying forms of relationships that exist in today's world among government, labor, and (for want of a better word) capital. Research conducted by the Organization for Economic Cooperation and Development (OECD) finds that, in the settled democracies and market economies of the West, two models work well.[10]

In the first model (which accords most closely with the pluralist political
model) the government stays out of labor/management negotiations and bargaining over wages and conditions is decentralized to firms. On the principle that "the
purpose of power [is] not to do good but to prevent the worst," the role of the state
is normally confined to mediating between different interest groups only when
these find themselves at loggerheads.[11] This is largely how things are done in the
United States, where unionization of the labor force is low and plant-level bargaining is common (though not universal), and where the government has little or
no control over bargaining between management and labor. A comparable situation pertains in Japan, where unionization is high but unions are *company* unions
and bargaining takes place, as it does in the United States, at the level of the firm.

Under the second model, "liberal corporatism" or "social partnership" as
practiced in Austria or Sweden, wage-bargaining is highly centralized. Government representatives meet regularly with a body representing *all* unions and a
body representing all or most employers. Together they set guidelines for labor
remuneration and working conditions across the whole economy (or at least a pre-
dominant part of it). Such a system is not common since it tends to work only
where there is mutual confidence between the parties and a recognition that they
share a common interest in economic and political stability and industrial harmony.

To say that these two arrangements "work well" is simply to observe that, according to the OECD, the evidence across a large number of capitalist countries in
recent years shows that both models—the one highly decentralized, the other
quite strongly centralized—are associated with greater success in maintaining relatively high levels of employment without accelerating inflation. This can be

compared with countries (such as the United Kingdom) where wage-bargaining is organized according to a third model—that is, by large-scale labor/management negotiations conducted on an industry-by-industry basis, with no coordination across industries. Here, the OECD found, the result tends to be constantly increasing real wages and high unemployment—in other words, the worst of both worlds.

Yeltsin Turns to "Social Partnership"

Relations among government, labor, and business are a potential source of instability in any society, but they assume particular importance in a society trying to make the transition to a market economy. Mikhail Gorbachev, whose overriding aim when he came to power in 1985 seemed to be to revitalize the flagging Soviet economy, had clearly concluded by the middle of 1986 that elite interests were so strongly entrenched in the USSR that economic reform could be realized only if it were preceded by political reform.

The political liberalization initiated under Gorbachev was seized upon with such avidity by some sections of Soviet society that, by 1989, observers were warning that the pendulum had swung too far and that political reform had been allowed to get too far out in front of economic reform. Even though the democratization of Soviet society was far from complete, political power had already devolved to such an extent that the Gorbachev leadership seemed to be deterred from embarking on radical economic reform at least partly by fear that popular opposition, sparked by declining living standards, might derail the entire transition process. Strong opposition to reform also appears, with hindsight, to have been put up by the USSR's "industrial lobby." This lobby represented the managers of state-owned industrial enterprises, many of them in the defense industry, whose prospects in a real market environment would be dim.

Boris Yeltsin faced the same problem in autumn 1991 when he announced his determination to launch Russia on the road to a market economy. It is hard for *any* reforming government to maintain popular support if it implements policies that lead to rising prices and increasing unemployment and that threaten, in the short term, to lower the standard of living of almost all members of society. Unless measures are taken to soften the blow for ordinary people, the population may become alienated from the reform program and reject the government's austerity measures. In these circumstances, could the transition be managed without the introduction of authoritarian political controls? Would the political pluralism that blossomed in the USSR during the Gorbachev era have to be halted if economic liberalization was to go ahead? What kind of trade-off would have to be made between maintaining political stability and enforcing financial stabilization? Looked at from this perspective, relations among government, labor, and employers in Yeltsin's Russia took on special importance.

The Yeltsin government was clearly concerned lest its efforts be derailed by popular opposition to reform. Yeltsin's close aide Gennadii Burbulis candidly admitted the government's apprehension in December 1991 when he appealed for the help of Russia's official trade unions in riding out the initial stages of the reform. Addressing a meeting of the Council of the Federation of Independent Trade Unions of Russia (the Russian initials of this successor to the old official Soviet trade unions are FNPR), Burbulis said: "We face an extraordinary situation—one in which the policies of the leadership, undertaken in the interests of the majority of the population, are not yet understood by the population."[12]

Yeltsin's government expended considerable effort on the creation of an institutional framework to ensure industrial stability. It seemed, in this respect, to be aiming quite consciously at what Schmitter would call a "liberal corporatist" approach to relations among government, labor, and business. On October 26, 1991, two days before he informed the Russian Congress of People's Deputies of his intention to launch the country on the road to the market, Yeltsin signed a presidential edict "On Guaranteeing the Rights of Trade Unions During the Transition to a Market Economy."[13] In that edict, Yeltsin promised that before adopting any major legislation on social or economic questions his government would consult with both the official Russian trade unions (the FNPR) and "other republican trade union associations" in order to work out "the soundest decisions and those that will be most acceptable to the workers."

On November 15, Yeltsin signed an edict "On Social Partnership and the Resolution of Labor Disputes," pledging that the Russian government would reach an annual agreement on social and economic questions with "representatives of republican trade union associations and employers."[14] To this end, Yeltsin undertook to form a tripartite commission empowered to review and set general and sectoral wage rates, monitor working conditions, and mediate industrial disputes. The commission was to be composed of representatives of the Russian government, the trade unions (both official and unofficial), and Russia's fledgling employers' associations. Yeltsin gave his government two weeks to settle the composition of the commission. In return for a role in top-level decision making, he indicated, organized labor would be expected to agree that as long as the government kept its side of any bargain struck between them the unions would not call their members out on strike.

Although Gennadii Burbulis was eventually assigned by Yeltsin to coordinate the activities of the tripartite commission, the main architect of Russia's social partnership was Aleksandr Shokhin, appointed minister of labor of the Russian Federation in August 1991, as the nominee of the Russian Social Democratic Party.[15] Shokhin, who has a background as an economist, was promoted to deputy prime minister in Yeltsin's government in November 1991 and was the person chiefly involved in setting the tripartite commission in motion.[16]

Shokhin told a conference in Moscow on December 9, 1991, that Yeltsin's government was determined to create "a civilized labor market" in Russia.[17] To this end, he said, new social mechanisms must be established, the most important of which were "institutions for cooperation among the various partners in the labor market." In its search for solutions, Shokhin said, the Russian government would be relying heavily on Western experience. He went on to outline the difficulties involved in trying to set up a Western type of institution in postcommunist Russia, explaining that a dispute was under way over the composition of the three equal-sized subgroups (one each for the government, unions, and employers) that were to make up the tripartite commission. The main questions, Shokhin said, were: "Who is to represent the employers, and who the workers?"

As far as the employers were concerned, the minister said, the problem was that in Russia employers' associations were at only an early stage of development. The state still owned the overwhelming majority of enterprises, many of which remained, at least formally, the property of government ministries. The government therefore found itself playing two roles at once: its own and that of the employer. Shokhin said this vastly complicated the resolution of labor disputes. Workers' demands over bread-and-butter issues such as wages could not be negotiated between management and workers' representatives purely on their merits and in the absence of government intervention; instead, negotiations tended to escalate almost immediately into political confrontations into which the government found itself dragged whether it wanted to be involved or not.

The problems regarding the representation of workers' interests were just as awkward, Shokhin went on, since the FNPR was demanding the exclusive right to speak in the name of Russia's workers on the tripartite commission. The FNPR is Russia's largest trade union center and is strong both organizationally and materially, but the word "independent" in its name is deceptive, since the regional and sectoral unions grouped under its umbrella are Russia's official, formerly communist-dominated trade unions.[18] Because of their communist past, these official unions are mistrusted by many workers and are rumored to be losing substantial numbers of members. The official unions, Shokhin said, could not claim to represent the interests of the entire working class; moreover, he continued, he was not convinced that the official unions retained enough influence over workers to prevent the outbreak of wildcat strikes.[19] Shokhin said some workers would prefer to support one or another of the truly independent new workers' organizations that had sprung up in Russia in recent years. He cited as an example the workers' committees that emerged from the 1989 miners' strike, though he noted that these committees were not yet officially recognized or registered as trade unions.

As a result of disputes over representation—and because of the inner turmoil that plagued the early months of the Yeltsin government—the tripartite commission did not get off the ground within the two-week period specified in Yeltsin's edict of November 15. A number of preliminary meetings were held in December, but the Russian Tripartite Commission on the Regulation of Social and Labor Relations (to give it its full title) came into official existence only on January 2, 1992.[20]

The problem of representation for the employers was partially resolved when it was decided that only enterprise directors would serve on the employers' subgroup and that the staff of government ministries would belong to the government subgroup, not the employers' one. Serving on the employers' subgroup were representatives of a number of employers' organizations, the most influential of which was the Russian Union of Industrialists and Entrepreneurs—Russia's largest employers' association. It is led by sixty-year-old Arkadii Vol'skii, a former Communist Party official who had served as economics adviser to General Secretaries Yuri Andropov and Mikhail Gorbachev. The organization was originally created on an all-union basis in summer 1990 as the USSR Scientific and Industrial Union. It claimed to represent plants accounting for 65 percent of the USSR's 1991 industrial output.[21] Following the collapse of the Soviet Union, the organization was reestablished as a Russian association. It is generally seen as the mouthpiece of Russia's massive state-owned military-industrial complex.

As for the controversy over who should represent workers' interests, both the FNPR and the unofficial unions expressed reservations about working together. The FNPR, forced to relinquish its demand for the exclusive right to represent hired labor, accused the government of fostering the unofficial unions in a deliberate effort to split and weaken the workers' movement.[22] The unofficial unions, for their part, feared that the FNPR would dominate the trade union subgroup because of its superior size. (In 1991, the FNPR claimed 66 million members—almost the entire Russian labor force.) Eventually, official and unofficial unions agreed to cooperate. The union subgroup had fourteen members: nine representatives from the FNPR; three from the Union of Socialist Trade Unions (Sotsprof); and one each from the Independent Miners' Union (NPG) and the independent union of civil aviation pilots. The fact that Sotsprof—an independent union set up in 1989 that claimed around 250,000 members—had as many as three representatives was much resented by the FNPR, which also grumbled about the Sotsprof leadership's close links with Shokhin. Indeed, Sotsprof often seemed to be acting as a kind of unofficial think tank on labor issues for the government, and its political influence was considerably greater than the size of its membership alone might have suggested.[23]

The tripartite commission met regularly from January 1992 onward. Decisions in the three subgroups were reached by qualified majority vote, but the commission as a whole made decisions only when all three constituent groups had achieved consensus, since each of the three sides had a veto. Representatives of the unions and the employers won the right to attend government meetings, and, in theory at least, the government was supposed to show drafts of new legislation to the members of the tripartite commission before submitting them to Parliament. However, the official unions complained frequently about the government's failure to do so.

Landmark Agreement

Following much argument, negotiations culminated in the March 25, 1992, signing of the General Agreement for 1992 by representatives of the Russian government, the official and unofficial Russian trade unions, and Russia's employers' associations.[24] Under the terms of this document (the first of its kind in Russian history[25]), the government made various promises concerning the provision of social safety nets (retraining programs, job creation schemes, unemployment benefits, and so on) during the reform process. In return, the trade unions and the employers' associations (including those representing major state-owned enterprises) assented to the government's plans to liberalize prices, privatize property, and create what the General Agreement called "a socially oriented market economy." The employers promised to refrain from mass layoffs and plant closures, and the unions promised that as long as the government and the employers observed their pledges they would not call their members out on strike.

From the point of view of the government, the main attraction of the General Agreement was that in signing it the trade unions and the managers of state-owned enterprises, both of whom represented constituencies likely to be adversely affected by the transition to the market, committed themselves publicly to helping rather than hindering the government in carrying out its reform program. According to Burbulis, the document meant that all three sides had become "co-authors of the reforms."[26] To obtain the agreement of the unions and the industrialists, however, the government had to make concessions on at least two major issues.

The first was wages. Under the terms of the agreement, the government promised to institutionalize a minimum wage, to review it every three months, and to use it as the yardstick against which minimum pensions and other allowances, such as student grants, would be measured. However, the agreement made no mention of any commitments on wages being assumed by the unions. That is, the unions were not required to give their public assent to any prolonged decline in real wages or to promise to be moderate in their wage demands. Yet without some such self-restraint on the part of the unions, the government's stabilization program (and therefore the rest of its program for economic transformation) was unlikely to be achieved. The silence of the General Agreement on this issue threatened to render the government very vulnerable at some future date.

The second issue concerned plant closures and worker layoffs. It is hard to imagine a successful transition to a viable economy (to say nothing of a viable economy per se) in which factories never go bankrupt and large-scale layoffs never occur. The fact that the employers promised, under the terms of the General Agreement, not to close plants or fire large numbers of workers implied that the managers of state-owned enterprises were expecting government subsidies to enable them to go on paying wages even to employees of unprofitable enterprises.

This clause in the General Agreement threatened to be a major obstacle to future economic reforms.

At first, the FNPR dragged its feet about signing the agreement, pointing out that many of the government's promises to provide social safety nets were incompatible with the pledges to get inflation under control and to reduce the budget deficit (by, among other means, scaling down unemployment benefits) that the Yeltsin government had made to the International Monetary Fund (IMF) only a few weeks earlier.[27] Eventually, however, the leadership of the FNPR announced that it was giving the General Agreement its official approval. The FNPR's decision to relent coincided with moves by the Yeltsin government that many observers interpreted as a dangerous concession to Russia's "industrial lobby." The leaders of the lobby had earlier been demanding softer credits and higher subsidies and had been threatening that if they did not receive them, they would ally themselves with organized labor to bring the Russian economy to a halt.[28]

"Social Partnership" in Action

Pessimists had predicted that the liberalization of prices, introduced by the Russian government on January 2, 1992, would provoke a violent explosion of popular anger. In any event, this did not happen: There were no riots; strikes and demonstrations were few. The relief of the Yeltsin government was palpable. Informing the Russian Congress of People's Deputies in April that strike activity had actually decreased in the first quarter of 1992 compared with the same period in 1991, Burbulis said the credit for this gratifying decline in workers' protests should go to the social partnership mechanism.[29] Government spokesmen claimed, too, that Russia's workers were beginning to turn increasingly to the tripartite commission when they had grievances and that this showed that the social partnership machinery was beginning to function as planned.

From a more skeptical viewpoint, it might be countered that what really happened was that the government purchased industrial harmony by the simple expedient of giving in to strikers' demands and granting wage increases even where these threatened to undermine its ability to curb inflation and cut the budget deficit. According to the Russian economist Grigorii Yavlinsky, "petty concessions [to workers] have so far made it possible to avoid mass strikes," but are putting "an ever heavier burden on the budget." In May, Yavlinsky accused the government of risking a general conflagration by tackling strikes piecemeal, like brush fires. "The government's cooperation with the unions," Yavlinsky wrote, "boils down to bargaining for pay raises for workers in one or another region, which usually precedes questions from other regions or sectors as to why they haven't been given the same thing."[30] Yeltsin's government insisted that it had not abandoned its strategic goals, yet the picture by the middle of 1992 was one of small tactical concessions, whose cumulative effect might, in the long run, be to destroy the entire reform effort.

Even before the General Agreement was signed, the government had made a number of concessions to Russia's coal miners. In January 1992, face workers in the coal mines of the Kuzbass threatened to strike unless they received higher wages to keep pace with retail price rises. Their demands were put forward by the official miners' union, which was affiliated to the FNPR, but were not supported by the workers' committees (the heirs of the workers' organizations set up during the 1989 miners' strike). On January 22, a delegation of miners traveled to Moscow, where they met with Yeltsin. Faced with the threat of a strike in a key industry, the Russian government capitulated and awarded the miners a threefold pay raise, backdated to the beginning of the year. The minimum monthly wage for a face worker went up from 2,000 rubles to between 5,000 and 7,000 rubles. Coal miners in the far northern cities of Vorkuta and Syktyvkar threatened to strike in February and March, respectively; both groups called off their strikes after Burbulis traveled to the region and promised them an increase in pay.

These awards cost the state 22 billion rubles. Although, in themselves, they did not represent a substantial proportion of Russia's officially projected gross national product (GNP) (6.5 trillion rubles in 1992, according to government forecasts of early 1992, though these were revised upward), the miners' wage concessions worsened the government's chances of balancing the budget and set off a wage-price spiral that spurred workers in other professions to demand raises too. The resultant strike threats, which began in mining regions, came mainly from employees in budget-financed institutions—teachers, doctors, and public transport workers.[31]

The tripartite commission made its first attempt to mediate a labor dispute shortly before the signing of the General Agreement. On March 12 Shokhin traveled to Kemerovo, capital of the Kuzbass, at the head of a delegation composed of representatives of all three groups in the commission. The Kuzbass region of western Siberia was the area where the 1989 coal miners' strike had its birth, but in March 1992 the call for a general strike came not from face workers but from surface and auxiliary mine workers. They were demanding wage hikes to compensate for the rises in retail prices that followed the January 1992 liberalization, and also because of the gap that had opened up since January, after the government's concessions, between their wages and those of face workers. Their wage demand was advanced by the official trade union federation of the Kuzbass, which was affiliated to the FNPR. It was not supported by the Kuzbass workers' committees, which issued a sharp statement in which they called the official unions "the last bastion of reactionary communist forces" and accused them of trying to wreck the economic reform.[32]

Demands for higher wages were granted by the government on this and subsequent occasions. At times the government gave in completely to the workers' wage demands, but at others it managed to achieve a compromise settlement. At the end of April, for example, medical workers throughout Russia began a strike; their demands for a tenfold wage hike to keep pace with inflation and for increased state spending on the health service were put forward by the official medical workers' union, which was affiliated to the FNPR. At that time, teachers in various parts of Russia had been on strike for several weeks, also demanding higher wages. On May 7, Yeltsin discussed the strikes with FNPR chairman Igor Klochkov and ordered the creation of a working group chaired by (then) First Deputy Premier Egor Gaidar and made up of representatives of government and unions (though not of the employers' organizations). Yeltsin gave Gaidar's team until May 12 to come up with proposals, which were then presented to the tripartite commission. The strikes were suspended on May 13, after the government agreed to more than double the wages of both teachers and medical workers.[33] The fact that it required the personal intervention of Yeltsin and Klochkov to resolve the dispute was said to have given rise to resentment on the part of those excluded (the unofficial unions and the employers' associations) and to have led to charges that tripartism was failing to function.

Wonderland Revisited

The evidence presented here suggests that, at least as far as labor relations are concerned, the Yeltsin government has been trying to move Russia less toward a classic pluralist system than toward some form of neocorporatism. However, Russia's path to social partnership is likely to be a thorny one. Corporatism is a system that works best in circumstances in which there is strong social consensus and shared values. In the Russian Federation today, such consensus is largely lacking. Rather, the incipient pluralism cutting through Russia's emergent political institutions suggests that successful attempts to introduce corporatist procedures may be difficult to achieve.

A major problem is created by the lack of clearly distinguishable interests in Russia. This is largely because privatization has not yet started in earnest and because over 90 percent of enterprises are still state-owned. The ambiguity of the present situation has been vividly described by Gennadii Semigin, who represents the Congress of Russian Business Circles on the tripartite commission.[34] Semigin has asserted that in creating the commission the government had expected to be able to play the entrepreneurs off against the unions. This had not happened, Semigin asserted: All the government had managed to do was to play the FNPR off against Sotsprof. Semigin said Shokhin complained constantly that all the unions wanted was higher wages and all the entrepreneurs wanted was lower taxes; but this, Semigin claimed, was not the whole story. More often than not, he said, the businessmen's lobby found itself on the same side as the unions, both ganging up against the government.[35]

This is not a situation that would long continue once genuine privatization took place, but it helps to explain why the Yeltsin government has so far found itself in so difficult a position. Until the country has undergone a privatization of state property that forces enterprises to fail or succeed and that facilitates the emergence of a genuine labor market, any tripartite mechanism is going to stand shakily on only one-and-a-half legs (the government and a divided trade union movement) instead of on three; and the system it seeks to regulate is, therefore, likely to be an unstable one.

The lack of clearly defined business interests is only part of a larger picture. The whole of Russian society is reinventing itself today: Civil society is gradually beginning to take shape. The atoms of the once atomized society are charging around, trying to link up. Constituencies, interests, and rules of the game are all fluid. Nothing is what it seems and everyone's role is provisional. Just such a situation has been observed by those who have studied countries in transition from authoritarian to democratic rule. Following their examination of Latin America and Southern Europe, Guillermo O'Donnell and Philippe Schmitter concluded that "during these transitions, ... it is almost impossible to specify *ex ante* which classes, sectors, institutions, and other groups will take what role, opt for which issues, or support what alternative."[36]

Indeed, as one observes postcommunist Russia, the image that comes most often to mind is that of Alice trying to play croquet in Wonderland:

> Alice thought she had never seen such a curious croquet-ground in all her life; it was all ridges and furrows; the balls were live hedgehogs, the mallets live flamingoes, and the soldiers had to double themselves up and to stand upon their hands and feet, to make the arches.
>
> The chief difficulty Alice found at first was in managing her flamingo: she succeeded in getting its body tucked away, comfortably enough, under her arm, but generally, just as she had got its neck nicely straightened out, and was going to give the hedgehog a blow with its head, it *would* twist itself round and look up in her face, with such a puzzled expression that she could not help bursting out laughing: and when she had got its head down, and was going to begin again, it was very provoking to find that the hedgehog had unrolled itself, and was in the act of crawling away: ... and, as the doubled-up soldiers were always getting up and walking off to other parts of the ground, Alice soon came to the conclusion that it was a very difficult game indeed.[37]

In Russia today there is a similar (almost surreal) situation in which roles seem to be provisional, multiple, and constantly shifting, with military officers serving in Parliament, businessmen forming political parties, and trade unions acting as entrepreneurs.[38]

The Road to Neocorporatism?

To return to the original question: Are industrial relations in Russia heading toward a corporatist or a pluralist framework? The answer, though not clear at present, may become so in the near term. The Swedish economist Anders Aslund warns that the vested interests of Russia's industrialists make the industrial lobby, at the present stage, a powerful political pressure group, threatening the ability of the Yeltsin government to implement its program of market reforms. Workers' organizations are still weak, and broadly based political parties have yet to take root. What is most needed in these circumstances, Aslund argues, is the formation of independent trade unions and political parties that would counteract the power of the industrial lobby and "provide the economic reforms with a satisfactory political base." The process of forming political parties in Russia lost impetus at the end of 1991 when Yeltsin announced that he was suspending local government and parliamentary elections for an indefinite period. If there are no elections to be fought, parties lose their salience. By the same token, Aslund argues, the calling of parliamentary elections under a new Russian Constitution could prove the most direct way of speeding up the process again.[39]

What will determine whether Russia moves toward corporatism or pluralism? Much will depend on what kind of constitution is adopted for Russia. At present, on the one hand, Yeltsin's battles with the communist and nationalist factions in the Russian Parliament seem to be inclining him to favor a presidential system for Russia—one modeled, most probably, on the French system, under which the president would have the power to dissolve Parliament and to override its decisions. Such a political system, characterized as it would be by a strong executive presidency and a Parliament that was relatively weak, might well favor the emergence of a neocorporatist or even an authoritarian corporatist framework. If, on the other hand, Yeltsin were to decide on early elections and a system under which Parliament was sovereign and the president was more or less a figurehead, the likelihood of the establishment of a smoothly operating corporatist system of any kind in postcommunist Russia would seem to be reduced. Meanwhile, the fluid and unstable character of political roles and social interests in the present, mutant state of the Russian economy makes the development of a functioning corporatist system, to say nothing of a functioning pluralist one, highly problematic.

Notes

The author is indebted to Sarah Ashwin, Walter Connor, Philip Hanson, Frank Hoffer, and Ben Slay for valuable advice.

1. David A. Dyker, "Comment to V. A. Naishul,' in *The Supreme and Last Stage of Socialism* (London: Centre for Research into Communist Economies, 1991), p. 41.

2. Vera Tolz, "Political Parties in Russia," Radio Free Europe/Radio Liberty (hereafter cited as RFE/RL), *RFE/RL Research Report,* no. 1 (1992).

3. For an overview of the development of the concept of pluralism and of its application to the study of the Soviet Union, see Susan Gross Solomon, "'Pluralism' in Political Science: The Odyssey of a Concept," in Susan Gross Solomon, ed., *Pluralism in the Soviet Union* (London: Macmillan, 1983), pp. 1–36.

4. Philippe Schmitter, "Still the Century of Corporatism?" *Review of Politics,* no. 36 (1974), pp. 85–131 at pp. 93–94; as quoted in Valerie Bunce and John M. Echols III, "So-

viet Politics in the Brezhnev Era: 'Pluralism' or 'Corporatism'?" in Donald R. Kelley, ed., *Soviet Politics in the Brezhnev Era* (New York: Praeger, 1980), pp. 1–26 at p. 4.

5. Schmitter, loc. cit.

6. See the definition of corporatism in Julius Gould and William L. Kolb, eds., *A Dictionary of the Social Sciences* (New York: Free Press, 1964), p. 141.

7. Bunce and Echols, op. cit.; Jerry F. Hough, "Pluralism, Corporatism, and the Soviet Union," in Solomon, op. cit., pp. 37–60; Archie Brown, "Pluralism, Power and the Soviet Political System: A Comparative Perspective," in ibid., pp. 61–107.

8. Bunce and Echols, op. cit..

9. "Social partnership" in the West European sense denotes more than just institutional frameworks for nationwide collective bargaining, being further typified by a number of components. These include (1) a degree of worker participation in enterprise management (e.g., Germany's system of codetermination); (2) "active labor market policies" that aim to keep unemployment low by promoting labor retraining and mobility; and (3) a degree of worker ownership of enterprises (e.g., Sweden's worker investment funds). See Gerald A. Dorfman and Peter J. Duignan, eds., *Politics in Western Europe,* 2d ed. (Stanford, CA: Hoover Institution Press, 1991).

10. The information contained in this section was provided by OECD economists at a conference in Moscow on December 9–10, 1991. The conference was jointly sponsored by the OECD's Center for Cooperation with European Economies in Transition, the U.S. Department of Labor, and the Russian Ministry of Labor and Employment.

11. Solomon, op. cit., p. 11.

12. *Rabochaia tribuna,* December 27, 1991.

13. For the text of the edict on trade union rights, see *Rabochaia tribuna,* October 31, 1991.

14. For the text of the edict on social partnership, see *Rossiiskaia gazeta,* November 19, 1991; for press commentary, see *Trud,* November 16, 1991; *Izvestiia,* November 18, 1991; and *Rabochaia tribuna,* November 20, 1991.

15. *Trud,* February 7, 1992.

16. In June 1992, Shokhin was shifted sideways and given responsibility for Russia's foreign economic relations.

17. Shokhin was addressing the conference referred to in note 10.

18. The official unions remain strong because they still control the distribution of social security funds to workers. These funds cover sickness and invalid benefits, maternity leave, and child-care allowances for low-income families; they are drawn from the state budget, but administered by the official unions. Russia's unofficial unions are contesting the official unions' monopoly over these funds, complaining that workers who do not join the official unions do not receive, or are threatened with not receiving, benefits to which they are entitled.

19. On the one hand, the FNPR, which claims at present to have more than fifty million members, has not resorted to strike action against the economic reforms of Yeltsin's government but did hold a few rather small demonstrations in Moscow in autumn and winter 1991–1992. These demonstrations were poorly attended, which suggested that the FNPR did not have real power to mobilize workers. The Independent Miners' Union, on the other hand, could boast only 4 percent of the miners of the former USSR as its members when, in spring 1991, it organized a two-month strike that crippled the Gorbachev leadership; the lesson did not escape Yeltsin's government. See Sarah Ashwin, "The 1991 Miners' Strike:

New Departures in the Independent Workers' Movement," *Report on the USSR*, no. 33 (1991).

20. *Trud*, December 31, 1991.

21. Elizabeth Teague, "Soviet Employers' Organization Celebrates First Birthday," *Report on the USSR*, no. 26 (1991).

22. The militant Moscow Trade Union Federation urged the FNPR not to enter into any kind of social partnership with the government, on the grounds that the unions would be required to sign away their right to strike and would become party to decisions that suited the government and employers but went against the interests of the workers (*Solidarnost'*, no. 16 (1991), p. 6).

23. The official unions have complained that Sotsprof "always sides with the government"; see *Trud*, March 14, 1992. Sotsprof clashed with the official unions, but scored an important victory for the unofficial ones in March 1992, when its version of a new Russian Federation law on collective agreements was adopted by the Parliament. (For the text, see *Ekonomika i zhizn'*, no. 21 [1992], p. 2.) In the past, annual agreements between management and the work force were negotiated and signed on behalf of the workers by representatives of the official trade unions. A draft law favored by the FNPR stipulated that the exclusive right to conduct negotiations would belong to the union with the largest membership at a given enterprise (which would almost invariably be the official union). Sotsprof's draft stated that workers might be represented by any union, regardless of the size of its membership. The FNPR objected to Sotsprof's draft at meetings of the tripartite commission in January 1992, but its protests were overruled, and Russia's unofficial unions for the first time won the legal right to negotiate with management.

24. Russian Television, March 25, 1992. For the text of the General Agreement, see *Ekonomika i zhizn'*, no. 17 (1992), p. 20.

25. In April 1991, the official trade union confederation of the USSR signed a bilateral agreement with the government of USSR Prime Minister Valentin Pavlov, under which the unions pledged to refrain from strikes as long as the government kept various promises it had made regarding economic reform. The 1991 agreement was not, however, a tripartite arrangement of the kind the Yeltsin government has tried to establish; nor was Pavlov a genuine reformer; and the agreement was consigned to the wastebasket as soon as the August 1991 putsch caused the collapse of the Soviet Union.

26. *Trud*, March 26, 1992.

27. *Trud*, March 28, 1992, and *Nezavisimaia gazeta*, March 31, 1992, commented on the "clear contradiction" between the General Agreement and the government's memorandum to the IMF. The former, *Nezavisimaia gazeta* noted, was "more humane" than the latter. The text of the memorandum to the IMF was published by TASS on March 4, 1992, and in *Ekonomika i zhizn'*, no. 10 (1992), pp. 4–5; for analysis, see Keith Bush, "Gaidar's Guidelines," *RFE/RL Research Report*, no. 15 (1992).

28. Philip Hanson and Elizabeth Teague, "The Industrialists and Russian Economic Reform," *RFE/RL Research Report*, no. 19 (1992).

29. *Radio Rossii*, April 14, 1992. The relative absence of workplace unrest was a source of great satisfaction to the Russian government. Indeed, the number of strikes in Russia actually decreased in the early months of 1992 in comparison with the first months of 1991. Whereas Russia lost 573,000 man-days through strikes in the first quarter of 1991, only half as much time (268,000 man-days) was lost in the first quarter of 1992 (*Ekonomika i zhizn'*, no. 17 [1991], p. 16, and no. 17 [1992], p. 14).

30. *Moscow News,* no. 22 (1992), p. 8.

31. *Izvestiia,* March 7, 1992; *Nezavisimaia gazeta,* March 18, 1992; *Moscow News,* no. 18 (1992), p. 9.

32. *Nezavisimaia gazeta,* March 7, 1992.

33. *Interfax,* May 16, 1992.

34. The Congress, whose head is the twenty-eight-year-old Semigin, represents Russia's new commercial banks, insurance companies, and commodity and stock markets.

35. *Trud,* April 22, 1992.

36. Guillermo O'Donnell and Philippe C. Schmitter, *Transitions from Authoritarian Rule: Tentative Conclusions About Uncertain Democracies* (Baltimore: Johns Hopkins University Press, 1986), p. 4.

37. Lewis Carroll, *Alice's Adventures in Wonderland* (London: Macmillan, 1949), pp. 109–10.

38. The FNPR has established a computer network linking *birzhi* (exchanges) throughout eastern Russia (author's interview, Moscow, December 1991).

39. Anders Aslund, "The Gradual Nature of Economic Change in Russia," paper presented at a conference on economic stabilization, sponsored by the Working Center of Economic Reforms of the Russian Government and held in St. Petersburg on June 21–24, 1992.

CHAPTER 7

State, Property, and Political Society in Postcommunist Russia: In Search of a Political Center

Michael E. Urban

In this chapter, I shall look at the constellation of political forces—parties, movements, and blocs—that has emerged in postcommunist Russia. These forces are analyzed according to categories that are basic to any political order, namely those of "state" and "property." The central thesis has two aspects: first, that discord on the issues of the basis of authority in the Russian state and on the appropriate form of property relations for the Russian economy has fractured political society in such a way as to retard, if not prevent, the development of a political center. Rather, these cross-cutting issues have provided a number of possible "centers" that various political forces have come to occupy. Second, by categorizing these same forces along the dimensions of state and property, I note that political society in Russia has, indeed, begun to take on an identifiable shape. That is, the confusing picture presented by the whole of political society should not be mistaken for random behavior at the level of its constituent parts. There seems to be a certain logic at work with respect to the programmatic positions adopted by political parties and the manner in which they have formed alliances with one another.

From these observations, two tentative conclusions appear to follow. On the one hand, as long as discord remains widespread on the questions of state and property, political society will lack any recognizable center. By that measure, politics will also remain volatile, as blocs are pitted against each other in both the legislature and in the larger society without the common ground required for reaching compromises and, thereby, engendering stability. On the other hand, should a center take shape in the future, its elements will be drawn from the fragmented forces that exist at present. Accordingly, these forces—whose politically promiscuous behavior doubtless offends all analysts who prize tidiness, predictability, and closure—represent important objects of research. Their study should prove indispensable to answering the question that future historians will ask: How was it that a political center formed—or failed to form—in postcommunist Russia? I begin my analysis with a discussion of the idea of a political center and of the problem attending this concept in the transition from communism.

The Communist Center and Its Collapse

During the last year or so of the Soviet order's existence, it was by no means un-common to find in Western analyses the adjective "centrist" alongside the name of Mikhail Gorbachev. At the same time, however, both analysts and activists in the USSR seemed much more inclined to employ descriptions such as "conserva-tive" or "rightist" when speaking of the Soviet president. Although the political orientations of Western commentators and their Soviet/Russian counterparts may have influenced the ways in which they viewed Gorbachev, this difference be-tween them with respect to his position on the political spectrum bespoke an even larger difference that separated the political phenomenology of one group from that of another. The issue of Gorbachev's alleged centrism could only be resolved by asking the simple question: Center of what? Since this was never defined, each group could cling to its own characterization. Moreover, each was, in its own way and depending on its own political phenomenology, correct. What were these po-litical phenomenologies and how did they produce the diverse characterizations of Gorbachev? The Western one, I would argue, was rooted in the discourse of Sovietology, wherein the upper levels of the Communist Party's hierarchy counted for the sum and substance of the political. From this perspective, success-ful party leaders, as Anthony D'Agostino has shown, have always been centrists.[1] Whether they had a program of their own, and no matter how rapidly they might exchange whatever problems they had for those earlier associated with their oppo-nents, the key to centrist politics in this milieu lay in the leader's ability to encour-age (and even create) contention around himself while simultaneously appearing as that force that alone could resolve oppositions within the party, thus both hold-ing it together and uniting it behind himself in one motion.

Gorbachev fit this pattern reasonably well. He assumed the position of general secretary without divulging any program of his own (unless we are to count such vacuities as "social justice" or "acceleration"). He did much to stimulate the emergence and development of a left-wing or progressive element in the party. He played this element off masterfully against the Brezhnevian apparatus that he had inherited, without ever becoming a captive of this tendency (as indicated, for in-stance, by his unceremonious dumping of Boris Yeltsin from the Politburo and leadership of the Moscow party organization). He compromised repeatedly on po-litical and economic reforms, maintaining a balance around himself fragile enough to prevent any serious thought of his removal from leadership. His many threatened resignations stand as eloquent testimony to this fact. However, what we in the West too often missed while focusing on the Communist Party qua polit-ical system was the reappearance of politics in Russia and the USSR. That is, we had lost sight of the fact that the order superintended by the general secretary was one in which politics, in any meaningful sense, had long since been excised.[2] And, when politics returned, we were rather slow to take notice. This return might be dated from the First Congress of People's Deputies of the USSR, at which a group of democratically oriented legislators, having concluded that it was senseless to pursue their agenda within a Congress dominated by an "aggressively obedient majority" controlled by the Communist Party apparatus, organized a parliamentary bloc outside the official structures.[3] This bloc, the Inter-Regional Deputies' Group (I-RDG), spent remarkably little time with parliamentary work, choosing instead to devote their efforts to the upcoming local and republic-level elections of 1990.[4] By October 1989, the I-RDG had linked itself with voter associations that were springing to life in most of Russia's larger cities, thus forming a nationwide campaign network, Election-90, that would field its own slate of candidates.[5] At the USSR's Second Congress of People's Deputies in December 1989, the I-RDG effectively served notice that it would quit the institutions of the Soviet state and instead focus its energies on the creation of a liberal-democratic order in Russia.[6]

The first step in this strategy was to take state power in Russia and then to take Russia out of the Soviet state. The plurality in Russia's Parliament won by Democratic Russia (the new name adopted by Election-90 in January 1990), the subsequent election of its de facto leader, Boris Yeltsin, to the position of Chairperson of Russia's Supreme Soviet, and the Russian Parliament's Declaration of Sovereignty (adopted on June 12, 1990) accomplished the initial phase of this project. As a consequence—since the Communist Party and the all-union structure gave no indication that they were prepared to fold their Russian tents—a situation of dual power, a "war of laws," developed between Russia and the USSR, each pressing its claim to sovereignty on Russian soil. The election of Boris Yeltsin to the Russian presidency in June 1991 and the defeat of the August coup d'état settled this issue.[7] But the manner in which this contest over sovereignty was resolved meant that the Russian polity would be divided by issues inherited from its struggle with the old union structures that would further disorganize its fledgling political institutions so as to all but preclude the possibility of forming a political center. My examination of these issues, and of Russian politics in general, will be facilitated by defining several key concepts. I do this in the next section.

State, Society, and Politics

Andrew Arato has developed some categories useful to our analysis of contemporary Russian politics: state, political society, and civil society.[8] Viewed from the vantage of communication, "state" refers to authoritative injunctions backed by coercive power. "Civil society" encompasses that sphere of life marked by a normative discourse aimed at reaching understanding among socially differentiated participants. "Political society," which mediates between the two terms given above, involves strategic communication intended to translate specific projects originating in civil society into policies adopted by the state.[9] From the perspective of organization, "state" is represented by hierarchically structured governmental bodies; "political society," by parties and Parliament; and "civil society" by voluntary associations based on specific interests. As an ideal type, these categories, as set out in Table 7.1, connote distinct spheres of action, as well as indicate ongoing interrelations among them. That is, what might emerge by way of associations and interest-based conflicts within the sphere of civil society would find specific media in political society capable of expressing, adjusting, and compromising conflicting claims, which then enter the sphere of state power as policies that can be thematicized again as objects of discussion and debate in political and civil society. Before applying this model to the political system that prevails in today's Russia, one might single out for particular attention that Janus-like phenomenon—social-political movements—that occupies the seam between civil and political society. Sociopolitical movements are born in civil society and commonly make claims on state power through the development of projects that enter the sphere of political society. But they also operate directly on the terrain of civil society itself—as, for example, the feminist movement in the West would indicate—attempting to establish a presence and an identity for themselves in the face of opposition from other actors.[10]

When one applies these categories to the Russian case, one notices a number of conditions impeding the formation of a political center. I might begin with the gulf that has developed between state and political society, in many respects the direct product of the Russian Revolution of 1991. First, the exigencies of this revolution—begining with the struggle for national liberation from communism and continuing with the government's decision to press for a rapid transformation of the economic system—have created circumstances favorable to the concentration of power in the executive. At the same time, the executive has remained largely uncoupled from the institutions of parties and Parliament. This has been, in part, because no relations of mutual obligation had been worked out between Yeltsin and Democratic Russia, his base of organized support, before Yeltsin's election as president.[11] Consequently, on assuming office, he turned almost exclusively to associates from his days in the apparatus of the Communist Party in order to fill key executive positions.[12] In their turn, those taking up these new duties have often been prepared to accommodate the career interests of the old *nomenklatura* stratum.[13] Not only have Yeltsin's erstwhile supporters from Democratic Russia been largely denied positions in the executive branch but also those very few appointments at national and regional levels awarded to them have carried the provision that party membership be suspended during the appointee's tenure in office. These appointments thus reduce the responsibility of executive offices to parties and Parliament, since appointments come not from party organizations but from the president's administrative apparatus.[14] Moreover, they retard the development of (already weak) parties, loading incentives on the side of the executive and simultaneously depriving parties of some of their leading activists, who have taken up duties in the executive branch. To be sure, forceful complaints from those parties that had worked for Yeltsin's election produced some concessions in the form of "protocols," signed on November 2, 1991, by the Russian president with

TABLE 7.1   Ideal-Typical Forms of Political Communication and Organization

Levels of System	Types of Communication	Forms of Organization
State	Authoritative	Hierarchical government bodies
Political society	Strategic	Parties and Parliament
Civil society	Normative	Voluntary associations

nine of the parties in question.[15] These protocols pledged Yeltsin to monthly meetings with party leaders, at which he would take into consideration their recommendations on questions of policy and personnel. In return, parties would work to organize support in society for the government's economic reform.[16] Within a few weeks, the protocols were supplemented by a pledge from the government to provide the parties with drafts of legislation that it intended to submit to Parliament.[17] However, despite these formal agreements, relations between the government and a would-be "governing coalition" of parties have remained estranged, with party leaders angrily contending that the government has only been honoring its protocols in the breach.[18]

Second, as Oleg Vite has pointed out, the defeat of the August coup was accomplished at the organizational level by masses of governmental officials sundering their ties with the USSR and transferring their loyalties to the Russian state. In the absence of party government, this meant that the armies of officialdom—the so-called "August bloc"—would serve as the immediate constituency and base of support for Yeltsin's government.[19] The conditions attending the birth of the Russian state therefore divided the "parties of power" (namely, groups of officials locked in competition with one another in the corridors of state power) from the "parties of society."[20] This gulf between state and political society has contributed to, and, in turn, has been reinforced by, the tendency of organized interests in civil society simply to bypass parties as political intermediaries and to seek their objectives through lobbying governmental officials directly.[21]

Parallel to the fault line dividing state from political society in Russia today, we find another such line separating political society from civil society. In large measure, the latter gap—inasmuch as social forces have no clear sense of how their respective projects might be translated into state action via the agencies of political society—would follow from the former. But other factors contribute as well. On one hand, the phenomenon of civil society, possessed of associations consciously formulating their respective interests, remains at a relatively low level of development in Russia.[22] Indeed, party leaders, conscious of this fact, admit that their task lies not so much in articulating interests on behalf of one or another social group as it does in pressing for macrolevel policies that would supply those hitherto absent structural differentiations—in particular, property—required for the very existence of civil society.[23] On the other hand, until quite recently, both Russia's democratically orientated political parties and emerging interest-associations characteristic of civil society have been enfolded in and around the mass movement. The primary focus of this movement, Democratic Russia, had been the overthrow of the communist system, a condition sine qua non for the emergence of civil and political society. As such, political and civil discourse gravitated toward the pole of the negative—"Down with the CPSU!", "'No' to the communist order!" This thereby reinforced black-and-white dichotomies inherited from the discourse of communism (albeit in inverted form) and contributed little to the development of political culture.[24]

As a result of this gap between state and political society in Russia, and because of the relatively low degree of differentiation that persists in Russian society, political parties have, in the main, been largely indistinguishable from one another. Differences among them have had more to do with such things as leadership style and organizational ethos—that is, factors pertaining to activist members rather than to would-be mass electorates—than with their formal programs of the social interests that support them.[25] Emerging as they have from the political vacuum of communism and the struggle against that order, this much is perhaps understandable. However, although party differentiation in some respects has progressed in the aftermath of communism's defeat, the conditions under which this differentiation has occurred would themselves seem to militate against the formation of a political center.

State and Property in Political Society

What are these conditions? I address this question by rearranging the categories displayed in Table 7.1 as a two-by-two figure, using "state" as the vertical axis and using that on which civil society is predicted—namely, the property order—as the horizontal one.[26] In so doing, it becomes possible to differentiate the various forces in political society according to the positions that they have taken on the fundamental issues of state and property.

One needs to avoid treating these categories as real, for they represent no more than a bundle of problems surrounding the ways in which people and groups stand, or should stand, in relation to one another. For instance, "state," as a term standing for authority relations within a given territory, subsumes in this case such issues as: the borders of this territory (and membership in the unit); relations between the unit and subunit (federalism); and relations among the various institutions that exercise authority (constitutionalism). Equally, "property" refers (at a minimum) to relations among individuals, as well as those obtaining between state and society because of the boundaries that it establishes on the basis of certain "rights."[27] Since my purpose is to deploy these concepts as categories that distinguish political forces in postcommunist Russia, I employ them not in an essentialist manner but in a phenomenological one. That is, I take them as they appear in the discourse of the actors themselves. Consequently, I note that in the course of political struggles one or another facet of each becomes activated such that, within a particular phase of these struggles, that facet represents for those concerned the issue of "state" or "property" at that moment. The relative replacement of one facet by another as an object of contention—in the case of "state" (as we see below) the replacement of membership in the unit by federalism, and federalism, in turn, by constitutionalism—represents a process contributing to the (re)formation of state and civil society. It simultaneously represents a process that (re)divides political society on the basis of the positions adopted by opposing forces with respect to the issues of state and property as they appear at a particular juncture. Figure 7.1 sets out schematically this division of political forces on the eve of the August coup. One can locate in cells 1 and 4 the poles of the struggle attending Russia's liberation from communism. Here, one finds those organized forces in political society committed to the maintenance of both a centralized state and a centralized property system arrayed in cell 1 and their opposite numbers in this contest grouped in cell 4. What is important to add is that, at this stage of conflict, certain elements within Democratic Russia have suspended their own disagreements over questions pertinent to the Russian state. They have done so in order to join together in a single movement aimed at the defeat of their common opponent, the Communist Party. Along with communism's defeat, then, these more or less latent differences would come to the fore.

The relations between the first and fourth quadrants of Figure 7.1 represent political society's analogue to the condition of dual power, as described above. Divided by these fundamental questions of state and property, it becomes obvious that the Soviet Union, in its final period of existence, contained no political center that Gorbachev or anyone else could have occupied. Equally, the word *revolution* seems apt in describing the resolution of these questions. Figure 7.2 utilizes the same axes of state and property to locate the various forces in political society in the immediate postcommunist period. One notes that rather than completing itself, this revolution seems to have moved on to another stage wherein a political center had not yet appeared.

If one focuses on the cells in Figure 7.2, one observes first a migration of parties from the fourth cell toward the third one.[28] This migration was induced by the defeat of communism, which obviated the need felt earlier by some parties to ally themselves with Democratic Russia. This movement was also induced by the specific form and consequences of that defeat, namely, Russia's national liberation, which simultaneously triggered similar aspirations for self-determination among non-Russian minorities within the Russian Federation. The first major migration was undertaken by the three parties—Democratic Party of Russia (DPR), Russian Christian Democratic Movement (RCDM), and Constitutional Democratic Party (CDP)—that had in December 1990 formed the bloc, Popular Consensus, within Democratic Russia.[29] The major partner in this bloc, the DPR, had itself split at its Second Congress in April 1991, in large measure over the issue of national self-determination for Russia's non-Russian minorities.[30] Although the DPR and its allies had muted their differences with others in Democratic Russia on the question of the state while the struggle with the Communist Party was the paramount issue, the rapid collapse of the USSR—portending in their view the

		State	
		Centralized	*Decentralized*
Property	*Centralized* (state-owned)	1. Part of CPSU (esp. Russian Communist Party) Parliamentary faction "Soyuz" United Front of Working People, Edinstvo, other neo-Bolshevik organizations	2. Null Set
	Decentralized (privately or cooperatively owned or leased)	3. Authoritarian non-Communist right-wing: Pamyat' and others	4. Democratic Russia and affiliated political parties

FIGURE 7.1   Axes of Conflict and Disposition of Political Forces in the Late Soviet Period

impending collapse of the Russian state—became of overriding importance for them in the wake of the August coup.[31] Popular Consensus, complaining of a "destructive" orientation present among many forces in the "democratic" camp, staged a dramatic walkout during Democratic Russia's Second Congress (November 10, 1992). It began to look for new coalition partners regardless of their positions on the issue of property; this search then split Popular Consensus. DPR leader, Nikolai Travkin, aroused strong disapproval within his own party for his zealous but unauthorized attempt to court new allies among Russia's "patriotic" movement.[32] As a result, when the other parties in Popular Consensus arranged with the Russian Social Union and others to stage a Congress of Civic and Patriotic Forces in early February 1992, the DPR decided against participating in it.[33]

This Congress, a rather unruly event, replete with elements of tragifarce, produced the Russian National Assembly, which appears at the intersection of cells 1 and 3 in Figure 7.2.[34] Its constituent units are split on the issue of property. But they have agreed to shelve this question in the interest of maintaining unity on what for them is the salient issue of the day—the establishment of a unitary Russian state.[35] However, long-term cooperation to achieve this end has already been rendered problematic by the matter of the putative boundaries of this state. Some participants, such as the RCDM and the CDP, consider these boundaries to be those of the former USSR.[36]

Interestingly, it was Russian vice-president Aleksandr Rutskoi who delivered the keynote address to the Congress of Civic and Patriotic Forces. The party he has led, the People's Party of Free Russia (PPFR),[37] however, declined participa-

| | | State | |
		Centralized	Decentralized
Property	Centralized (state-owned)	1. Reorganized Communist forces: Working Russia, the Socialist Party of Working People, "Justice, Nationality, Statehood, Patriotism"	2. Null Set
	Decentralized (privately or cooperatively owned or leased)	Russian National Assembly —— 3. Russian Movement for Democratic Reform Popular Consensus Conference of Public Forces Social-Liberal Association New Russia	4. Democratic Russia Radical Faction of Democratic Russia Liberal Union Liberal Free Market Bloc

FIGURE 7.2   Axes of Conflict and Disposition of Political Forces in Russia's Immediate Postcommunist Period

tion in the affair because of the "red-brown" (communist-fascist) hues evident on the guest list.[38] Rutskoi has, of course, been an active player at the state level, as well.[39] He has been widely reputed to be the leader of one of the main "parties of power." The eclipse of his faction resulted from conflict with the chief of Yeltsin's administration, Russia's secretary of state and deputy prime minister, Gennadii Burbulis.[40]

As one after another of the doors along the corridors of power began slamming in his face, Rutskoi turned to political society in search of allies. Fittingly, since his party had refused to attend the Congress of Civic and Patriotic Forces, he found his first partner in the other sizable party that was eschewing participation. In mid-March 1992, the PPFR and DPR held a joint meeting, a Conference of Public Forces, focusing on the issue of establishing a Russian state and a united voting bloc for the upcoming Sixth Congress of People's Deputies (cell 3 of Figure 7.2). The views of the two parties have coincided on the question of the state.[41] But the DPR's rather strident anticommunist past and its continuing opposition to all the "parties of power," which Travkin regards as nothing less than the perpetuation of the old *nomenklatura* system,[42] have raised questions about the longevity of this self-conscious attempt to create a "centrist bloc."[43] What is more, the respective orientations of the PPFR and the DPR differ, at least by degree, on the pace and costs of Russia's transition to a market economy based on private property. This suggests that if the issue of establishing a Russian state were solved, the question of property might then surface to divide these parties.[44]

The second major rupture within Democratic Russia occurred at a plenary session of its governing council of representatives in January 1992. On the surface, the issue of contention was the same one that had dogged the movement since the furor over the "nine-plus-one" accords of April 1991, which set in motion the process of reaching a new union agreement for the USSR, namely, the issue of support for Yeltsin's government.[45] In present circumstances, the question of support has ineluctably raised the root issues of state and property, splitting the movement along these axes.

The minority position—represented by Yurii Afanas'ev, Leonid Batkin, and Yurii Burtin—has been based on "conditional" and "critical" support for the Russian government.[46] What is conditional and critical in this context is the idea of self-determination for non-Russian minorities within Russia and prohibitions against holding governmental office while simultaneously engaging in private business.[47] (The latter issue touches on the question of property—the so-called "*nomenklatura* privatization"—discussed below.) The minority, which appears as the radical faction of Democratic Russia in cell 4 of Figure 7.2, has endorsed these points, but the majority (straddling cells 3 and 4 in the figure) has not. The property question in this respect does not involve the form of property per se, but the future recipients of it. The minority view has called for an egalitarian approach that would commence the process of privatization by awarding shares in enterprises to all citizens. The majority view, however, has favored the purchasing of shares by private individuals in order to concentrate ownership in a few hands, under the assumption that this would lead to rapid economic growth.[48] The intensity of these conflicts has led to the minority suspending its membership in Democratic Russia, thus raising the prospect of the movement's further dismemberment and ultimate collapse.

As I have already noted with respect to the exit of Popular Consensus from the movement, the dismemberment of Democratic Russia has been largely coextensive with the decisions taken by its constituent parties to form coalitions with like-minded partners. Perhaps the earliest efforts in that direction were mounted by the Social Democratic Party of Russia (SDPR) and the Republican Party of Russia (RPR), both of whose orientations initially could be described as "social democratic."[49] Close relations between their respective elites—traceable to joint work in the (preparty) "informal" movement and continuing in the form of legislative alliances in the Parliament and city councils of Russia—promised to lead to a SDPR-RPR merger in February 1991. Reluctance on the part of provincial delegates to the conference called to ratify the agreement worked out by Moscow-based SDPR and RPR leadership postponed the merger.[50] Following another six months of negotiations toward this end, the RPR—now evolving away from a social democratic orientation and toward a liberal one[51]—decided to drop the idea of a merger altogether.[52]

The RPR has tended to subordinate the issue of state construction in Russia to that of pursuing the course of economic reforms.[53] However, the SDPR, by virtue of the leading role played by Oleg Rumyantsev, then party cochairperson on the Constitutional Commission of Russia's Supreme Soviet, perforce was more concerned with the question of federal relations within the new Russian state.[54] Perhaps more important, however, major differences emerged between the SDPR and the RPR on the subject of property relations. A majority in the RPR has endorsed the approach associated with the reform orientation of First Deputy Prime Minister Egor Gaidar. Gaidar's approach promises to concentrate property in a few hands, thus generating "effective investments." The SDPR, however, has consistently viewed such a policy as tantamount to *"nomenklatura* capitalism," whereby yesterday's ruling stratum would convert their positions and privileges into private property, thus reconstituting themselves as tomorrow's ruling class.[55] As a result, most of the RPR gravitated toward a number of small parties forming the Liberal Union[56] or Liberal Free Market bloc[57] (cell 4 of Figure 7.2). Another section of the RPR, however, moved toward the Social-Liberal Association of the Russian Federation (in cell 3 of Figure 7.2).

The Social-Liberal Association resembles a political version of a Russian *matrioshka* doll: The largest doll is New Russia[58] consisting of moderate-left and left-populist parties; the next is the Social-Liberal Association, itself composed of left-oriented elements of Democratic Russia. Several political parties constitute New Russia—the SDPR, the People's Party of Russia,[59] and the Peasant Party of Russia.[60] They differentiate themselves from the neoliberal tendencies in Democratic Russia, which they regard as needlessly setting loose centrifugal forces on the question of the state and as socially destabilizing on the issue of property distribution. They also distinguish themselves from forces found in cell 3 of Figure 7.2; they regard these groups as overly authoritarian on the state question and as insufficiently attentive to considerations of "social justice" on the matter of property relations. With its varying degrees of limited national sovereignty, plus the widest possible distribution of state property, federalism represents the crux of New Russia's position on the state/property axes. Moreover, consensus within this left-center bloc seems sufficiently high to suggest that New Russia's member parties may soon drop their separate labels and fuse into one party.[61]

Another political force active among the "parties of society"—the Russian Movement for Democratic Reform (RMDR)—appears near the top of cell 3 in Figure 7.2. This group was initially organized by such perestroika-era luminaries as Eduard Shevardnadze, Aleksandr Yakovlev, Gavrill Popov, Anatolii Sobchak, and Arkadii Vol'skii as the Movement for Democratic Reform (MDR).[62] It had appeared as a would-be center, attempting to position itself between those groups located in cells 1 and 4 of Figure 7.1. As such, the MDR was regarded by Democratic Russia as a rather odious competitor, even though a number of prominent members of Democratic Russia, such as Vyacheslav Shostakovskii and Stanislav Shatalin, had entered its ranks.[63] Given its support within the state apparatus of Russia, the MDR could have been regarded, much like Rutskoi's PPFR, as the manifestation in political society of one of the "parties of power," jockeying for position within the government.[64] Indeed, its critics within the democratic movement charged that the creation of the MDR was a project hatched in the Central Committee of the Communist Party for the purpose of establishing an authoritarian regime, designed to protect the "post-*nomenklatura* bourgeoisie."[65] Owing to both its unsavory reputation among most elements in the "democratic" camp and the disappearance of such figures as Shevardnadze and Yakovlev from its leadership, by February 1992 the ranks of the MDR shrank considerably.[66] It then reconstituted itself as the RMDR, in the wake of the USSR's disintegration.[67]

In its new incarnation, the RMDR appeared as a political party opposed to the current government but bereft of political allies.[68] Its chairperson, Gavrill Popov, called for new elections to the legislature. At all levels the legislature's authority would be sharply delimited in order to establish those strong executive institutions that Popov regards as essential for instituting a private property system based on individual ownership.[69] Moreover, this positive orientation toward executive power is complemented by the RMDR's position on federal relations within the Russian state. The constitutional draft that the RMDR prepared for Russia's April 6, 1992, convening of the Sixth Congress of People's Deputies was conceived as an alternative to that produced by the Supreme Soviet's Constitutional Commission. Whereas the latter's draft retained the institution of autonomous national republics, the RMDR's eliminated them, thus elevating the unitary principle over the federal one in Russian state construction.[70]

One Center or Many?

Most of those forces depicted in cell 1 of Figure 7.2—with notable exceptions such as the Socialist Party of Working People—represent what might be called "antipolitical society." Whether they are of the variety of the Black Hundreds, the neo-Bolsheviks, or the orthodox-Stalinists, the orientation of these groups and parties is fundamentally opposed to Russia's new political and economic order and calls for a return to an essentially prepolitical past. For present considerations, however, their importance lies less in their particular goals and activities than in their simple presence in political society—especially within the Congress of People's Deputies—and the way in which that presence has been construed and made use of by those parties and coalitions examined in the preceding section.

In preparation for Russia's Sixth Congress of People's Deputies ultranationalist and reconstituted communist organizations, having joined forces in street demonstrations opposing Yeltsin's government, assembled a parliamentary bloc (Russian Unity). Its announced purpose was to bring down the government and roll back the economic reform. Given the severe social and economic dislocations brought on by the government's freeing of prices, as well as the voting strength commanded by Russian Unity at the congress itself, concerns grew among supporters of reform.[71] They feared that the deputies might reverse the reform, strip Yeltsin of his power, and adopt constitutional provisions that could further exacerbate the already strained relations between Russia and its partners in the CIS, and in federal relations within Russia itself.[72]

To counter this perceived "red-brown" threat, some two thousand representatives of parties, groups, and movements supporting Yeltsin and the general idea of market reform (if not the government's specific program for it) gathered as the Assembly of Democratic Forces during the two days preceding the Sixth Congress. Its purpose was to work out a common program and strategy. The assembly proved a harbinger of new cleavages within the democratic camp, which would again rearrange the constellation of political forces in the aftermath of the Sixth Congress. Above all, the assembly was split by a resolution prepared by the leadership of Democratic Russia. This resolution would protect the process of reform from the conservative threat by dissolving the Congress of People's Deputies, wherein the opponents of reform held a sizeable plurality. The Congress of People's Deputies had been elected in spring 1990 while the Communist Party still maintained its monopoly on political power. Perhaps this explained the size of the conservative contingent within it. This strategy could be easily couched in terms of "democratic" values. Nonetheless, ten of the parties and groups in the Assembly of Democratic Forces (including four of its organizers[73]) staged a walkout in protest of the decision calling for a referendum that would dissolve the Congress and adopt a new Constitution, leading, in turn, to new national elections.[74]

The divisions manifest at the meeting of the Assembly of Democratic Forces were effectively contained in the Sixth Congress. Here the "democratic" camp tended to vote as a bloc in support of Yeltsin's government and its reform program.[75] But the divisions surfaced anew in the immediate aftermath of the Sixth Congress of People's Deputies. This triggered another round of realignment among parties and groups, which can be described in terms of four "centers" that have appeared in the wake of the Sixth Congress.

The Right-Center. This grouping is anchored in the Russian National Assembly (discussed above). The National Assembly seems to be staking its political future on the collapse of the economic reform program pursued by Yeltsin's government. If the program were to collapse, the group would likely seek to form some sort of "government of national unity" around itself, drawing in elements from both Russian Unity and the "opposition-center" (see below). In June 1992, it actively supported Russian Unity's petition to conduct a national referendum to recall Boris Yeltsin from the presidency.[76] At the same time, however, considerable friction appeared within the ranks of member parties—the RCDM and the CDP—

regarding further cooperation with "communists and chauvinists,"[77] and half of the CDP's twelve-member directorate resigned over this issue.[78]

The Left-Center. This center is based on New Russia, a coalition headed by the SDPR. The issue of support for the economic course pursued by Yeltsin's government sharply divided this party at its Fourth Congress in mid-May 1992.[79] By the end of that month, however, the SDPR had signed formal protocols with Deputy Prime Minister Anatolii Chubais, committing it to support the government's program on privatization, while the government, in turn, agreed to incorporate the SDPR's suggestions on implementing this policy.[80] As in the case of the right-center, the fortunes of this political orientation seem to depend on mobilizing larger constituencies adversely affected by the government's economic policies. Consequently, as New Russia associates itself more with the government, it may be that it will be replaced as a left-center group by a new coalition organized around the recently formed Party of Labor, which has been attempting to marshal trade union support behind a program emphasizing social assistance, job protection, and a decentralization of state power.[81]

The Presidential-Center. This term is used to designate the coalition of Democratic Russia and the RMDR. The coalition was formed at the Assembly of Democratic Forces in order to spearhead a petition drive leading to a national referendum on the dissolution of the Congress of People's Deputies and the adoption of a new Constitution. The fact that these erstwhile competitors have chosen to join forces is in large part explicable in terms of the disintegration of both Democratic Russia and the RMDR's parent body, the MDR. These disintegrations were brought on in part by the stand taken by each groups' dominant faction, which were in favor of strengthening executive institutions at the expense of legislative ones.[82] The presidential-center coalition also seems to have been cemented by associates from one of the parties of power grouped around Gavrill Popov.[83] Popov resigned as mayor of Moscow in June 1992 in order to devote himself fully to political work as leader of the RMDR.[84]

Although Yeltsin initially endorsed a referendum regarding the dissolution of the Congress of People's Deputies and the creation of a new Constitution, in the face of widespread criticism of the idea he apparently reconsidered his position.[85] Similarly, the coalition promoting the idea decided to carry forward the project in scaled-down form.[86] It is noteworthy that this presidential-center coalition is not necessarily coupled to the president himself; it represents a support base for Yeltsin, which he may or may not choose to occupy at a given time. He seems to have planted one foot (rather gingerly) on it, while shifting his political weight toward the fourth of these centers.

The Opposition-Center. it appears that Yeltsin was able to parry the attacks launched by the conservative opposition on his government at the Sixth Congress of People's Deputies. He did this by reaching an agreement with parliamentary factions, such as the Industrial Union and Smena, which held the balance of power between supporters and opponents of economic reform.[87] Before the Sixth Congress, the "opposition-center" was made up of the DPR-PPFR alliance, which took the position of supporting market reform in general (hence, "center") yet opposing the monetarist orientation toward it hitherto displayed by its architect, Egor Gaidar (ergo, "opposition"). In the aftermath of the Sixth Congress, the co-alition was joined by a new political party, Renewal. Renewal was founded in late May by the parliamentary factions of Smena and the Industrial Union and by Arkadii Vol'skii's powerful Russian Union of Industrialists and Entrepreneurs.[88] On June 21, the coalition of these forces was consummated as Civic Union. It is a broad front opposed to the referendum sponsored by Democratic Russia and the RMDR and against the specific economic policies hitherto pursued by the government.[89] Of perhaps greater moment for the future, however, has been Civic Union's formation of a shadow government based strictly on party lines.[90] Civil Union would probably slow the pace of economic reform by redirecting government expenditures toward the vast bulk of the population impoverished by the hyperinflation that has accompanied Gaidar's policies.[91] It would also fundamentally alter the previous relations between state and political society by introducing party responsibility as the condition for membership in government.

Conclusion

I have outlined some of the turbulence present in Russian political society that has been manifest in a seemingly endless number of organized ruptures, in the formation of new parties and coalitions, and in their subsequent splintering and regrouping. In the face of this confusion, students of Russian political life may wonder whether theirs are not just morbid preoccupations with extinct species, observing and cataloging them as they pass out of existence. The point to remember in this respect, however, is that these moments of extinction and regeneration represent phases in the process through which Russian political society has been constituting itself. Rather than waiting for things to settle down and assume clearer institutional shapes, observers are obliged to determine as best they can what it is that has "settled down," as well as how (and from what) institutionalization has come about.

This study has traced this kaleidoscopic character of Russian political society to the conditions surrounding the defeat of communism and to the root issues of state formation and property relations that have emerged in the wake of that defeat. On the one hand, I have noted how these conditions—an "overdeveloped" executive wherein function the "parties of power" and an "underdeveloped" civil society wherein function social differentiation and interest formulation with political parties—have tended to minimize the mediating role associated with political parties. In Russia, these conditions appear to have had little impact on the direction of governmental policy and little to represent by way of extant constituencies. On the other hand, the overriding issues of state and property have carved up the party system in such a way as to preclude the formation of a single political center and the arraying of political forces along a single continuum. "Patriots" have been pitted against "patriots" on the issue of property, just as "liberals" have been pitted against "liberals" on the issue of the state.

Although one may argue that these issues may fracture the political spectrum at present, one might also argue that Russian political society has begun to take on a degree of coherence and shape. A certain amount of progress in this respect is evident in the programmatically meaningful blocs depicted in Figure 7.2. Perhaps even more progress can be seen in the various centers that have formed in the wake of the Sixth Congress of People's Deputies. The present situation does not inspire thoughts of stability in political society. But one would do well to recall the situation a short time ago. Then party programs had been hardly distinguishable one from another. All attention among the democratic forces had been focused on bringing down the communist system in order to usher in the liberal-democratic millennium.

This development in programmatic orientation from the abstract to the concrete promises to accelerate as the issue of the state moves toward resolution, with the conclusion of the federal agreement between the Russian government and the country's separate republics and regions. It may be hastened even more by the adoption of a new Constitution, prospects for which seem likely in the months ahead. The focus thereafter may shift toward the matter of property relations. Should the current economic reform not wash away in a wave of resentment and hostility induced by the alarming level of deprivation and dislocation that it has induced, this focus would then confine itself to matters of "to whom?" and "how much?" should the state divest itself, rather than to the obdurate issue of "what kind of property system, state or private, should we have?" The uncertainty still surrounding the fundamental questions of state and property prohibits predictions on the future shape of Russian political society. Nonetheless, one might make the conjecture that in the context of the apparent momentum toward resolving these matters, future national elections (the first since Tsarist times to be contested by political parties) may well help the Russians complete the search for a political center.

Postscript

The tumult that has characterized Russian political life between the time this study was completed and the opportunity to update it as this volume goes to press would not alter fundamentally the general outlines of the foregoing analysis. To be sure, a new round of political regrouping was occasioned by the national referendum of April 25, 1993, and its results that pointed in the direction of new elections, perhaps at all levels of government. But with small exception, the electoral blocs that have formed in anticipation of such elections coincide in most instances in their memberships and programmatic orientations with the four "centers" discussed in this chapter.[92] In the face, then, of some thirteen months of political turbulence that both has deepened the crisis in federal relations and has opened a full-blown constitutional crisis among the branches of the national government, the correspondence that obtains between our "centers" and these electoral blocs suggests at one level that a remarkably high degree of continuity has already become evident in Russian politics.

But it would be foolish at the moment to make more of this continuity than the fact that it has persisted even under extremely inclement conditions. That is, too many contingencies remain, too many unknowns have popped up, for us to draw any analytic conclusions about the valences of attraction/repulsion that might characterize Russia's political forces, much less hazard any conjectures about the potentials for forging new political bonds among hitherto separate parties and groups. The list of these contingencies and unknowns is, indeed, a formidable one. How will the process of adopting a new constitution play itself out? What will the final draft look like, and what method will be employed to secure its formal adoption? What concessions will be offered to obtain the consent of Russia's regions who have been bidding up the price of their allegiance to Moscow with insistences that their own sovereignty be duly recognized? Relatedly, how will the struggle over the issue of property unfold if the cost of regional adherence to a new national constitution turns out to be regional proprietorship over state property? Will enterprise directors and regional governments use their combined shares in newly "privatized" firms to erect some form of sub-national state capitalism? And, finally, how will the new national parliament be organized and under which electoral system—single-member district, proportional representation, or some mix of the two—will its members be chosen? These questions alone would render moot the question of Russian political society's future shape. Moreover, even were we to have knowledge of their eventual outcomes, we still would remain fully ignorant about the decisions adopted by the political actors themselves, decisions taken in response to what other actors have decided, decisions taken often enough on the basis of anticipated responses of other actors, all in one glorious blur of mutually determinate indeterminacy that makes the study of politics as frustrating as it is stimulating. Yet for all that obscures our vision at the moment, certain shapes on Russia's political landscape are detectable, even if these remain in transition to yet other forms.

Notes

My thanks to Isebill Gruhn and to David Powell for their helpful comments on an earlier draft of this study.

1. Anthony D'Agostino, *Soviet Succession Struggles* (Boston: Allen and Unwin, 1988).

2. Sheldon Wolin called attention to this facet of Leninism long ago by noting how the organizational forms developed by Lenin and perfected by his successors assiduously occluded a political moment. More recently, Jadwiga Staniszkis has made an analogous observation that Leninism's "state principle" always excluded a "social principle." Wolin's view can be found in *Politics and Vision* (Boston: Little, Brown, 1960), pp. 421–429; those

of Staniszkis appear in "Forms of Reasoning as Ideology," *Telos,* no. 66 (Winter 1985–1986), pp. 67–80.

Another approach to the "end of politics" in Russia can be found among those who argue that state socialism's peculiar social structure has resulted in an absence of autonomous social forces capable of both formulating their own interests and pursuing these in opposition to others. Examples of this view appear in M. V. Malyutin, "Perspektivy demokratii v Rossii" (Report to the Higher Consultative-Coordinating Council under the chairperson of the Supreme Soviet of Russia, August 1991); and Sergei Mitrokhin, "Novye partii v politicheskom spektre Rossii" (Moscow: Institute for Humanist-Political Research, June 1991).

Finally, those concerned with the communicative aspects of politics—particularly the abilities of would-be political subjects engaged in what Juergen Habermas has called "discursive will formation"—have been led to the same conclusion. See, for instance, Michael E. Urban, "Conceptualizing Political Power in the USSR: Patterns of Binding and Bonding," *Studies in Comparative Communism* 18 (Winter 1985), pp. 207–226; idem, "From Chernenko to Gorbachev: A Re-Politicization of Official Soviet Discourse?" *Soviet Union* 13 no. 2, (1986), pp. 131–161; Maria Markus, "Overt and Covert Modes of Legitimation in Communist States," T. H. Rigby and F. Feher, eds., *Political Legitimation in Communist States* (New York: St. Martin's Press, 1989), pp. 82–93.

3. This phrase belongs to one of the leaders of the Inter-Regional Deputies' Group, Yurii Afanas'ev. My argument here is not, or course, to deny that as early as 1988 substantial numbers of individuals had been preparing for postapparatus careers by enrolling in courses of study in politics and business or that tens of thousands more had not by then become active to one degree or another in the "informal" movement. On "defectors" from the apparatus, see O. V. Grigor'ev and M. V. Malyutin, *Vlast' i sobstvennost' v Rossii osen'yu 1991: Kto pobedil i chto dal'she?* (Moscow: Public Center of Moscow City Soviet, 1991), p. 7. On the development of the "informal" movement, see V. V. Igrunov, "Public Movement: From Protest to Political Self-Consciousness," *Problema Vostochnoi Evropii,* nos. 27/28 (1990), pp. 1–14; and Michael E. Urban, "Popular Fronts and 'Informals'," *Detente,* no. 14 (1989), pp. 3–8, 27.

4. Brendan Kiernan, *New Soviet Politics* (Boulder, CO: Westview Press, 1993), chap. 8.

5. Vladimir Pribylovskii, "Pouchitel'naia istoriya Moskovskogo narodnogo fronta," *Panorama* (Moscow), no. 28 (Jul. 1991), pp. 6–7.

6. Interview with Vladimir Lepekhin (15 May 1991). On the split between the I-RDG and the Soviet order evident in the speeches delivered by I-RDG leaders to the USSR's Second Congress of People's Deputies, see Michael E. Urban and John McClure, "Discourse, Ideology, and Party Formation in the USSR," M. E. Urban, ed., *Ideology and System Change in the USSR and Eastern Europe* (London: Macmillan, 1992), pp. 92–120.

7. For an analysis of this election, its relevance to the defeat of the August coup, and the politically disorganizing effects of the Russian presidency, see Michael E. Urban, "Boris Yeltsin, Democratic Russia, and the Campaign for the Russian Presidency," *Soviet Studies* 44 no. 2 (1992), pp. 187–207.

8. Andrew Arato, "Social Movements and Civil Society in the Soviet Union," J. B. Sedaitis and J. Butterfield, eds., *Perestroika from Below* (Boulder, CO: Westview, 1991), pp. 197–214.

9. A discussion of these types of communicative action can be found in Juergen Habermas, *Communication and the Evolution of Society* (Boston: Beacon, 1979); idem, *The Theory of Communicative Action,* vol. 1 (Boston: Beacon, 1984).

10. On the subject of movements, see Jean L. Cohen, "Strategy or Identity: New Theoretical Paradigms and Contemporary Social Movements," *Social Research* 52 (Winter 1985), pp. 663–716; Alain Touraine, "An Introduction to the Study of Social Movements," ibid., pp. 749–787.

11. Interview with Lev Ponomarev, cochairperson of Democratic Russia (30 May 1991).

12. Stephan Kiselyov, "How to Capture the 'White House'," *Moscow News* (29 Sept.– 6 Oct. 1991), pp. 8–9. See also the interviews given by Yurii Petrov, the head of the president's administration, to G. Shipit'ko, *Izvestiia,* 9 Oct. 1991 and Tat'yana Malkina in *Nezavisimaia gazeta,* 14 Feb. 1992, pp. 1–2.

13. Mikhail Kislyuk, interviewed by Aleksandr Ermakov, "Kuzbass vybiraet svobodu," *Rossiskaia gazeta,* 6 Jan. 1992, pp. 1, 3; Aleksei Golovkov, interviewed by Aleksei Zuichenko, "Eto pravitel'stvo—nadolgo," *Nezavisimaia gazeta,* 22 Jan. 1992, pp. 1–2; "Nomenklaturnoe podpol'e beret pod kontrol' administratsiiu prezidenta Rossii," ibid., 24 Jan. 1992, p. 2; Ivan Rodin, "Stolichnoe pravitel'stvo ekonomicheskikh reform nachalo rabotu," ibid., 25 Jan. 1992, p. 1.

14. This situation received eloquent testimony at a meeting of the board (*pravlenie*) of the Republican Party of Russia convened on 19 November 1991. On the matter of the party's role—or lack of it—in staffing government offices, one member remarked: "We can't recommend anyone to Yeltsin's team. They [Yeltsin's circle] have the right [somehow] to decide whom to include." The other members of the board nodded in assent and moved on to the next item on their agenda.

Sergei Filatov, the first deputy chairperson of Russia's Supreme Soviet, offers a similar analysis of the effects of executive appointments on party strength and cohesion in Parliament. See his interview with Ol'ga Burkaleva, "Klyuchevoi vopros—priniatie konstitutsii," *Rossiiskaia gazeta,* 19 Mar. 1992, p. 2.

15. The parties signing these protocols included: the Democratic Party of Russia, the Social Democratic Party of Russia, the Republican Party of Russia, the Russian Christian Democratic Movement, the People's Party of Russia, the Party of Free Labor, the People's Party of Free Russia, the Constitutional Democratic Party, and the Peasant Party of Russia. The text of the protocols can be found in *Gospodin narod,* no. 15 (1991), p. 1.

16. Vladimir Zorich, "Partii i Yeltsin dogovorilis'," *Nezavisimaia gazeta,* 28 Nov. 1991, p. 1; Evgennii Krasnikov, "Partii khotiat upravliat' Rossiei, a Yeltsin—partiiami," *Kommersant,* no. 43 (4–11 Nov. 1991), p. 23.

17. Yulii Lebedev, "Novogodnii podarok rossiiskim partiiam," *Nezavisimaia gazeta,* 4 Jan. 1992, p. 2.

18. Vladimir Todres, "'Partiia Rustkogo' podderzhivaet svoego lider," *Nezavisimaia gazeta* 7 Dec. 1991, p. 2; Konstantin Medvedev, "V Rossii vozmozhno smena kursa," ibid.; Anna Kraeskaia, "NPSR verna protokolu," ibid., 16 Jan. 1992, p. 2; Elena Musatova, "Ne za gorami," *Rossiiskaia gazeta,* 29 Feb. 1992, p. 1. Boris Orlov (SDPR chairperson), interviewed by Pavel Anokhin, "Zachem nas Yeltsin sobiral vtoroi raz," ibid., 1 Apr. 1992, p. 6

As far as Yeltsin is concerned, he has not kept to his monthly schedule of meetings with party leaders; instead, he merely summons them when he feels the immediate need for their support. See the interview given to Stanislav Rotsinskii by Valerii Khomoyakov, "Otsenku postviat vybory," *Demokraticheskaia gazeta,* no. 14 (Apr. 1992), p. 2.

19. Oleg Vite, "'Ekonomicheskii' krizis demokraticheskogo dvizheniia," *Nezavisimaia gazeta,* 27 Feb. 1992, p. 2.

20. These terms are employed by Grigor'ev and Malyutin, *Vlast' i sobstvennost' v Rossii.*

21. Mikhail Karpov, "Mnogopartiinost' ne speshat finansirovat'," *Nezavisimaia gazeta,* 13 Feb. 1992, p. 2.

22. Malyutin, "Perspektivy demokratii v Rossii."

23. Interview with Igor' Yakovenko, member of the Board of the Republican Party of Russia (19 Nov. 1991). See, in particular, the remarks of Pavel Kudyukin, one of the leaders of the Social Democratic Party of Russia, in the round-table talks conducted by O. Bondarenko and G. Koval'skaia, "Sotsial-Demokraty v Rossii; Byli. Kazhetsya est'," *Demokraticheskaia Rossiia,* no. 4 (12 Apr. 1991), p. 5.

Steven Fish has made this same point in "The Emergence of Independent Associations and the Transformation of Russian Political Society," *Journal of Communist Studies* 7 (Sept. 1991), pp. 299–334. Although Fish's analysis of Russia's emerging political society, with its "overdeveloped" state and "underdeveloped" civil society in the Soviet period, largely coincides with the one presented here, it nonetheless differs on two important questions. First, Fish tends to treat political and civil society as coextensive categories. Second, in his discussion of associations that articulate, aggregate, and represent interests in civil society, he employs the conventional categories found in the field of comparative politics, which contain a tacit Western bias. In this case, the bias is evident in the assumption that associations have more or less ready-made interests—generated by a civil society—that they would articulate, aggregate, and represent. In my view, it is precisely the relative absence of such structures that accounts for the still primitive and confused state of what could be called "interest formulation," the generation of interests in the first instance. Civil society, then, could be counted as weak not only because of the movement-like displacement that Fish has rightly noted but also because of the lack of social differentiation and concomitant patterns of interest formulation on which the concept of civil society is predicated.

24. A discussion of these problems can be found in Michael E. Urban, "Party Formation and Deformation on Russia's Democratic Left," R. T. Huber and D. R. Kelley, eds., *Perestroika-Era Politics* (Armonk, NY: M. E. Sharpe, 1991), pp. 129–150. On the formation of Democratic Russia and the political parties that founded it, see "Itogi uchreditel'nogo s"ezda dvizheniia 'Demokraticheskaia Rossiia'," *Demokraticheskaia Rossiia,* no. 5 (Nov. 1990), p. 1.

25. Sergei Mitrokhin and Michael E. Urban, "Social Groups, Party Elites and Russia's New Democrats," David Lane, ed., *Russia in Flux* (Aldershot, UK: Edward Elgar, 1993).

26. Boris Volkhovskii has used a similar scheme in "'Tret'ya sila': Problemy i perspektivy," *Nezavisimaia gazeta,* 8 Feb. 1992, p. 2. Although I am borrowing Volkhovskii's basic idea, I am also amending it in certain respects, especially with regard to the disposition of the property axis in postcommunist Russia.

27. Steven Gilham, "State, Law, and Modern Economic Exchange," D. Willer and B. Anderson, eds., *Networks, Exchanges, and Coercion* (New York: Elsevier, 1981), pp. 129–151.

28. Excluded from the discussion that follows are the occupants of the first cell in Figure 7.2. This exclusion is based on two considerations. First, the parties and groups involved seem to represent a marginal phenomenon in political society, supported by neither powerful interests nor a sizable public following. Second, should this situation change, I

would expect a polarization—as depicted in Figure 7.1—to accompany it, indicating a movement away from politics and toward civil war.

29. See the joint statement of these parties, "Deklaratsiia konstruktivno-demo-kraticheskogo bloka 'narodnoe soglasie,'" in *Demokraticheskaia gazeta*, no. 5 (1991), p. 2.

30. Nikolai Travkin, "O raskole kotoryi nam prorochat," *Demokraticheskaia gazeta*, no. 5 (1991), pp. 1–2.

31. Vladimir Todres, "Glavnym dlia DPR ostalsia vopros gosudarstvennosti," *Nezavisimaia gazeta*, 10 Dec. 1991, p. 2.

32. Vladimir Zorich, "Nikolai Travkin prizval na miting storonnikov soyuza," *Nezavisimaia gazeta*, 12 Dec. 1991, p. 2; and Zorich, "Travkinu ugrozhaiut vykhodom iz DPR," ibid., 17 Dec. 1991, p. 2.

33. Evgenii Krasnikov, "V fevrale Rutskoi stat' tenevym prem'erom," *Nezavisimaia gazeta*, 18 Jan. 1992, p. 2.

34. Inna Murav'eva, "Patrioty kakogo tsveta spasut Rossiiu," *Rossiiskaia gazeta*, 10 Feb. 1992, p. 1.

35. See the interview given by Sergei Baburin to Vladimir Todres, "'Situatsiiu vzryvaet natsional'naia ushchemlennost' russkikh'," *Nezavisimaia gazeta*, 9 Jan. 1992, p. 2.

36. Ibid. See also Olga Bychkova's interview with Baburin in *Moscow News*, no. 7 (16–23 Feb. 1992), p. 14. For an outline of the Russian National Assembly's member organizations, leadership, and program, see Vladimir Todres, "Patrioty v verkhovnom sovete trubyat sbor," *Nezavisimaia gazeta*, 25 Feb. 1992, p. 2.

37. This party first developed as a splinter from the parliamentary faction "Communists of Russia" at Russia's Third Congress of People's Deputies in March 1991, at that time taking for itself the name "Communists for Democracy." After the August coup, it dropped the word "Communist" from its appellation and took its current name at its founding Congress (26–27 October 1991). On its development, membership, and political orientation, see: V. S. Lipitskii, "K reformirovannoi partii," *Izvestiia TsK KPSS*, no. 1 (1991), pp. 37–40; I. Elistratov, "'My sozdaem partiiu dlia liudei'," *Izvestiia*, 22 Jul. 1991; Nikolai Kas'yanov, "Demokraty-Kommunisty nakonets-to ob"edinilis' v rabochee vremia," *Soiuz*, no. 13 (14–21 Aug. 1991), p. 6; Yulii Lebedev, "Rutskoi posledoval sovetu Meidzhora i Tetcher," *Nezavisimaia gazeta*, 29 Oct. 1991, p. 2.

38. Vladimir Todres, "Rutskoi ne soglasen so svoei partiei," *Nezavisimaia gazeta*, 31 Jan. 1992, p. 2.

39. The only ministerial posts in the Russian government awarded to members of political parties before late spring 1992, have gone to the PPFR (the Ministry of Social Security and the Ministry of Industry). Krasnikov, "Partii khotiat upravliat' Rossiei ... "

40. See in particular the interview given by Rutskoi to Andrei Karaulov, "'V Rossii net ni vlasti ni demokratii'," *Nezavisimaia gazeta*, 18 Dec. 1991, pp. 1–2.

41. Maksim Sokolov, "Chechenskii krizis i rossiiskaia vlast'," *Kommersant*, no. 44 (11–18 Nov. 1991), p. 5.

42. See the interview with Nikolai Travkin, "Tekhnologiia vlasti'," *Demokraticheskaia gazeta*, no. 8 (Jul. 1991), p. 2. See also the comments made by Travkin on the floor of Russia's Supreme Soviet in October 1991, quoted in ibid., 31 Oct.–6 Nov. 1991, pp. 2–3.

43. Natal'ya Gorodetskaia, "Vozmozhen novyi forum politicheskikh sil," *Nezavisimaia gazeta*. 27 Feb. 1992, p. 2.

44. The DPR acknowledged its differences with the PPFR on the issue of property; hence, the "conditional" nature of the coalition itself at the time that the alliance was struck. "DPR-NPSR: shagi k konstruktivnomu dialog," *Demokraticheskaia gazeta*, no. 11 (Mar. 1992), p. 2. Indeed, the speeches delivered at the conference by the respective party leaders made these differences readily apparent. Travkin emphasized tax reductions in order to stimulate business activity; Rutskoi called instead for market regulations and the reinstitution of price controls for basic goods. Excerpts from these speeches can be found in Stanislav Rotsinskii, "Ostanovit raspad Rossii," ibid., no. 12 (Mar. 1992), pp. 1–2.

45. Sergei Mitrofanov, "Yeltsin predlozhil bastuyushchim krasivo vyiti: Oni ne khotiat," *Kommersant*, no. 17 (22–29 Apr. 1991), p. 12; "Zaiavlenei '9 + 1'; mnenie 'Demrossii'," *Demokraticheskaia Rossiia*, no. 7 (10 May 1991), p. 3.

46. "U SvDPR svoya politika," *Nezavisimaia gazeta*, 4 Feb. 1992, p. 2; Tat'yana Malkina, "'DemRossiya' prikazala dolgo zhit'," ibid., 17 Mar. 1992, p. 2.

47. Galina Skoptsov, "Byt' DemRossii ili ne byt'," *Rossiiskaia gazeta*, 25 Jan. 1992; Tat'yana Malkina, "Prezhnei DemRossii bol'she net," *Nezavisimaia gazeta*, 21 Jan. 1992, pp. 1–2.

48. Malkina, "Prezhnei DemRossii ... "; Yuri Afanasyev, "Government and Society Must Unite," *Moscow News*, no. 11 (15–22 Mar. 1992), pp. 10–11.

49. See Urban, "Party Formation and Deformation," pp. 135–39.

50. Interview with Dennis Pankin, executive secretary of the SDPR (23 Apr. 1991). On the history of the SDPR/RPR merger attempts, see V. Lyzlov, "Ob"ediniaemsya," *Al'ternativa*, no. 6 (Mar. 1991), p. 3.

51. It seems that this change of ideological direction was to some degree the product of a change in the socioeconomic status of RPR leaders and activists. The RPR had formed out of the democratic platform that left the CPSU at its 28th Congress in July 1990. On leaving the CPSU, many of the leaders and activists in the democratic platform were fired from their jobs in the academic world and turned to commercial and entrepreneurial activities. Gradually, then, a social democratic orientation gave way to a liberal one with the RPR. On this ideological metamorphosis, see the interview given by one of the party's leaders, Vyacheslav Shostakovskii, to Vladimir Todres, "Pravitel'stvo ne koketnichat' 'oblikom vremenschchika'," *Nezavisimaia gazeta*, 6 Feb. 1992, p. 2.; and V. P. Gaidek and S. S. Shulakshin, "O chem umolchala 'Pravda'," *Gospodin narod*, no. 4 (1991), p. 10.

52. Aleksandr Verkhovski, "Demokraty na poroge novoi epokhi," *Panorama*, no. 28 (Jul. 1991), pp. 4–5.

53. This is evident in the relative emphasis devoted to these questions in the RPR's position paper, prepared for the Sixth Congress of People's Deputies—"Pozitsiia Koordinationnogo Soveta Respublikanskoi partii Rossiiskoi Federatsii k VI s"ezdu narodnykh deputatov RF" (unpublished document, Moscow, March 1992). "Respublikanskaia partiia o situatsii vokrug Kryma," *Nezavisimaia gazeta*, 1 Feb. 1992, p. 2.

54. For example, see the interview given by Oleg Rumyantsev to Andrei Sharapov, "Poslednii shans vozrodit' edinuiu gosudarstvennost' Rossii," *Rossiiskaia gazeta*, 15 Jan. 1992, p. 3.

55. For a short, recent description of the differences between the SDPR and RPR on this issue, see G. Bondarev and V. Smirnov, "Sobstvennost' khotiat poluchit' vse. No kazhdyi po-svoemu." *Rossiiskaia gazeta*, 13 Mar. 1992, p. 2. The first major statement of the SDPR's position on property redistribution appeared as "Situatsiia v strane," *Al'ternativa*, no. 3 (Sept. 1990), pp. 1–2. More recently, see Oleg Rumyantsev, "Politika reform—dloe

obshchee," *Rossiiskaia gazeta,* 7 Dec. 1991, p. 2; and the SPDR's extension of its critique of "*nomenklatura* capitalism" to include the "democratic *nomenklatura* ... organically growing within the old corrupt connections" maintained by state officials, which appeared as "'Demokratiia pod ugrozoi'," ibid., 28 May 1992, p. 2.

56. Konstantin Katanyan, "Znakomye vse litsa," *Kuranty,* 10 Aug. 1991, p. 2.

57. This bloc, together with its affiliated parties, is outlined in the "Statement of the Political Committee of the Party of Constitutional Democrats" (not to be confused with the CDP) that appeared in *Rossiiskaia gazeta,* 28 Feb. 1992, p. 2.

58. Mikhail Karpov, "Ne putaite s 'liberal-demokratami' Zhirinovskogo," *Nezavisimaia gazeta,* 28 Jan. 1992, p. 2.

59. The People's Party of Russia (PPR) was formed by a number of Russian political notables—Tel'man Gdlyan, Tat'yana Koryagina, Nikolai Ivanov, Oleg Borodin, and Igor Chubais—positioned on the radical-populist wing of Democratic Russia. From its inception, the PPR's orientation has pitted it against the *nomenklatura.* Its views also oppose those elements in the democratic movement—represented by, for instance, those in the Liberal Free Market bloc—whose stance on the property question, PPR leaders argue, means in practice to transfer property back to the *nomenklatura* via a privatization process in which the overwhelming majority of citizens could not participate. On the PPR's founding, see Vladimir Todres, "Radikaly ovladevaiut massami?" *Nezavisimaia gazeta,* 21 May 1992, p. 2; M. Volodina and V. Pribylovskii, "Narod i narodnaia partiia Tel'mana Gdlyana—ediny," *Panorama,* no. 28 (Jul. 1991), p. 7.

60. The Peasant Party of Russia emerged in 1990 out of that wing of the agrarian deputies group in the Soviet Parliament committed to a program of peasant proprietorship. See Don Van Atta, "Political Mobilization in the Russian Countryside: Creating Social Movements from Above," in Sedaitis and Butterfield, op. cit., pp. 43–71; "Krest'yanskaia partiia Rossii," B. I. Koval', ed., *Rossiia segodnia* (Moscow: Mezhdunarodnye otnosheniia, 1992), pp. 215–228.

61. On the New Russia coalition, see Pavel Anokhin, "'Novaia Rossiia'—esche odna popytka demokratov sozdat' svoi blok," *Rossiiskaia gazeta,* 26 Feb. 1992, p. 2; Vladimir Todres, "Partii levogo tsentra ob"edinilis'," *Nezavisimaia gazeta,* 16 Jul. 1992, p. 2; idem, "Rossiiskie partii nedovol'nyi Gaidarom," ibid., 14 Jan. 1992, p. 2.

I might note in passing the political distance traveled by the parties in New Russia in order to combine forces. As late as December 1991, for example, the PPR regarded social democracy, in the context of a poor country like Russia, as an incipient form of their archenemy, Bolshevism. See Mikhail Tarasov, "Narodnaia partiia Rossii," *Rossiiskaia gazeta,* 27 Dec. 1991, p. 2.

62. On the organization, leadership, and support-base for MDR, see "Za ob"edinenie sil demokratii i reform," *Izvestiia,* 2 Jul. 1992; "Zaiavlenie v podderzhku 'Dvizhenie demokraticheskikh reform'," *Izvestiia,* 9 Jul. 1991; "Dvizhenie demokraticheskikh reform gotovit svoi s"ezd," *Izvestiia,* 13 Jul. 1991.

63. Nikolai Kras'ianov, "'Dviznenie demokraticheskikh reform': istoki, politika, perspektiva," *Soiuz,* no. 28 (10–17 Jul. 1991), p. 6. See also Valerii Vyzhutovich's interview with Yuri Afanas'ev, Lev Ponomarev, and Gleb Yakunin, "My podderznivaem El'toina uslovno," *Izvestiia,* 7 Oct. 1991.

64. Grigor'ev and Malyutin, *Vlast' i sobstvennost' v Rossii ...* , pp. 8–11; Vite, "Ekonomicheskii krizis ... "; Verkhovskii, "Demokraty na poroge ... "; D. A. Levchik et

al., "Putch 18–21 avgusta 1991g. i mestnye organy vlasti," (Report to the Kras-
nogvardeiskii Raion Soviet, City of Moscow, 17 Oct. 1991), pp. 15–19.

65. See the interview given by the SDPR leader, Boris Orlov, to Alla Struchkova,
"Raskol neizbezhen," *Rossiiskaia gazeta,* 6 Jan. 1992, p. 2; and "Liberly ne priznaiut
DDR," *Nezavisimaia gazeta,* 17 Dec. 1991, pp. 1–2.

66. At its official founding in mid-December 1991, the MDR claimed a membership of
over one million, Galina Mashtakova and Mikhail Tarasov, "Delegaty raz'ekhalis': Chto
dal'she," *Rossiiskaia gazeta,* 17 Dec. 1991, pp. 1–2.

67. Whereas Democratic Russia supported the agreement worked out on 8 Dec. 1991
by the leaders of the three Slavic republics, which led to the formation of the Commonwealth of Independent States, the MDR condemned it as "national-state nihilism" and
continued to back Gorbachev's notion of a renewed union. Tat'yana Malkina,
"Praviashchaia partiia nesostoiavshegosia gosudarstva?" *Nezavisimaia gazeta,* 14 Dec.
1991, p. 2; idem, "DemRossiia privetstvuet SNG," ibid.

68. An intimation of this occurred in St. Petersburg in mid-November 1991, when the
regional section of the MDR organized a conference in support of the mayor's economic
reform program. Although the mayors of St. Petersburg and Moscow—Anatolii Sobchak
and Gavrill Popov, respectively,—were featured speakers, all democratic organizations of
any size boycotted the proceedings. See "Otkryti Peterburgskoe otdelenie DDR,"
Nezavisimaia gazeta, 16 Nov. 1991, p. 2. A contingent of the RPR, led by party
cochairperson, Vyacheslav Shostakovskii, attended the RMDR's founding congress, as did
a large group from the PPFR, comprising 20 percent of all delegates. The RPR, however,
walked out, but the PPFR decided to reconsider at the next meeting of its Central Committee whether to maintain its membership in the RMDR. See Galina Mashtakova,
"Nizhegorodskie radeteli," *Rossiiskaia gazeta,* 17 Feb. 1992, p. 1.

69. Galina Mashtakova, "Metamorfozy vnutri dvizheniia," *Rossiiskaia gazeta,* 20 Feb.
1992, p. 2.

70. Vladimir Todres, "Tvaricheskii dvorets protiv belogo doma," *Nezavisimaia
gazeta,* 14 March 1992, p. 2.

71. On the eve of the Sixth Congress, the information center, RF Politika, reported to
the president and the government of Russia that whereas some 300–350 deputies could be
counted as their firm supporters, another 400–450 should be regarded as staunch opponents. This report put the swing vote at 250–350. This memorandum appeared as "O
rasstanovke sil v deputatskom korpuse i vozmozhnykh stsenariiakh razvitiia sobytii na VI
s"ezde narodnykh deputatov RF," *Nezavisimaia gazeta,* 1 Apr. 1992, p. 2.

72. Anna Ostapchuk, "Levo-pravye razrabotali disositsiiu," *Nezavisimaia gazeta,* 7
Apr. 1992, p. 2; idem, "Vozrozhdenie SSSR," *Nezavisimaia gazeta,* 16 Apr. 1992, p. 2.

73. These four included: DPR, SDPR, RPR, and PPFR.

74. The statement issued by these parties and groups cited the "destabilizing" effect
that this referendum would have on the "social-political situation in Russia, opening up an
opportunity for subverting the existing constitutional order." See "Zaiavlenie
politicheskikh partii i organizatsii," *Demokraticheskaia gazeta,* no. 16 (Apr. 1992), p. 2.
This "destabilizing" effect has been understood as a delegitimation of legislative institutions, generally; the dangerous precedent of adopting a constitution via plebiscite; and the
holding of new elections. All by-elections to the Congress of People's Deputies, staged in
winter 1992, failed to attract more than a 30 percent turnout. New elections would likely

not attain the required turnout of 50 percent and, therefore, would be invalid, leaving the country without a legislature.

75. Igor Yakovenko outlined the voting patterns on major issues at the Sixth Congress of People's Deputies in "Esli Kommunisty Rossii—'za', Demokraticheskaia Rossiia—'protiv'," *Nezavisimaia gazeta,* 24 Apr. 1992, p. 2.

76. Inna Murasheva, "Chtoby ne rukhnuli poslednie nadezhdy," *Rossiiskaia gazeta,* 9 Jun. 1992, p. 1; for an account of the major points adopted at the Russian National Assembly's second congress (12 Jun. 1992) see Dmitrii Slobodyanyuk, "Russkii natsional'nyi sobor poidet drugim putem," ibid., 15 Jun. 1992, p. 2.

77. "Krizis v partiiakh kadetov i demokhristian," *Nezavisimaia gazeta,* 29 Apr. 1992, p. 2.

78. "Partiia kadetov: krizis nazrel?" *Demokraticheskaia gazeta,* no. 16 (Apr. 1992), p. 2; Ernst Chernyi, "Ne povtorim oshibku," *Rossiiskaia gazeta,* 3 Apr. 1992, p. 6; idem, "Vzlet i padenie kadetov," ibid., 21 May 1992, p. 2.

79. One high-level functionary reports that "unity" in the party on the question of supporting the government's economic policies was only achieved via an exceptionally general statement pledging support (thus accommodating the party's right wing), without any practical provisions (therefore assuaging the center), and permitting the party's left wing to enter a formal dissent.

80. Mikhail Karpov, "Esdeki na puti ot belova doma k kremlyu," *Nezavisimaia gazeta,* 30 May 1992, p. 2. The fruition of this compromise has appeared in the government's revised scheme for privatization that awards a check to each citizen, which can then be used to purchase shares in enterprises or sold on the open market. Vasilii Kononenko, "Osen'ya rossiiskie grazhdane dolzhny poluchit' privatizatsionnye cheki," *Izvestiia,* 11 Jun. 1992.

81. Liliya Shevstvova has noted the "relative vacuum" on the left-center. She expects this to be filled soon, probably by the Labor Party (Berkeley-Stanford Workshop on Political Parties in Post-Communist Russia, Stanford, California, 30 Apr.–2 May 1992). On the emergence of the Labor Party, see Anna Ostapchuk, "Partila truda prognoziruet aprel'skii krizis vlasti," *Nezavisimaia gazeta,* 18 Mar. 1992, p. 2. On the coalescence of the Labor Party with others on the "democratic left" around a program calling for mixed economy and the "defense of the social rights of the citizenry in the epoch of great reforms," see Evgenii Krasnikov, "Protiv demokratov-kapitalistov, patriotov-shovinistov i kommunistov-totalitaristov," ibid., 5 Jun. 1992, p. 2.

82. On the rift between the RMDR and the MDR induced by this issue, see Elena Tregunova, "Mezhdunarodnye i Rossiiski demreformatory na grani ssory," *Nezavisimaia gazeta,* 28 Apr. 1992, p. 2. On the opposition to the referendum registered by the RPR— the only sizable party still affiliated with Democratic Russia—see "Zaiavlenie Respublikanskoi partii Rossii," ibid.

83. Popov had been a leader of Democratic Russia until he suspended his membership in May 1990. However, he retained a strong base within the organization, composed of individuals such as Vladimir Bokser, whom he employed on his staff while mayor, and Lev Ponomarev, with whom he had worked closely in politics since 1989. With the departure of the radical faction from Democratic Russia in early 1992, the organization seems to have fallen under the direction of the Bokser-Ponomarev group, thereby facilitating cooperation with Popov's RMDR.

84. Andrei Sharapov, "Mer-politik ustupaet mesto meru-khoziaistvenniku," *Rossiiskaia gazeta,* 11 Jun. 1992, p. 1.

85. Vladimir Kuznechevskii, "Referenduma vse-taki ne budet?" *Rossiiskaia gazeta,* 23 May, 1992, p. 1.

86. The idea of dissolving the Congress was dropped from the project, leaving three issues on the proposed referendum: (1) awarding to the president the right to call referenda; (2) the institutions of private property in land; and (3) the convening of a constituent assembly to draft a new Constitution.

87. These groups delivered their votes to Yeltsin on key issues taken up at the Sixth Congress; he, in turn, appointed a number of their members to the Cabinet named in the weeks that followed. Mikhail Berger, "Novye naznacheniia Yeltsin—veroiatnost' 'abalkanizatsii' pravitel'stva Gaidara," *Izvestiya,* 3 Jun. 1992, p. 2.

88. On the formation of Renewal, see Sergei Parkhomenko, "Vol'skii sozdaet partiiu pragmatikov," *Nezavisimaia gazeta,* 13 May 1992, p. 2; the interviews given, respectively, to Parkhomenko and G. Melikyants by Alexandr Vladislavlev, the second figure in the Russian Union of Industrialists and Entrepreneurs, "'Cherez Kakoe-to vremia Vol'skii dolzhen privesti novoe pravitel'stvo'," ibid., 2 Jun. 1992, p. 2; and "'Promyshlennoe soslovie' vykhodit na politicheskuiu stsenu," *Izvestiya,* 22 Apr. 1992; and "Sozdan vserossiiskii soyuz 'Obnovlenie'," *Rossiiskaia gazeta,* 13 May 1992, p. 1.

89. Evgenii Krasnikov, "Zarozhdenie 'novoi oppozitsii?'," *Nezavisimaia gazeta,* 26 May, 1992, p. 2; Sergei Nikitin, "Pod flagom obnovleniia," *Rossiiskaia gazeta,* 2 Jun. 1992, p. 2.

90. Evgennii Krasnikov, "Novyi prem'er Rossii: Vol'skii, Vladislavlev, ili Saburov?" *Nezavisimaia gazeta,* 6 Jun. 1992, p. 2.

91. This observation is based on two considerations, one pertinent to the state, the other to political and civil society. Regarding the former (as noted above) Yeltsin's reshuffle of his Cabinet following the Sixth Congress of People's Deputies has already provided a sizable base in government for members and supporters of Civic Union. With respect to the latter, this new "center" has begun to draw in new members previously associated with other groupings. Also its "middle class" constituencies—older directors of state enterprises, younger private businessmen, and state officials—represent strategically positioned groups on whom the success of the economic reform is predicated. On Civic Union's attraction of new members from other blocs and parties, see Igor' Surikov and Vladimir Todres, "Aksyuchits i Astaf'ev teriaiut storonnikov?" *Nezavisimaia gazeta,* 3 Jun. 1992, p. 2. On the second point, see Georgii Ivanov-Smolenskii, "Grazhdanskii soiuz: oppozitsiia no konstruktivnaia," *Izvestiia,* 22 Jun. 1992.

92. As of July 1993, the following correspondences can be noted between the four "centers" outlined in this chapter and the electoral blocs that began to form in the wake of the referendum of 25 April 1993: the "presidential center"—Russia's Choice (*Vybor Rossii*); the "opposition center"—Civic Union; the "left-center"—Entrepreneurs for a New Russia; the "right-center"—a bloc forming between two poles of the Front for National Salvation and, at the other end, an alliance among the Communist Party of the Russian Federation, Russian Unity, and the Agrarian Union. Although the formation of these blocs has involved a measure of political regrouping—for instance, the DPR at this writing has all but defected from the Civic Union while a splinter from the SDPR, calling itself the Social Democratic Center, has joined it—there remains an overall correspondence between our "centers" and the more recently constituted electoral blocs.

CHAPTER 8

Conclusion: Today's Russia, Pluralism, and Social Science Theory

Anthony Jones and Carol R. Saivetz

The contributors to this volume have raised many more questions than they have answered. This is due in large measure to the confusing and volatile situation that currently exists in the former Soviet Union. Even as post-Soviet leaders tout democracy, the very process of democratization seems to propel Russia and the other successor states into chaos. For example, there is clearly no firm agreement on the division of powers within the government; moreover, the legislators who will likely decide this issue were elected under rules initiated by the ancien régime. With glasnost and democratization, voice was given to ethnic groups— many of whom have demanded sovereignty, if not outright secession, from the existing state structures. This political picture is further complicated by the precipitous economic decline that seems to doom to failure the attempts at democratization in Russia and the rest of the Commonwealth of Independent States (CIS). And although high—and often dramatic—politics are played out in Moscow, equally significant dramas can be seen at the local levels. The contributors deal with all these issues and raise questions about the future of the former Soviet Union.

We can attempt to make some order out of this chaos by systematizing our inquiry. One way to do this is to look at analyses of the political transitions from authoritarianism to democracy in Latin America and Southern Europe (especially in Spain and Portugal). Another is to explore what we might call classic democratic theory. We must also continue to gather data on the contemporary situation in Russia and the other successor states.

When the wave of democratization spread to Eastern Europe and the USSR, some analysts were tempted to use transition theories to offer predictions and recommendations. Although some scholars thought that the experiences of the Soviet bloc were of an entirely different order, others saw enough similarities to justify applying the existing models to postcommunist Eastern Europe and the former Soviet Union.[1]

Ironically, even the transition theorists agree that each transition is unique to the country in which it occurs. Nevertheless, they see similar variables at work in all transitions. These include how the transition process is initiated; the duration and characteristics of authoritarian rule; and the financial and military resources available to both the old and the new regimes.[2] Thus, as one reads the transition literature, there are times when the analyses of the Latin American or southern European transitions ring true as well for the former Soviet Union. For example, Guillermo O'Donnell and Philippe Schmitter, in writing about the origins of the transition process, distinguish between liberalization and democratization. In their terminology, liberalization refers to the process of redefining and extending rights, initiated by the authoritarian rulers. Democratization (not to be confused with Gorbachev's use of the term) refers to a process whereby the rules and procedures of "citizenship" are applied to political institutions and are expanded to include persons previously excluded.[3] It is implicit in this formulation that there are agreed upon rules of the game that bind officials and the populace alike.

This demarcation between two distinct processes means that liberalization can occur without true democratization. Moreover, an authoritarian leader may well use liberalization to relieve pressures upon the system, without changing its basic structures and without introducing accountability.[4] This, it would seem, is precisely what Gorbachev did under the rubrics of perestroika and glasnost. Clearly, liberalization does not necessarily portend democratization or democracy. As was the case in the last days of Gorbachev's Soviet Union, it could lead to a backlash, an antidemocratic reaction, and an attempt to replace the liberalizing and reforming leadership.[5]

Approaching the question somewhat differently, Samuel P. Huntington has suggested that transitions can be of three types: "transformation," which occurs when the elites in power take the lead in establishing democracy; "replacement," when the opposition takes the lead and the regime collapses; and "transplacement," which involves the creation of democracy by the regime and its opponents jointly.[6] This last category includes the so-called "pacted democracy," as outlined by O'Donnell and Schmitter.[7] According to this typology, the Soviet experience could be said to be a case of both transformation and transplacement. Gorbachev, as head of the ruling elite, began the process and then Boris Yeltsin co-opted it, bringing about the collapse of the old system.

With regard to the duration and characteristics of authoritarian rule, most observers would agree that Stalinist totalitarianism was different from Latin American authoritarianism. The differences become less clear-cut when we look at the Brezhnev era and beyond, especially if we characterize that period as bureaucratic authoritarianism. If we are to use the six classic features of totalitarianism, then, in the Brezhnev period, institutionalized terror was minimal and the role of the dictator was reduced. Until Gorbachev, the ideological justification of the system remained, and the Communist Party maintained its monopoly on the media, the military, and the economy. By late 1991, new political thinking had taken hold in both domestic and foreign policies, the monopolies on the military and police were disintegrating, and only the economy remained more or less under state control. We should note as well that the Soviet system was unique in its fusion of state and party. Moreover, communist ideology and demographic policies had legitimated the maintenance of a multiethnic state, and with the rejection of communism there was no alternative basis on which to preserve ethnic coexistence, save for reasons of practicality. Most strikingly, economy and polity were merged to an extent that was not true anywhere else.

When we get to the question of the resources available to the state and to the opposition, the situation is further complicated by the close connections between the political and economic transitions. The slowness with which the state-owned economy has been privatized, the monopoly that many state-owned enterprises continue to enjoy, the continuing power of industrial managers and former bureaucrats, and the precipitous decline in economic production have certainly made it difficult for private groups to acquire the resources necessary for political organization and action. If anything, Arkadii Vol'skii's Civic Union (as Michael Urban points out) has become a powerful political force that is opposed to certain aspects of economic reform precisely because it currently enjoys a near-monopoly on economic power with which it can challenge the reformist government. Also, for a population not accustomed to the hardships of transition, economic problems have tended to overwhelm the public's interest in the formation of new political structures.

As for military or police resources, the disintegration of the Red Army, the apparent independence of certain regional commanders, the existence of rebel militias, and even the current crime wave occurring in major cities would all seem to indicate that no one possesses sure authority over the instruments of force. It would seem safe to say, for the moment, that Boris Yeltsin's government has at its disposal preponderant military force; but, we cannot forget, for example, that Ruslan Khasbulatov, the chair of the Supreme Soviet, possesses a five-thousand-man private army.

The existing literature is helpful in that it pinpoints the beginnings of the transition process away from authoritarianism. Yet, as noted above, there are clear differences between the Latin American and Soviet brands of authoritarianism. The literature tells us that the former Soviet Union is stuck somewhere on the transition route, yet it cannot provide a basis for an analysis of the problems currently facing Boris Yeltsin, the other republican leaders, and the reformers. Finally, the existing transition literature does not provide an answer to the question, transition to what?

It is implicit in most of the literatures that democracy is the end point of the transition, but there are, of course, no guarantees. As several of our contributors noted, there seem to be both prerequisites for and thresholds of democracy. Many theorists would argue that democracy requires a specific level of industrialization.[8] Indeed, many well-known specialists on the USSR such as Jerry Hough and Moshe Lewin have argued that the increasing complexity of Soviet society was itself a mechanism for producing pluralism.[9] Increasing social and economic differentiation involves the creation of new and conflicting interests, the bearers of which can be expected to desire access to the political process. Hough even went so far as to posit the Communist Party of the Soviet Union (CPSU) as a mediator among competing interests in society. By this, he meant not a mass pluralism, but instead pressure from a limited number of interest groups, such as ministries, scientists, and enterprise managers.[10] Lewin, for his part, predicated the reforms of the Gorbachev era on increased education, urbanization, and economic stratification.[11]

The main question is whether modernization necessarily implies a well-developed capitalist economy, and whether this, in turn, is a prerequisite for democracy. In *Politics and Markets,* Charles E. Lindblom noted that it was historically the middle classes that promoted democracy as a means of protecting their property.[12] And, although the middle class is not necessarily a guarantor of democracy, O'Donnell and Schmitter wrote that during a transition to democracy the property rights of the bourgeoisie are inviolable. But what happens when the bourgeoisie has been erased, when there are no middle-class interests to protect? Russia and the other successor states seem to lack the entrepreneurial middle class that triggered democratization in Europe.[13] Moreover, we have already noted that the lack of privatization limited the resources available to reformist groups and went a long way toward explaining the strength of the Civic Union. Thus, economic instability, coupled with the low level of industrialization, would not seem, thus far, to be fertile ground for the development of democratic pluralism.

Other theorists have noted the difficulties inherent in establishing pluralism in multiethnic societies. They argue that mediation and accommodation among competing interests is easier when they are not reinforced by tribal and national strife. This is consistent with the argument of Dankwart Rustow, who stressed that democratization is easier in an ethnically homogeneous society.[14] For example, the former Soviet Union faces overwhelming ethnic and national problems that seem to confound efforts to create governments recognized as legitimate by those over whom they preside.

Finally, democratic theorists, most notably Robert Dahl, take participation and true contestation as the central features of democracy.[15] In the Soviet period, participation, as David Lane has reminded us, involved the mobilization of the populus in the implementation of policies decided at the top. It did not mean providing inputs to the system. Support for the regime was sought not through popular access to power-holders, but through the managed charisma of leaders, through an elaborate system of rituals and symbols, and through the promise of security and economic growth. Politics was underpinned by the assumption of a "systematic unity of interest between [the] masses and the political elite."[16] The citizenry were mobilized (i.e., they participated), but their conflicting interests were not permitted expression until the Gorbachev period.

With the liberalization and the tentative democratization of the late Gorbachev period, the nature of participation changed. Individuals and groups fought for access to the decision makers and the political process. By 1990, many groups were voicing their concerns, as evidenced by the proliferation of associations calling themselves movements and parties.[17] We can still question, however, whether these groups actually enhance participation. Are they truly representative? Do they aggregate interests and thereby provide access to the system? Are they accountable? What kind of participation is guaranteed to those not affiliated with these political groups? These issues are clearly related to the concept of contestation. Here we must ask two questions: Are would-be participants in the political process permitted real choices? And do these groups mentioned above actually compete for power? The answer to the first question is a qualified "yes." Even in the first—obviously controlled—elections, the people exercised choice by voting out of office many Communist Party officials who were running uncontested. By the same token, as Jeffrey Hahn notes, there were no party symbols visible when the electorate went to the polls in Yaroslavl' and there was nothing to differentiate clearly among the candidates. Once in power, these deputies whether at the local or national levels seemed to "float." Groupings coalesced and faded without much regard to institutionalized competition between or among them.

Underlying all these questions is concern about the "procedural minimums" of democracy.[18] Asked in another way, are there agreed upon rules of the game, that is, a framework within which participation and contestation occur? On the list of such minimums are secret ballots, universal suffrage, regular elections, associational freedom, accountability, and competition.[19] Another question that needs to be addressed is whether the loser still has a stake in the ongoing system, that is whether he will continue to abide by the rules and accept their outcome. In some respects, Russia and some of the other successor states seem to meet the test, yet as we have seen, there are also crucial elements lacking.

One important factor that needs to be included in this discussion of the potential for democratic pluralism in Russia and the other successor states, and one that is missing from the transition literature, is political culture. Scholars have long discussed the degree to which Russian political culture has inhibited the development of Western-style democracy.[20] They point to the support historically given to the centralized state, to the lack of toleration for diverse opinions, and to the absence of compromise. Russians, though supportive of democracy in the abstract, are said to long for a firm hand to reestablish order. A survey conducted in Russia in late 1992 indicated that there is more popular support for a government that "strove toward security" and the "protection of the population" than one which "protected individual liberties."[21] At the same time, political discussions seem to devolve into shouting matches because of intolerance. As Peter Rutland has noted: "It is very hard to make compromises and build consensus in a political system where mutual suspicion is so pronounced. If one side regards their opponents as holdovers from a past regime now collapsed and discredited, and the other side sees their adversaries as agents of a foreign power, it is not surprising that the political system is in deadlock."[22] To the extent that these judgments are correct, the creation of adequate rules of the game will require dramatic changes in cultural beliefs.

The question of political culture relates as well to the issue of systemic legitimacy. In the Soviet period, some Western scholars argued that the system had achieved legitimacy because it provided for the economic needs of its citizens. What many of these same observers missed was the lack of affective legitimacy—*compliance* was mistaken for *support.* In the absence of instrumental legitimation, because of the severe economic crisis, affective legitimacy acquires ever greater importance. And it is particularly this component that requires a supportive political culture. Pluralism would seem to be predicated on the acceptance by the population of competing groups, their right to participate in the political process, and the acceptance of the outcomes of that process. In the current situation in Russia, people's lack of toleration and the impatience with indecision renders the government vulnerable to a loss of legitimacy.

Although public opinion polling can shed some light on these issues, we still lack firm data on the content of contemporary Russian political culture. Nevertheless, it would seem safe to posit that this culture will condition the rules of the game that are finally implemented. This point stands out all the more clearly when we contrast Russian political life with that of the Central Asian states. There, as Peter Clement points out, the traditional culture—Islamic values and the existence of clans—seems to inhibit the growth of pluralism.

The linkages among the transition process, the prerequisites of democracy, and pluralism lie in what O'Donnell and Schmitter have referred to as the resurrection of civil society. By their use of the term "resurrect," O'Donnell and Schmitter refer in part to the elements of civil society that may have existed before the imposition of authoritarian rule. However, in the Soviet case, "create" would be a more appropriate term. During the Tsarist period, civil society was relatively weak, and of course over seventy years have passed since then. Nevertheless, as we mentioned in the Introduction, there were rudimentary elements of a unique kind of pluralism in the post-Stalinist era. Therefore, what the post-Soviet successor states need to do is to build on these groups, and on the new ones that began to flourish in the late Soviet period. Following the repeal of article 6 of the Soviet Constitution—that guaranteed the leading role in society to the CPSU—movements and parties sprang up and competed for parliamentary seats. The Congress of People's Deputies and the local soviets contain factions composed of former communists, industrialists, nationalists, and erstwhile democrats. The existence of these factions explains much of what we have seen in the debates in the Congress of People's Deputies and the struggles for power in Moscow and in the provincial capitals. The problem lies in the fact that these debates seem to occur in a vacuum, since there is no link to broad constituencies in the society at large.

A major reason for this lack of connection is that pluralism in Russia has developed more fully at the top and is still exceptionally weak at the grass-roots level. Many of these groups proliferated with the collapse of the Soviet Union in December 1991, but they are currently little more than shifting coalitions without strong links to the people.[23] The public opinion poll cited above asked the respondents about the relative popularity of political figures. It was immediately apparent that many had never heard of Gennadii Burbulis or even Arkadii Vol'skii.[24] So, whose interests really were represented in the debate about Egor Gaidar's tenure as acting prime minister? Who will benefit or lose in the future constitutional reform? The government has functioned based on the ability of a few individuals who are either powerful enough to pursue policies on their own or who are able to garner enough votes to legislate a particular program. In effect, these political battles are among individuals and cliques and not among representatives of clearly defined constituencies.

It would appear, therefore, that for the post-Soviet transition to move forward, more permanent parties and autonomous groups need to be created. Once Gorbachev opened up the political process through liberalization, a mobilization of the population took place, to a limited extent. We can point to the emergence of such groups as the green movement, Pamiat', Memorial, and the several national independence movements that sprang up, particularly in the Baltic republics.[25] Yet, in many respects, these groups remain informal associations, different from interest groups in the Western sense of the term. They lack the clear definition, the self-consciousness, and the organization that would enable them to form the basis of effective political parties.

At the moment in the former Soviet Union, it would seem that there is a variety of nascent pluralisms. In fact, we would argue that any discussion of pluralism in the post-Soviet context must be broadened to include cultural, social, economic, and political pluralisms. Most of our discussion has touched on the political dimension; nonetheless, knowledge of these other areas is necessary to give us a complete picture of the current situation in the former Soviet Union. *Cultural* pluralism refers to the existence of and tolerance for a diversity of ideas. *Social* pluralism encompasses the existence of multiple informal and formal associational groups that may or may not have political agendas. Finally, *economic* pluralism involves a variety of forms of production, employment, and ownership.[26]

Each of these exists to a greater or lesser extent in contemporary Russian society. But as our contributors stress, the main questions revolve around the *institutionalization and interrelation* of these pluralisms. For example, Mervyn Matthews has described the proliferation of newspapers but has questioned whether they can survive without legislative guarantees. Theodore Friedgut has reminded us that the existence of many groups alone does not ensure pluralism and that there is a clear differentiation between fragmentation and pluralism.

This volume is among the first attempts to create new models of post-Soviet politics and to measure progress toward democratization. As we have seen, existing transition theories contribute to our understanding of the initiation of the transition process, and democratic theory points to the necessary conditions for the institutionalization of democratic structures and behavior. Yet both types of theories must be considered in light of the Soviet legacy. What is created will certainly be strongly influenced by what has gone before, and so explaining the present and future will require our continued attention to the past. In our opinion, attempts to apply mechanically to Russia and the successor states theories developed for other societies can only lead to failure. Therefore, as specialists on the former Soviet Union we must continue to collect data on and to analyze this tumultuous phase in Soviet and post-Soviet politics.

As we continue our analyses of the post-Soviet era, we might find that so-called modernization theory, first devised to explain political processes in the developing countries, will add to our understanding of contemporary Russian politics. Some of that literature emphasized the need to create stability in the new states and it is this feature that may well be relevant to our postcommunist studies. For example, Huntington, in *Political Order in Changing Societies,* focuses on the need for governmental institutionalization to keep up with the increasing and ever-widening demands for participation that are placed upon the system.[27] In the Russian context, this may help us to unravel the factors surrounding the role of associational groups in the creation of a new political system. This approach also raises the question of whether the current governmental institutions—the Congress of People's Deputies and the Supreme Soviet—are adequate to meet increasing demands from ethnic groups and others within the Russian republic.

Two other themes that strike us as important elements in the Russian context are the tight interrelationship between the economic and political transitions and the questions surrounding the role of political culture. Until the collapse of the Soviet Union and its empire in Eastern Europe, no country had ever made the transition from communism to democracy and a market economy. More precisely, no country had undertaken the transformation of its economy and polity simultaneously. The two transitions are interconnected, with each one having a direct impact on the other. This creates instability in both processes. Moreover, we need to address the question of whether one type of transition should precede the other. Put differently, is democracy the best way to achieve the transition from a centrally planned economy to capitalism?

As for political culture, we need to undertake more systematic studies of what people are thinking and their attitudes toward leaders and institutions. Recent polls illustrate that people are increasingly in favor of greater security for society, to the detriment of greater political freedom: This seems to suggest that the majority would, in the words of one analyst, "look favorably on mitigation of the reform policy and the pace of its implementation."[28] Yet we need information on people's affective allegiances, as well. For example, we don't know whether people's current political apathy is a result of political culture (i.e., traditional attitudes toward the state and politics) or of their frustration at the practical difficulties of everyday life. The same analyst cited above feels that the shift away from support for democracy was due to frustration with political infighting at the top, in the face of economic decline.[29] But we do not know for certain. Thus every poll we take adds to our knowledge of contemporary attitudes, and we need to continue gathering more data and asking more varied kinds of questions.

In the final analysis, whatever our specific research agenda, we must recognize that because we are dealing with an ever-evolving situation, our theories must by definition be dynamic. We need, in the words of O'Donnell and Schmitter, to introduce uncertainty as a variable in our search for pluralism.[30]

Notes

1. See, for example, Samuel P. Huntington, "How Countries Democratize," *Political Science Quarterly* 106, no. 4 (Winter 1991–1992).

2. See, for example, the way the transition literature was applied in the Romanian case, Mary Ellen Fischer, "The New Leaders and the Opposition," in Daniel N. Nelson, *Romania After Tyranny* (Boulder: Westview Press, 1991), p. 47.

3. Guillermo O'Donnell and Philippe C. Schmitter, *Transitions from Authoritarian Rule: Tentative Conclusions About Uncertain Democracies* (Baltimore: Johns Hopkins University Press, 1986), pp. 7, 8.

4. Ibid.

5. Huntington, op. cit., p. 597.

6. Ibid., p. 583.

7. O'Donnell and Schmitter, op. cit., pp. 37–47.

8. See, for example, the argument in Robert Dahl, *Polyarchy: Participation and Opposition* (New Haven: Yale University Press, 1971).

9. For an interesting survey of the literature on modernization and pluralism as applied to the Soviet Union, see Catherine Merriman, "Perestroika and Political Pluralism: Past and Present," in Catherine Merriman and Christopher Ward, eds., *Perestroika: The Historical Perspective* (New York: Edward Arnold, 1991), pp. 16–33.

10. Jerry Hough, *The Soviet Union and Social Science Theory* (Cambridge: Harvard University Press, 1977).

11. Moshe Lewin, *The Gorbachev Phenomenon: A Historical Interpretation* (Berkeley and Los Angeles: University of California Press, 1988).

12. Charles E. Lindblom, *Politics and Markets* (New York: Basic Books, 1977).

13. Russell Bova, "Political Dynamics of the Post-Communist Transitions," *World Politics* 44 (October 1991), p. 134.

14. See, for example, Dankwart A. Rustow, "Transitions To Democracy: Toward a Dynamic Model," *Comparative Politics* 2 (April 1970).

15. According to Robert Dahl, these are the hallmarks of true pluralism. See Dahl, op. cit.

16. David Lane, *State and Politics in the USSR* (New York: New York University Press, 1985), p. 256.

17. There has been considerable attention paid to the emergence of civil society during the Gorbachev period, and there is now a large literature on the subject. See, for example, Jan Feldman, "Perestroika and the Uneasy Status of Private Interests," in Anthony Jones,

ed., *Research on the Soviet Union and Eastern Europe* (Greenwich, CT: JAI Press, 1990), pp. 155–166; Victoria E. Bonnell, "Voluntary Associations in Gorbachev's Reform Program," in A. Dallin and G. Lapidus, eds., *The Soviet System in Crisis* (Boulder: Westview Press, 1991), pp. 151–160; Gail W. Lapidus, "State and Society: Toward the Emergence of Civil Society in the Soviet Union," in Dallin and Lapidus, op. cit., pp. 130–150;

18. O'Donnell and Schmitter, op. cit., p. 8.

19. Ibid.

20. See, for example, Archie Brown, *Political Culture and Communist Studies* (London: Macmillan, 1984).

21. Mark Rhodes, "Political Attitudes in Russia," Radio Free Europe/Radio Liberty (hereafter cited as RFE/RL) *RFE/RL Research Report* 2, no. 3 (January 15, 1993), p. 43.

22. Peter Rutland, *Arguments and Facts International,* August–September, 1992, as cited in Vera Tolz, "Russia: Westernizers Continue to Challenge National Patriots," *RFE/RL Research Report* 1, no. 49 (December 11, 1992), p. 1.

23. An invaluable guide to these organizations is Vera Tolz, *The USSR's Emerging Multiparty System* (New York: Praeger, 1990). Despite the intervening years, relations among parties, associations, and movements remain as vague and unsystematic as they were before.

24. Rhodes, op. cit., p. 43.

25. For an account of the political involvement of interest groups in the emerging private economy, see Darrell Slider, "The First Independent Soviet Interest Groups: Unions and Associations of Cooperatives," in Judith Sedaitis and Jim Butterfield, eds., *Perestroika from Below: Social Movements in the Soviet Union* (Boulder: Westview Press, 1991), pp. 145–164; Anthony Jones and William Moskoff, *KO-OPS: The Rebirth of Entrepreneurism in the Soviet Union* (Bloomington: Indiana University Press, 1991).

26. For a recent survey of these types of pluralisms see Sedaitis and Butterfield, op. cit..

27. Samuel P. Huntington, *Political Order in Changing Societies* (New Haven: Yale University Press, 1968).

28. Rhodes, op. cit., p. 44.

29. Ibid.

30. O'Donnell and Schmitter, op. cit., p. 3.

About the Book

Building innovatively on Western social-science theory and on older models of Soviet politics, the authors review recent changes in the former USSR in order to assess the prospects there for democratic pluralism. Chapters focus on the first competitive elections, the new legislative bodies at state and local levels, and the newly freed press, exploring the extent to which these institutions can be described as democratic or pluralistic. Other chapters trace the complex linkages between a plurality of political-economic interests—explaining why Russian labor, government, and business may be moving toward a corporatist coalition and how political activists' sharply divergent attitudes toward the state and property keep them from forming a broad-based party.

Although it is difficult in this period of dramatic flux to predict the future, these thought-provoking analyses will provide a deeper understanding of the transformations under way and will stimulate further exploration.

About the Editors
and Contributors

Peter Clement is a Russian affairs analyst with the Office of Slavic and Eurasian Affairs at the Central Intelligence Agency.

Theodore H. Friedgut is professor and acting chair (1992–1993), in the Department of Russian and Slavic Studies, The Hebrew University in Jerusalem. He is the author of numerous works, including *Political Participation in the USSR* (1979); his most recent works are *Iuzovka and Revolution, Vol. I: Life and Work in Russia's Donbass, 1869–1924* (1989) and *Vol. II: Politics and Revolution in Russia's Donbass, 1869–1924* (forthcoming).

Jeffrey W. Hahn is a professor of political science, specializing in Russian domestic politics, at Villanova University. He is the author of *Soviet Grass Roots: Citizen Participation in Local Soviet Government* (1988). He is currently engaged in a long-term research project studying Russian political culture and institution-building at the local level of government in Russia.

Anthony Jones is a fellow at the Russian Research Center, Harvard University, and associate professor of sociology at Northeastern University. He is the coeditor of *Soviet Social Problems* (1991), part of the Olin Series of the Russian Research Center, and coauthor of *KO-OPS: The Rebirth of Entrepreneurism in the Soviet Union* (1991).

Mervyn Matthews is a reader in Russian Studies at the University of Surrey. He is the author of numerous books on Soviet society and Soviet social problems. His latest study on passport controls in the Soviet Union will be out in late 1993.

Carol R. Saivetz is a fellow at the Russian Research Center and a lecturer in social studies, both at Harvard University. She is author of numerous works on Soviet policy in the Third World, including *The Soviet Union and the Gulf in the 1980s* (Boulder: Westview Press, 1989) and editor of *The Soviet Union in the Third World,* part of the Olin Series of the Russian Research Center. She is currently working on *Central Asia's Emerging Relations with the Middle East* and a book on Russian foreign policy.

Elizabeth Teague has been an analyst of Soviet and Russian politics with Radio Free Europe/Radio Liberty in Munich since 1981. She has written widely on Russia's evolving political system.

Michael E. Urban is associate professor of politics at the University of California at Santa Cruz. He is the author of numerous articles and books on Soviet and Russian politics, including *More Power to the Soviets* (1990), and *Ideology and System Change* (1992). His current research focuses on political parties and movements in the new Russia.

Stephen White is professor of politics and a member of the Institute of Russian and East European Studies at the University of Glasgow. His most recent works include *Gorbachev and After,* 3d ed. (1992) and *The Politics of Transition: Shaping a Post-Soviet Future,* which will appear in 1993.

Index

Adalat (Uzbekistan), 92
Adamov, B. I., 53
Afanas'ev, Yurii, 134, 142(n3)
Agrarian Union (Russia), 150(n92)
Agzybirlik (Democratic Party of
    Turkmenistan), 96
Akayev, Askar, 94–95
Alash (Kazakhstan), 94
Aleph, 55
Almond, Gabriel, 8
Ancient Law (Maine), 6
Ancient Society (Morgan), 6–7
Arato, Andrew, 127–128
Argentina, 110
Argumenty i fakty, 32, 39
Aristotle, 49
Ashar (Kyrgyzstan), 95
Ashkabad earthquake (1948), 13
Aslonov, Kadriddin, 98
Aslund, Anders, 120–121
Assembly of Democratic Forces, 137, 138,
    148–149(n74)
Austria, 110, 111
Azat (Kazakhstan), 94

Badakhstan, 102
Bakaev, V. N., 72
Baker, James, III, 95, 96, 98
Baltic republics, 16. *See also* Minorities;
    Soviet collapse
Batkin, Leonid, 134
Bendix, Reinhardt, 47
Bentham, Jeremy, 48
Birlik (Uzbekistan), 91, 92, 93
Bodin, Jean, 48
Bokser, Vladimir, 149(n83)
Boldyrev, Iurii, 52

Borodin, Oleg, 147(n59)
Brezhnev, Leonid, 5, 8, 27, 48, 110, 152.
    See also Soviet system
Bukharin, Nikolai, 13
Burbulis, Gennadii, 113, 117, 133, 157
Burks, R. V., 6
Burtin, Yurii, 134
"Businesses, Like People, Are Not
    Forever" (Galbraith), 48

Carnegie, Dale, 13
CDP. *See* Constitutional Democratic Party
Center for Jewish Education and Culture,
    55, 57
Center for the Study of Public Opinion,
    78, 85(n54)
Central Asia, 86–98
    natural resources, 104–105
    political life, 90–98
    and Soviet collapse, 90–91
    and Soviet system, 86, 87–90
    See also Tajikistan
Central Committee of the Communist
    Party, 12, 28, 32–33
Christian Democratic Party, 18
Christian-Democratic Union of Russia, 34
Chronicle of Current Events, 29
Chubais, Anatolii, 138
Chubais, Igor, 147(n59)
CIS. *See* Commonwealth of Independent
    States
Civic Union (Russia), 139, 150(nn 91–92),
    153, 154
Civic violence, 46–47, 59(n6)
Civil society, 5, 17, 48, 56, 120
    definition of, 127–128
    Donetsk, 55–57, 58, 61(nn 44–45)

separation from political society, 129–130, 144(n23)

weakness of, 156–157

See also Labor movement; Political participation; Political parties; Press

Committee of Constitutional Supervision, 14

Committee for the Defense of Free Speech and the Rights of Journalists, 31

Committee for Glasnost, Citizens' Rights, and Appeals, 35

Commonwealth of Independent States (CIS), 15–16, 88, 137, 148(n67)

Communist Party of the Russian Federation, 150(n92)

Communist Party of the Soviet Union (CPSU)

absence of pluralism under, 5, 45, 46

Central Asia, 91, 93, 95, 97, 99

and coup attempt, 19–20, 57, 73, 82(n16)

and elections, 65, 66

Gorbachev reforms, 11–12, 15

and labor movement, 114, 122(n18)

leadership, 53

and local government, 62, 68, 70–71, 73

as mediator, 154

and new parties, 50, 136

and press, 32–33, 37, 39, 44(n40)

public support for, 17, 18

and Soviet collapse, 16, 25(n67)

Comte, Auguste, 6

Confederation of Independent Trade Unions of the Ukraine, 56

Conference of Public Forces, 133

Congress of Civic and Patriotic Forces, 132–133

Congress of Russian Business Circles, 119, 124(n34)

Constitution, 19

Constitutional Democratic Party (CDP), 131, 132, 137–138, 149(n79)

Convergence theory, 6

Corporatism, 109–111, 119, 120–121, 122(n9)

Council of Ministers, 11

Council of the Federation of Independence Trade Unions of Russia (FNPR), 113, 117, 119, 122(n19), 123(n22), 124(n38)

and unofficial unions, 114, 115, 118, 123(n23)

Coup attempt (Aug. 1991), 15, 61(n47)

and Central Asia, 90, 91, 95–96, 97–98

and Communist Party, 19–20, 57, 73, 82(n16)

and fragmentation, 45, 46

and labor movement, 123(n25)

and local government, 73, 82(n16)

and press, 19, 35–39, 43(n34), 44(n40)

public opinion, 20–21

and rule of law, 19

and Russian sovereignty, 127, 129

CPSU. *See* Communist Party of the Soviet Union

Criminal justice system, 14, 28, 29–30, 41–42(n8)

Czechoslovakia, 5, 8

Dahl, Robert, 7–8, 46, 62–63, 154

Darwin, Charles, 7

Democracy, 62–63

and industrialization, 153–154

transition theories, 151–153

See also specific topics

Democraticheskaia Rossiia. *See* Democratic Russia

Democratic Party, 18

Democratic Party of Russia (DPR), 18, 131, 133–134, 146(n44), 150(n92)

Democratic Party of Turkmenistan. *See* Agzybirlik

Democratic Party (Turkmenistan), 95, 96

Democratic Platform, 51

Democratic Rukh, 51

Democratic Russia, 51, 67, 128, 139, 147(n59), 148(n67)

and Movement for Democratic Reform, 135–136, 138, 149(n83)

negative focus of, 129–130, 131

public support for, 18, 127

See also Inter-Regional Deputies' Group

Democratic Union Party (Russia), 34

Democratic Yaroslavl', 67
Deutsch, Karl, 8
Dewey, John, 47
Dialog, 32
Discursive will formation, 142(n2)
Doctor Zhivago (Pasternak), 13
Donetsk, 45, 49–59
   civil society, 55–57, 58, 61(nn 44–45)
   and coup attempt, 45, 46, 57, 61(n47)
   economic crisis, 53–54
   leadership, 52–55, 60(nn 36–37)
   monism in, 49
   political parties, 49–52, 59(n18),
      60(n23)
Donetskie novosti, 55
DPR. *See* Democratic Party of Russia
Dubcek, Alexander, 8
Dyker, David, 109

Eastern and Central Europe, 5–6, 8, 16
East Germany. *See* German Democratic
   Republic
Eckstein, Alexander, 8
Economic crisis
   Donetsk, 53–54, 60(n36)
   and leadership, 54, 60(n36)
   and press, 37–38, 44(n41)
   and Soviet collapse, 16
Ednannia, 57
Egypt, 90
Ehrlich, Stanislaw, 47
Ekos, 13
Ekspress-khronika, 31
Election-90, 127. *See also* Democratic
   Russia; Inter-Regional Deputies'
   Group (I-RDG)
Elections
   Central Asia, 91, 96
   Gorbachev reforms, 9–10, 65–66
   Yaroslavl', 65–69, 77–78, 80
   See also Political participation
Elitism, 63
Engels, Friedrich, 6, 7
Entrepreneurs for a New Russia, 150(n92)
Environmental issues, 87, 93
Erk, 91, 92, 93
Ethnicity, 86–87. *See also* Minorities

Evolutionary theories, 6–7, 23(n9)

Fainsod, Merle, 8
Fascism, 110
Federalists, 47, 53, 103
Federalist structure, 46, 135, 136
Fedotov, Mikhail, 36–37
Filatov, Sergei, 143(n14)
Fish, Steven, 144(n23)
FNPR. *See* Council of the Federation of
   Independence Trade Unions of Russia
Fragmentation, 45–47, 59(n6), 102
Free Donetsk Medical Association, 56
Front for National Salvation, 150(n92)
Fundamentals of Criminal Law, 28, 29–30

Gaidar, Egor, 119, 135, 139, 157
Galbraith, John Kenneth, 48
Gdlyan, Tel'man, 147(n59)
Gellner, Ernest, 86–87, 102
Gemeinschaft und Gesellschaft (Toennies),
   6
General Federation of Labor, 56
German Democratic Republic, 17
German Federal Republic, 110
Germany, 122(n9)
Gidaspov, Boris, 15
Glasnost. *See* Gorbachev reforms; Press,
   freedom of
Glasnost, 31
Gorbachev, Mikhail, 16–17, 36. *See also*
   Gorbachev reforms
Gorbachev reforms, 5–6, 9–15
   and Central Asia, 90
   Communist Party, 11–12, 15
   criminal justice system, 14
   elections, 9–10, 65–66
   and government/labor/business
      relationships, 112
   and local government, 62, 71–72,
      83(n35)
   and modernization, 6, 8–9
   and political centers, 126, 131
   and political participation, 155
   and political parties, 50, 131–132,
      133(figure), 144–145(n28)
   and press, 12–14, 29–30

process of, 14–15
"socialist rule-of-law state," 14
soviet system, 10–11
and transition theories, 152
See also Gorbachev, Mikhail
Gorod, 55
Goskomizdat, 28, 34
Government/labor/business relationships
and corporatism, 109–111
models for, 111–112
and privatization, 119–120
Russia, 112–121
See also Russian Soviet Federated
Socialist Republic
Green Bud, 77, 84(n52)
Green movement, 157
Grigoriants, Sergei, 31
GUOT. *See* Main Administration for the
Preservation of State Secrets in the
Press and Other Mass Information
Media

Habermas, Juergen, 142(n2)
Hegel, G. W. F., 48
Homosexuals, 13, 21–22
Hough, Jerry, 153–154
How to Win Friends and Influence People
(Carnegie), 13
Huber, Robert T., 75
Human rights, 93
Huntington, Samuel P., 8, 49, 91, 103, 152,
158

Ikramov, Maksud, 98
Independent Miners' Union (NPG), 115,
122(n19)
Industrialization, 86–87, 153–154. *See
also* Modernization theories
Industrial Union, 138, 150(n87)
Inflation, 44(n41)
International Monetary Fund (IMF), 117,
123(n27)
Inter-Regional Deputies' Group (I-RDG),
11, 67, 126–127, 142(nn 3, 6). *See
also* Democratic Russia
Ippolito, Dennis, 63–64
Iran, 90

I-RDG. *See* Inter-Regional Deputies'
Group
IRP. *See* Islamic Renaissance Party
Iskandarov, Akbarsho, 100
Islam, 90, 92, 94, 101, 102–103. *See also*
Islamic Renaissance Party
Islamic Renaissance Party (IRP), 90, 92,
97, 98, 102
Istina, 51
Italy, 110
Ivanov, Nikolai, 147(n59)
Izvestiia, 19, 32, 38

Japan, 111

Kalugin, Oleg, 32
Kariera, 34
Karimov, Islam, 91, 92, 93, 104
Karnakov, L. L., 71–72, 73
Kasparov, Gary, 18
Kazakhstan, 88, 89, 90, 93–94. *See also*
Central Asia
KGB, 16, 32, 34, 91
Khangel'dyev, Khandurdy, 96
Khasbulatov, Ruslan, 37
Khodzha-Mukhamed, Durdymurad, 96
Khrushchev, Nikita S., 8, 14, 27
Khudonazarov, Davlat, 98
Klochkov, Igor, 119
Kolbin, Gennadi, 89
Kolson, Kenneth, 63–64
Kommersant, 32
Komsomol'skaia pravda, 39
Korbonski, Andrzej, 6
Koryagina, Tat'yana, 147(n59)
Kozakhmetov, Hasan, 94
Kozyrev, Andrei, 101
Kravchenko, Leonid Petrovich, 19, 35
Kravchuk, Leonid, 45, 46, 52
Kruglikov, L. L., 71–72, 73, 75
Kunayev, Dinmukhamed, 89
Kuranty, 36
Kyrgyzstan, 88, 94–95. *See also* Central
Asia
Kyrgyzstan Democratic Movement, 95

Labor movement
  and coup attempt, 123(n25)
  General Agreement, 116–117, 118,
    123(n27)
  government concessions to, 117–119,
    123(n29)
  miner's strike, 56–57, 61(n44),
    122(n19)
  official vs. unofficial unions, 114, 115,
    119, 122(n18), 123(nn 22–23)
  tripartite commission, 113–115, 118
  See also Civil society; Government/
    labor/business relationships
Labor Party, 149(n81)
Lane, David, 154
Language, 57, 87, 101
Laski, Harold, 46, 49
Law on Elections (1988), 66
Law on Local Elections, 66
Law on Public Associations (1990), 20
Law on State Enterprises (1987), 30
Law on the Press (1990), 19
Leadership, 52–55, 60(nn 36–37)
  Central Asia, 89–90
  and economic crisis, 54, 60(n36)
Lenin, V. I., 6, 48, 69, 70, 141(n2)
Lewin, Moshe, 9, 154
Liberal Free Market bloc (Russia), 135
Liberal Union (Russia), 135
Lindblom, Charles E., 154
Literaturnaia gazeta, 32
Local government. See Yaroslavl' local
  government; specific topics
Loshenkov, Fedor Ivanovich, 67, 71

Madison, James, 53, 103
Main Administration for the Preservation
  of State Secrets in the Press and Other
  Mass Information Media (GUOT),
  33–34, 36
Maine, Henry, 6
Makhkamov, Kakhar, 97, 98
Makhmudov, Alexander G., 52
Malyutin, M. V., 142(n2)
Marx, Karl, 6, 7, 69
Masaliyev, Absamat, 95
Maxwell, Robert, 39

Mayo, H. B., 65
MDR. See Movement for Democratic
  Reform
Media, 96. See also Press
Medvedev, Roy, 8
Megapolis ekspress, 32, 36
Memorial, 57, 61(n47), 77, 84(n53), 157
Mezey, Michael J., 75
Michels, Roberto, 48
Military resources, 153
Miloserdtsy, 77
Minorities, 12, 131, 154
  Central Asia, 87, 88–89, 93, 100, 101,
    104
  Donetsk, 57, 58, 61(n45)
  and political parties, 51, 134
  public opinion, 21–22
  See also Ethnicity
Mirakhimov, Mirbobo, 98
Mir-Saidov, Abdi, 104
Mitrokhin, Sergei, 142(n2)
Modernization theories, 6–9, 23(n9), 101,
    158
Montesquieu, 46, 47
Morgan, Lewis Henry, 6–7
Moscow Journalists' Union, 31, 34
Moscow News, 36
Moscow Trade Union Federation,
    123(n22)
Moskovskie novosti, 32, 97
Movement for Democratic Reform
  (MDR), 135–136, 138, 148(nn 67–
  68). See also Russian Movement for
  Democratic Reform
Mussolini, Benito, 110

Nabiyev, Rakhmon, 89, 98, 99–100, 102,
    103
Narodno-Trudovoi Soiuz (NTS), 32
National Democratic Party (Kazakhstan).
  See Zheltoqsan
National Unity Party (Kyrgyzstan), 95
Navzhuvanov, Mamadfayez, 98–99, 102
Nazarbayev, Nursultan, 88, 89, 93, 94
NDP. See People's (National) Democratic
  Party of Uzbekistan
Nenashev, Mikhail Fedorovich, 35

Nevada-Semipalatinsk movement, 93
New Russia, 135, 138, 147(n61), 149(n80)
New Russia Company, 49
Nezavisimaia gazeta, 32, 38
Nicholls, David, 47, 49
Niyazov, Saparmurad, 95, 96–97, 104–105
North Caucasus, 97
Novocherkassk incident (1962), 13
Novosti Press Agency, 35
NPG. *See* Independent Miners' Union
NTS. *See Narodno-Trudovoi Soiuz*

Obshchaia gazeta, 36
O'Donnell, Guillermo, 120, 152, 154, 156, 159
Ogonek, 32
Onishchuk, G. I., 50, 52–53
"On the Press and Other Mass Information Media" (1990), 33
Osh Aimagy, 95
Osh riots, 94, 95

Pakistan, 90
Pamiat', 51, 157
Pamir, 99
Pareto, Wilfrid, 48
Parsons, Talcott, 7, 23(n9)
Participation. *See* Political participation
Party for Democratic Renaissance of the Ukraine, 51
Party of Labor (Russia), 138
Party system. *See* Political parties
Pasternak, Boris, 13
Pavlov, Valentin, 123(n25)
Peasant Party, 18
Peasant Party of Russia, 135, 147(n60)
People's (National) Congress Party (Kazakhstan), 93–94
People's (National) Democratic Party of Uzbekistan (NDP), 91–92, 93
People's Party of Free Russia (PPFR), 18, 132–134, 136, 145(n39), 146(n44), 148(n68)
People's Party of Russia (PPR), 135, 147(n59), 147(n61)
Perestroika. *See* Gorbachev reforms
Perestroika (Gorbachev), 14

Perón, Juan, 110
Pervaia liniia, 55
Pipes, Richard, 6
Pittsburgh-Donetsk Friendship Society, 57
Pluralism
    case study method, 64, 82(nn 15–16), 83(n18)
    conditions for, 17, 46–48, 63–64
    vs. corporatism, 109–111, 119
    definitions of, 5, 46, 47, 104, 109–110
    and democracy, 62–63
    democratic theory, 153–156
    vs. fragmentation, 45–46
    multiplicity, 157
    and uncertainty, 158–159
    See also specific topics
Podrabinek, Andrei, 31
Poland, 17
Political centers, 125, 136–139, 150(n91)
    and Gorbachev reforms, 126, 131
Political culture, 155–156, 158–159
Political Order in Changing Societies (Huntington), 91, 158
Political organization, 127–128, 129(table)
Political participation, 49, 154–155
    and elections, 77–78
    and local government, 75–79, 84–85(nn 52–53)
    See also Civil society; Elections; Political parties; Public opinion
Political parties
    Central Asia, 91–92, 93–94, 95, 97–98
    and civil society, 129–130
    Donetsk, 49–52, 59(n18), 60(n23)
    and elections, 68, 121
    and Gorbachev reforms, 50, 131–132, 133(figure), 144–145(n28) //historical inheritance, 22
    and local government, 67–68
    and minorities, 51
    new parties, 17–19, 50
    public opinion, 20, 53
    Russian coalitions, 132–136, 146(n44)
    turbulence, 139–141
    Yeltsin's exclusion of, 128–129, 143(nn 14, 18), 145(n39)

See also Communist Party of the Soviet
   Union
Political society, 127–128, 129–130. *See*
   also Political parties
Politics and Markets (Lindblom), 154
Poltoranin, Mikhail, 37
Polyarchy, 62
Pomper, Gerald, 65, 68
Ponomarev, Lev, 149(n83)
Popov, Gavrill, 135, 136, 138, 148(n68),
   149(n83)
Popular Consensus (Russia), 131–132, 134
Popular Democratic Party of Uzbekistan,
   91
Popular Front of the Ukraine, 51
PPFR. *See* People's Party of Free Russia
PPR. *See* People's Party of Russia
Pravda, 19, 28, 32, 37, 38, 39, 44(n40)
Pravda vostoka, 92–93
Press, 27–39
   Central Asia, 92–93
   commercialization, 37–39, 44(nn 41,
      44)
   Donetsk, 55–56
   output, 40(table), 41(table)
   under Soviet system, 27–29, 41–42(n8)
Press, freedom of
   and coup attempt, 19, 35–37, 43(n34),
      44(n40)
   and Gorbachev reforms, 12–14, 29–31
   legal developments, 13, 19, 27, 29–30,
      33–34, 35
   and new press, 13, 30–33
   repression, 34–35
Presthus, Robert, 63, 83(n18)
Privatization, 119–120, 134, 135,
   147(n59), 154
Property, 134, 136, 146(n44), 147(n59)
Prostor, 13
Proudhon, Pierre Joseph, 47
Public opinion
   Communist Party, 17, 18
   coup attempt, 20–21
   Gorbachev, 16–17
   lack of knowledge, 157
   and local government, 78–79, 79(table),
      85(n54)

minorities, 21–22
political parties, 20, 53
Yeltsin, 17, 112
See also Political participation;
   Systemic legitimacy
*Public Opinion and Responsible
   Democracy* (Ippolito, Walker &
   Kolson), 63–64
Pulatov, Abdurakhim, 92, 93
Putsch. *See* Coup attempt (Aug. 1991)
Pye, Lucian, 9

Rabochaia tribuna, 32
Radio Liberty, 29, 31
Rakhmonov, Imomali, 101
Ranney, Austin, 63
Rashidov, Sharaf, 104
Rastokhez (Tajik National Front), 97, 98,
   99
RCDM. *See* Russian Christian Democratic
   Movement
Red Cross, 57
Religion
   Central Asia, 90, 92, 94, 97, 98, 101,
      102–103
   Russian Orthodox Church, 77
Renewal party (Russia), 139
Republican Party, 18
Republican Party of Russia (RPR), 134–
   135, 143(n14), 146–147(nn 51, 53,
   55), 148(n68)
RMDR. *See* Russian Movement for
   Democratic Reform
Romania, 59(n6)
Roman law, 22
Rossiia, 36, 39
Rossiiskaia gazeta, 36, 39
Rothschild, Joseph, 86
RPR. *See* Republican Party of Russia
RSFSR. *See* Russian Soviet Federated
   Socialist Republic
Rukh, 51, 57
Rule of law, 19–20
Rumiantseva, Tatiana P., 73, 78
Rumyantsev, Oleg, 135
Russian Christian Democratic Movement
   (RCDM), 131, 132, 137–138

Russian Federation Law on the Press, 37
Russian Movement for Democratic
    Reform (RMDR), 135, 136, 138, 139,
    148(n68). *See also* Movement for
    Democratic Reform
Russian Orthodox Church, 77
Russian Social Union, 132
Russian Soviet Federated Socialist
    Republic (RSFSR)
    and Central Asia, 88, 100–101
    concessions to labor, 117–119, 123(n29)
    Congress of People's Deputies
        dissolution proposals, 137, 138,
        150(n86)
    corporatism, 119, 120–121
    election suspension, 121
    General Agreement, 116–117, 118,
        123(n27)
    minorities, 131
    political centers in, 136–139, 150(nn
        91–92)
    political coalitions, 132–136, 146(n44)
    and press, 30, 33, 34, 35, 36, 37, 39,
        43(n34)
    privatization, 119–120, 149(n80)
    public support, 136–137, 148(n71)
    sovereignty declaration, 127, 129, 131
    tripartite commission, 113–115, 118
    Yeltsin's exclusion of political parties,
        128–129, 143(nn 14, 18), 145(n39)
    See also Commonwealth of Independent
        States; Yaroslavl'; Yeltsin, Boris;
        specific topics
Russian Tripartite Commission on the
    Regulation of Social and Labor
    Relations, 113–115, 118
Russian Union of Industrialists and
    Entrepreneurs, 115, 139
Russian Unity, 136–137, 150(n92)
Russian Workers' Front, 51
Russia's Choice, 150(n92)
Rustow, Dankwart, 154
Rutland, Peter, 155
Rutskoi, Aleksandr, 18, 20, 89, 132–133,
    136, 146(n44)

Sakharov, Andrei, 66

Salikh, Muhammed, 91, 92
Samizdat movement, 29, 30, 31
Samusev, Anatolii, 84(n47)
Saudi Arabia, 90
Scandinavian countries, 110, 111, 122(n9)
Schmitter, Philippe, 110, 113, 120, 152,
    154, 156, 159
SDPR. *See* Social Democratic Party of
    Russia
SEC. *See* State Emergency Committee
Semigin, Gennadii, 119, 124(n34)
Shamshev, Boris, 67
Shaposhnikov, Evgenni, 100
Shatalin, Stanislav, 136
Shchakhberdyev, Nazarly, 96
Shevardnadze, Eduard, 135
Shevstvova, Liliya, 149(n81)
Shokhin, Aleksandr, 113, 114, 115, 118
Shostakovskii, Vyacheslav, 136, 148(n68)
Smena, 138, 150(n87)
Sobchak, Anatolii, 21, 36, 135, 148(n68)
Social Democratic Center (Russia),
    150(n92)
Social Democratic Party, 18, 51, 60(n23)
Social Democratic Party of Russia
    (SDPR), 134, 135, 138, 146–
    147(n55), 150(n92)
Socialist Party, 18
Socialist Party (Kazakhstan), 93, 94
Socialist Party of Working People
    (Russia), 136
"Socialist rule-of-law state," 14
Social-Liberal Association of the Russian
    Federation, 135
Society. *See* Civil society
Society of Ukrainian Law Scholars, 56
Sociopolitical movements, 128. *See also*
    Civil society
Soiuz trudiashchikhsia Donbassa, 56
Solidarity, 17
Solzhenitsyn, Aleksandr, 13
Sotsialisticheskii Donbass, 55
Sotsprof. *See* Union of Socialist Trade
    Unions
Sovetskaia Rossiia, 19
Soviet collapse, 15–16, 20, 25(n67)
    and Central Asia, 90–91

and labor movement, 123(n25)
and political parties, 131–132, 136
See also Coup attempt (Aug. 1991)
Soviet Peace Committee, 57
Soviet system
  Central Asia under, 86, 87–90
  crisis orientation of, 48–49
  elections, 65
  fragmentation in, 45
  and Inter-Regional Deputies' Group,
    126–127, 142(nn 3, 6)
  irrelevance of pluralism to, 5
  local government, 65, 69–71, 84(n40)
  monism in, 48–49
  and political center, 126, 141–142(n2)
  political participation under, 76
  press under, 27–29, 41–42(n8)
  totalitarian model of, 3–4
  and transition theories, 152–153
  See also Gorbachev reforms; Stalinism;
    specific leaders
Soyuzpechat' network, 28, 38
Stalinism, 8, 27, 48, 152. *See also* Soviet
  system
Staniszkis, Jadwiga, 141(n2)
State Committees for Publishing, Printing,
  and the Book Trade. *See* Goskomizdat
State, definition of, 127, 130–131
State Emergency Committee (SEC), 19,
  45, 46. *See also* Coup attempt (Aug.
  1991)
State Inspectorate for the Defense of the
  Freedom of the Press and Mass
  Information, 36
State Television and Radio Company, 35
Suetnov, A., 30
Supreme Soviet, 10, 14
Svetlichnyi, Evgenii, 51–52
Svobodnoe slovo, 34
Sweden, 111, 122(n9)
Systemic legitimacy, 16–17, 21, 35
  as condition for pluralism, 46, 47–48
  and fear of civic violence, 46–47,
    59(n6)
  and political culture, 155, 156
  Russia, 136–137, 148(n71)

Tajikistan, 97–103
  civil war, 87, 88, 93, 100–101
  and coup attempt, 97–98
  ethnic divisions, 100, 101–102, 104
  political life, 98–100
  religion, 90, 97, 98, 101, 102–103
  See also Central Asia
Tajikistan Democratic Party, 97, 98, 99
TASS, 33
Television, 55
Tema, 13
Tocqueville, Alexis de, 46, 47
Toennies, Ferdinand, 6
Tolz, Vera, 109
"Towards a Humane, Democratic
  Socialism," 15
Transition theories, 151–153, 157–158
Travkin, Nikolai, 18, 133, 146(n44)
Tret'ya sila, 32
Trotsky, Leon, 13
Trud, 39
Turajonzoda, Akbar, 103
Turkey, 90
Turkmenistan, 88, 90, 95–97, 104–105.
  See also Central Asia

Ukraine, 25(n67), 57, 91. *See also* Donetsk
Ukrainian Language Association, 57
Ukrainian Republican Party, 51
Union of Independent Journalists, 31
Union of Medical Workers (Ukraine), 56
Union of Socialist Trade Unions (Russia),
  115, 119, 123(n23)
Union of Toilers of the Donbass. *See Soiuz
  trudiashchikhsia Donbassa*
United Kingdom, 112
United States, 95, 96, 98, 111
Uzbekistan, 88, 91–93, 104
  religion, 90, 92, 97
  See also Central Asia

Valynko, Nikolai, 51
Vasiliev, Sergei, 51
Vechernii Donetsk, 45, 55
Velsapar, Mukhamed, 96
Verbitskii, Iurii I., 84(n46)
Vestnik khristiyanskoi demokratii, 34

Vite, Oleg, 129
Vol'skii, Arkadii, 115, 135, 139, 153, 157
Volunchunas, Victor V., 72, 84(nn 40, 46)
VTsSPS. *See* General Federation of Labor

Walker, Thomas, 63–64
Wolin, Sheldon, 141(n2)

Yakovlev, Aleksandr, 135
Yaroslavl' local government, 62, 64–80, 82(n15)
  and coup attempt, 73, 82(n16)
  elections, 65–69, 77–78, 80
  legislative behavior, 69–75, 81, 83(n36), 84(nn 40, 46–47)
  political participation, 75–79

Yaroslavl' Popular Front (YPF), 67–68, 69, 71, 72, 77, 80
Yavlinsky, Grigorii, 117
Yeltsin, Boris, 11, 22, 39, 121, 127
  and coup attempt, 19, 36, 37, 73
  and political parties, 128–129, 138, 143(nn 14, 18), 150(n87)
  public support, 17, 112, 136–137, 148(n71)
  See also Russian Soviet Federated Socialist Republic
YPF. *See* Yaroslavl' Popular Front
Yugoslavia, 5
Yusupov, Shodmon, 97, 98

Zheltoqsan, 94
Zhizn', 55
Zviagil'skii, E. L., 52